THE PENGUIN FREEZER COOKBOOK

Helge Rubinstein and Sheila Bush write
as practical housewives and enthusiastic
cooks. Both have families; one lives in
London and the other in the country;
and 'travel, entertaining and greed', they
say, have been a spur in helping them,
on limited budgets, to aim at a high
standard of cooking.

HELGE RUBINSTEIN AND SHEILA BUSH

The Penguin Freezer Cookbook

ILLUSTRATED BY
SUSAN CAMPBELL

PENGUIN BOOKS

Penguin Books Ltd, Harmondsworth, Middlesex, England
Penguin Books Inc, 7110 Ambassador Road, Baltimore, Maryland 21207, U.S.A.
Penguin Books Australia Ltd, Ringwood, Victoria, Australia
Penguin Books Canada Ltd, 41 Steelcase Road West, Markham, Ontario, Canada
Penguin Books (N.Z.) Ltd, 182–190 Wairau Road, Auckland 10, New Zealand

—

First published 1973
Reprinted 1973, 1974 (twice), 1975, 1976

—

—

Made and printed in Great Britain
by Richard Clay (The Chaucer Press) Ltd,
Bungay, Suffolk
Set in Monotype Garamond

For our families,
with love and gratitude for
their patience, their criticisms and
their occasional praise

CONTENTS

INTRODUCTION

THIS book is designed to help the housewife to make the most of her freezer, by using fresh raw materials when they are at their best, cheapest and most plentiful in the garden or in the shops and markets. It does not deal with the more technical aspects of home freezing, which are very fully covered by several books on the market (we would particularly refer readers to *Fresh from the Freezer* by Marye Cameron-Smith, also published in Penguin, which answers clearly and concisely questions about buying and maintaining a freezer and freezing raw materials). Ours is a more personal approach. We have found that owning a freezer has not only cut down our household costs enormously, but has enabled us to produce a wider range of delicious and – paradoxically, perhaps – fresher food with far less time spent shopping or at the stove.

Our plan is to devote one chapter to each month of the year, listing the foods available, with brief freezing instructions for each and a number of seasonal recipes. Obviously, since nature herself is bountiful in fits and starts, this means that some months are fat and full, and others slender. Also, since almost every kind of food is becoming more readily available all the year round, our choice of month is necessarily arbitrary at times; but we have tried to pick in every case the month when the food in question is most abundant.

One of the interesting facts about home freezing is that, since it is still in its infancy, there is a great deal of uncertainty among the experts about what can and cannot be done. In our view almost anything can be done, so long as it doesn't involve safety risks. So don't be put off by being told that such-and-such can't be frozen, or that this or that is the only way of freezing it: experiment for yourself. Above all don't allow the freezer to become a tyrant or a chore; use it to suit your particular needs and way of life. We hope that this book will help you to do so, and to *enjoy* your freezer.

Basic Guide-Lines

ORGANIZING THE FREEZER

THE first decision to be made when you choose a freezer is whether to buy an upright or a chest model. For the pros and cons of the two types, and a list of suppliers, see *Fresh from the Freezer*. Whichever type you choose, one basic rule applies – subject to space, *always* buy a size larger than you think you will need.

Our own feeling is that, though upright freezers take up less floor-room than the chest ones, it is much more difficult to store food compactly in them and to use every inch of space. There is no difficulty with square or rectangular packages and containers; it is when you want to store large or awkwardly shaped things, or to pack food in really tight, that the trouble starts. However, upright freezers are easier for anyone who has difficulty in bending or lifting.

A chest freezer will hold considerably more so long as you pack the food carefully. The first rule is to divide up the space in the most economical way possible. One method is to use vertical dividers; the disadvantage of these is that they only come half-way up the freezer, and food cannot be lifted out in them.

The best method is to use baskets. These are available in many different sizes, and can be stacked one on top of the other, so that they fill the freezer. In this way every inch of space can be used, and food can be put in or taken out with the minimum of trouble. Moreover, baskets make the rather tiresome business of defrosting easier, since they can be taken out and wrapped individually in blankets or newspapers. Make sure they are a reasonable size, so that when they are filled they are not too heavy to handle. You can use these baskets to store the food according to categories or dates of freezing – choose whatever method will make it easiest for you to find any particular item later on.

Hamster Baskets, Much Marcle, Ledbury, Herefordshire, make excellent baskets. They are manufactured to order, and can be made in 6,360 different sizes. They are strong, inexpensive and easy to handle.

Tough cardboard cartons are an excellent cost-free alternative, but they are not so easy to lift out and they will need to be replaced from time to time.

Big coloured batching bags, which are available from Lakeland Plastics (see p. 15), are another useful way of keeping different categories of food separate.

PACKAGING MATERIALS

There are so many different types of containers and material for packaging frozen food that it is often difficult for anyone starting off with a freezer to know which are best. Although some of them are quite expensive, you will need to buy a basic trousseau; but you will also gradually acquire a useful supply of storage containers in the course of your ordinary shopping. Once you have a freezer, never throw away any of the waxed, plastic or foil containers in which you buy cream, yogurt, mousses, cottage cheese, pies, etc.

We have concentrated here on the forms of packaging which we have found the most satisfactory.

Plastic containers with lids: it is useful to have a store of these in various sizes, for freezing almost every kind of food. Though the initial cost is high, they can be washed and re-used almost indefinitely.

Foil containers: keep a stock of these also – shallow ones for tarts, deeper ones for stews and puddings. One of the advantages of foil containers is that food put into them freezes and thaws quickly. Another is that they are easy to clean if they have been used for strong-smelling food; so if you are freezing something with a very persistent smell, such as red cabbage or a dish containing pimentoes, use a foil container in preference to a plastic or waxed one.

Polythene bags: these are cheapest of all, and if they are fairly tough they can be used a second time, so long as they are washed thoroughly and tested to see that there are no holes in them.

Aluminium foil: This is virtually indispensable for wrapping all kinds of frozen food, especially meat and cooked dishes such as cakes and pastry. Buy it in the largest roll possible, even if this seems extravagant at the time, for in the end it will be much more economical. And choose a fairly heavy quality, as otherwise it will tear easily.

Moisture-vapour-proof tissue and polythene film: These are sold under various brand names and are useful alternatives to foil, especially if they are of the self-clinging variety. But they must not be exposed to heat.

Lakeland Plastics, Alexandra Road, Windermere, Westmorland, sell an excellent range of products for packaging frozen food. Their goods are the cheapest of the various firms whose prices we have examined, and the quality is excellent. They only deal direct with the public, not through shops. They also run an advisory service, and we have found them extremely cooperative and efficient.

WRAPPING FOR THE FREEZER

The cardinal rules of wrapping for the freezer can be summarized as follows:

1. Food must always be quite cold before it is wrapped.

2. As much air as possible must be excluded before the container is sealed. If this is not done, the food will become dehydrated and the flavour, colour and texture will suffer. If you are using a polythene bag you can suck out the air with a straw before tying the neck. But don't try this method with meringues or pastry cases, which will collapse if you suck too

hard. Rigid containers can if necessary have a piece of foil laid over the food, below the lid, to protect it from the air. Awkwardly shaped food is best wrapped in foil, polythene film or moisture-vapour-proof tissue, which can be moulded tightly round a chicken, for instance, or a joint of meat. It is advisable to put the parcel in a polythene bag, as it may otherwise be punctured when it is moved about in the freezer.

3. If you are using a polythene bag, make sure that the neck is absolutely clean before you secure it.

4. One disadvantage of freezing food in polythene bags is that the packages may be an awkward shape. To overcome this, fit the unfilled bag into a square or rectangular container, such as a plastic box or an empty sugar packet, pour in the food, seal the bag and freeze. When the food is quite hard the polythene bag can be lifted out of the container, and you have a neat package to store in the freezer.

5. Plastic containers are extremely practical for storing all kinds of food during the initial period of freezing. Pour in the food as soon as it is cold, cover, and freeze for 24 hours. Then ease the food out of the container – if necessary by dipping the latter in hot water for a few seconds – wrap in foil or a polythene bag, and return to the freezer. In this way a small supply of plastic containers can be used over and over again.

6. If you are using rigid containers, always leave a little head-space between the food and the lid – $\frac{1}{2}$ inch is about right, rather less for containers with very wide necks and rather more for narrow ones. If you don't do this, the contents will ooze out as they freeze and expand, creating a sticky mess and cross-flavours in the freezer.

7. Label every package clearly with details of the contents, including the date of freezing, and the weight and method used if you are freezing fruit or vegetables.

8. For quick and easy identification use coloured stick-on labels and coloured bags. You can plan your colour code according to types of food, dates of freezing or whatever other system seems most practical.

METHODS OF FREEZING PÂTÉS,
CASSEROLES, MOUSSES AND PUDDINGS

Food which needs to keep a certain shape can be frozen in a number of ways. There is no problem if you can spare the dish in which the food has been prepared but this is not usually possible, so here are some alternative methods.

1. *Foil containers* are best for food which is prepared and cooked in layers, such as pies, moussakas and fruit crumbles. They can also be used for cooking pâtés.

Wrap the container before freezing, and if the food needs to be cooked or reheated before serving place it straight from the freezer into the oven.

2. *Lining the dish with foil* is a practical way of cooking and freezing food which will later be served or heated in the same dish. It is useful therefore for pâtés, moussakas, crumbles and mousses. This method is not suitable for casseroles or other food which you will wish to stir during cooking.

Line the dish carefully with foil before putting in the food. If the food has been cooked, allow it to cool. Freeze for 24 hours. Then lift the food in its foil wrapping out of the dish, and put it into a polythene bag before returning it to the freezer. To serve, strip off the foil, replace the food in the original dish, and either put in the oven or leave to thaw.

3. *Lining the dish with polythene film or moisture-vapour-proof tissue:* this method is similar to the previous one, and has the advantage that these materials do not tear as easily as foil. However, they are not heat-proof, and so cannot be used for food which is to be cooked before freezing. This method is most useful, therefore, for mousses and other cold puddings.

4. *Hot-water method:* this is an alternative to the two previous methods and is chiefly for those who, like one of the authors, is all thumbs when it comes to lining dishes with foil. It can be used not only for mousses and puddings, but also for casseroles when you want to replace the food straight from the freezer into the original casserole dish for reheating and serving.

If the food has been cooked, allow it to cool.

Cover the container and place it in the freezer for 24 hours. Then stand it in a few inches of fairly hot water – the depth will depend on the height of the container, but the water should not be allowed to come over the top. In a few seconds it should be possible to work a knife round the edge and loosen the contents. Turn out, wrap well and replace in the freezer.

METHODS OF FREEZING TARTS AND FLANS

Tarts and flans can be frozen in foil flan-cases or in any of the following ways:

1. If the tart or flan is to be frozen uncooked (filled or unfilled), dust the flan-tin with flour before lining it with the pastry. Freeze for 24 hours. The pastry will then slip out of the tin quite easily, and can be wrapped before returning to the freezer.

2. If the tart or flan is to be frozen cooked (filled or unfilled), you can use a tin with a loose base or with a cutter. The tart should then come out quite easily when it has cooled, and can be wrapped and frozen. However, if it sticks to the tin, freeze it for twenty-four hours, and it should then slip out without difficulty. If it still sticks, you can always try the hot-water method – but take care that the water doesn't come over the edge of the tin.

3. Another method for tarts which are to be cooked before freezing is to line the tin with foil before putting in the pastry. After cooking, freeze the tart for 24 hours, then lift it out of the tin in its foil wrapping and put it in a polythene bag before returning it to the freezer. Strip off the foil before serving or reheating.

STORAGE TIMES

There are no hard and fast rules as to how long food may be stored in the freezer. In our experience most food keeps well for 6 months or longer, and every recipe in this book has been tested for at least this length of time, with the exception of ices and mousses, which deteriorate in taste and texture if they are frozen for more than a month or so. In the rare cases where it is not advisable to freeze for so long we have said so.

Some basic raw materials, such as good-quality meat, keep perfectly well for a year or more, and if you buy, say, a whole side of beef it may well last you this long. But there is nothing to be said for long-term storage for its own sake – however well pheasant or hare may keep, for instance, it is not going to seem very appetizing in July. And if you don't eat up your summer vegetables and fruit before the winter is out, you will miss half the joy of tasting the new season's garden produce. So freeze only what the household really enjoys eating, and keep a steady turnover.

QUANTITIES

When it comes to cooking for the freezer, remember that the more you cook at any one time, the more you will rejoice later on. Get into the habit of cooking at least twice as much as you are likely to want immediately, and freeze half; or if you have a couple of hours to spare make two or three stews for the freezer, or a big batch of cakes or pastry. This cuts down the total time spent in preparing food and is a big economy in fuel.

The quantities for most of the recipes in this book can be multiplied almost indefinitely, the only limitations being the size of your saucepans, oven, freezer and pocket. So that the amounts should not seem too daunting we have as a general rule given enough for 6 to 8 people. But this can only be a rough guide. As that great cook, Alice B. Toklas, said tetchily when asked how many people a particular recipe would serve, 'How should I know how many it serves? It depends – on their appetites, what else they have for dinner – whether they like it or not . . . Such questions! Typically home economics . . . so finicky.'*

MEAT

Meat is usually the most expensive item in any family's food budget, and buying meat in bulk is probably the biggest saving that can be made by freezer owners. But it is also likely to entail the greatest outlay in money, so consider carefully what your particular needs are and shop around before buying.

There are many deep-freeze depots or cash-and-carry stores which sell frozen meat in quantity at wholesale or reduced prices. These have the advantage that you can spend just as much or as little as you want, and that you need buy only the particular cuts that you are used to cooking and know your family likes. They are probably the best places to buy meat of which you are unlikely to want very much, such as veal. But don't necessarily buy the cheapest quality – it is no economy to buy a huge slab of stewing steak that you will end up feeding to the cat.

Most families will want to have a variety of cuts for different occasions, and for them the most economical way is to buy a whole, a half or a quarter of a carcass. More and more butchers are now catering for people with freezers. Find a butcher whom you can trust to sell you only first-quality meat, and if possible one who will allow you to watch him cut it up. A good butcher will be able to tell you the best way to cook the less familiar cuts, and you will be able to tell him exactly what size you want your joints to be; bear in mind, however, that the larger the joint the better it will cook. As he wraps the meat, you may find it useful to write labels yourself so that you can make a note

* *Aromas and Flowers of Past and Present*, Harper & Bros., New York, 1958.

of various ways of cooking a particular cut. See that you have just the right quantity of meat in individual packages – there is nothing more annoying than having to prise two lamb chops off an amorphous frozen lump.

Many butchers have their own freezing units, and you will need to take advantage of these if you are buying large quantities of meat, as you should not put into the freezer more than one tenth of its capacity of unfrozen food in any 24-hour period. So if possible ask the butcher to freeze the meat for you, and then get it home as quickly as possible. A little thawing is of course inevitable, and some 'bleeding' does no harm, but the meat should not be allowed to get soft. This means in effect that an interval of 2 to 3 hours between freezers for a large quantity of meat is perfectly acceptable, but it should not be very much longer than this.

You can also buy meat direct from a farm. This is probably the cheapest way of all, but it is only recommended for those who know enough about meat to be able to choose a good carcass and to cut it up properly themselves.

Beef: At its best in early autumn. See general notes on beef on p. 237.

Lamb: See general notes on p. 91.

Pork: The price and quality of pork do not fluctuate very much, so we have not given any particular time of the year for buying it in bulk. However, it is sometimes a little cheaper in the summer, as there is less demand for it in hot weather.

Veal: This is so expensive that few people will want to buy a whole carcass. Probably the best way, as we have said, is to buy a small quantity at a deep-freeze depot.

Bacon: In common with other cured meats, bacon does not freeze properly at the temperature of domestic freezers. However, it keeps perfectly well in the freezer for several weeks, especially if it is in one piece rather than in rashers; so take advantage of any special offers of whole gammons or other cuts.

Poultry: This is not really seasonal, but you will sometimes find

21

special offers in January or February, when everyone is tired of poultry after Christmas, or at the beginning of winter when the demand also drops as most people turn to more robust meat. These offers are usually of battery chickens, and while they cannot be compared for flavour or texture with fresh free-range chickens, they are excellent for casseroles. Avoid buying for the freezer just before Easter and Christmas, when prices rise steeply.

Some general rules for the cooking of frozen meat

1. It is usually thought that meat is more tender if it is thawed before roasting, but in our experience the difference in tenderness is only marginal, at any rate for beef and lamb. The disadvantage of roasting straight from the freezer is that it is difficult to gauge the length of time needed. As a rough guide, allow at least half as long again. Beef may be cooked semi-thawed in order to minimise 'bleeding'. Pork should always be thawed first, as it is very unpalatable if undercooked.

2. Meat to be fried or grilled is more tender if it is allowed to thaw first. If you need to thaw chops or steak quickly, place the meat in the unopened bag in a bowl of warm water.

3. Meat that is to be marinaded or simmered slowly can be used straight from the freezer, and there is a positive advantage in doing so as none of the juices are lost in the thawing.

4. Poultry should always be thawed before cooking, as otherwise it tends to become rather tough.

5. If you are cooking or reheating meat straight from the freezer, and are in a hurry, you can speed up the process by pushing a metal skewer through the centre of the joint. This will conduct the heat to the uncooked part of the meat. In the case of poultry you can cut down the cooking or reheating time by carving the bird as soon as it has thawed sufficiently, and then continuing to heat through.

7. It is better to cook a joint that may be bigger than you need immediately and freeze what remains than to cook a small piece of meat.

8. Do not freeze cooked meat which contains a lot of fat, as cooked fat goes rancid quickly.

FISH

Fish is really only worth freezing if it practically jumps out of the sea into the freezer. Since very few people can get it as fresh as this, we have confined ourselves to a few recipes for cooked fish dishes, which freeze well.

Salmon is the one fish which is, in our experience, worth freezing raw, especially as the price fluctuates so greatly (see p. 149).

VEGETABLES

If you have a garden, and plan carefully what to grow and what to freeze, you need hardly ever buy vegetables again – and the saving will be startling. While some vegetables freeze better than others, most of them stand up very well to freezing, and it is a joy to have a dish of your own baby peas on Christmas day, or delicious green vegetables in the very early spring when they are a ruinous price in the shops.

Nearly all vegetables should be either blanched or cooked before they are frozen: methods of freezing are given for each vegetable in the month when it is at its best. (For fuller instructions see *Fresh from the Freezer* by Marye Cameron-Smith.) It is worth experimenting with the different methods, and also with the various ways of cooking vegetables when they come out of the freezer, to find out what suits you.

The following points may be helpful:

1. Vegetables should be picked when they are young and tender, and should be frozen as soon as possible after picking.

2. Blanch them in small quantities, so that the blanching water is off the boil for the shortest possible time.

3. When you plunge them into cold water after blanching,

23

the addition of some ice-cubes will help the vegetables to cool quickly.

4. Freeze them in small quantities too. Two or three small bags of vegetables will cook or heat through much more rapidly and evenly, and therefore taste better, than one big lump.

5. If you freeze any vegetables that you may later want to use in recipes, write the weight on the label.

6. When you take vegetables out of the freezer, they should always be cooked or heated while they are still frozen. (Sweet corn is the one exception.) If they have been blanched remember that the blanching will have partially cooked them, so they will not need more than about two thirds of the usual time.

7. Vegetables which are cooked before freezing should in general be frozen with their cooking liquid – this assumes that you cook them simply in a little butter and water. The liquid can be used during the reheating, and very little more, if any, should need to be added.

8. Vegetables with a high water content, such as marrows, will only freeze satisfactorily if they are cooked first.

9. Salad vegetables, such as watercress, lettuce and cucumber, will be no good for eating raw after freezing. They can, however, be frozen cooked.

10. We do not recommend freezing new potatoes, as the texture and flavour suffer.

FRUIT

Most fruit freezes excellently, and if you have a garden, or access to cheap, fresh supplies of soft and stoned fruit, they are among the most rewarding of all foods to freeze. The following points are worth remembering:

1. Only ripe, good-quality fruit should be used.

2. Fruit should be frozen as quickly as possible after picking.

3. If syrup is used, it must be quite cold before it is poured over the fruit.

4. If the fruit is likely to be used in recipes afterwards, it is

helpful to write on the label of each packet the weight of the fruit and the amount of sugar used.

5. Bananas and avocado pears do not freeze well; pears are excellent frozen cooked, but are not good frozen raw; melons tend to become rather insipid, but they can be frozen in small quantities in either sugar or syrup for adding to fruit salads; grapes are only worth freezing in the form of juice.

Whether you freeze fruit sweetened or unsweetened is a matter of preference. Some people prefer to freeze soft fruit without sugar, because it keeps its shape better. On the other hand, if sugar is added the fruit keeps longer and has a better flavour and colour. This is especially true of soft fruit, which forms a delicious natural juice with the sugar as it thaws; it is not so important for the tough-skinned varieties, such as gooseberries, which do not form a juice. Stoned fruit is excellent frozen in syrup. Fruit which is slightly over-ripe or otherwise not quite perfect can be made into a purée before freezing.

The thawing of fruit is extremely important. It should be thawed slowly and exposed to the air as little as possible, to conserve the delicacy, colour and freshness of taste: so do not undo the wrapping until you are ready to use it. And never leave it longer than necessary: eat as soon as possible after it has lost its edge of coldness. Soft fruit, in particular, tends to collapse and lose its shape and flavour if it is allowed to thaw too much. A 1-lb. bag of fruit frozen with sugar will take 2 to 4 hours to thaw at room temperature, rather longer if it has been frozen in syrup, and at least double this time in a refrigerator. But no hard and fast rules can be laid down about times, which vary considerably according to the temperature, the type of fruit and so on.

We have not given the exact quantities of syrup needed for each pound of fruit, because so much depends on the size and type of fruit and the shape of the container. It is useful to keep a jug of syrup in the refrigerator ready for using straight away without the need for allowing it to cool first. Equally the quantities of sugar recommended can only be approximate, since tastes in sweetness vary so much. It is better to freeze with too little sugar than too much, since more can always be added when you come to eat or cook the fruit. For this reason we have given minimum quantities. Bear in mind, however, that fruit tends to lose a little of its sweetness during freezing.

After freezing most fruit tends to produce more juice, so allow for this in making puddings, and especially pies and tarts.

It goes without saying that any food put into the freezer should be scrupulously clean; on the other hand, when soft fruit is washed it inevitably loses some of its juice and flavour. So it is best to use common sense about this. It is important to wash soft fruit which has been lying around in shops, or if there is any risk that it might have been sprayed shortly before picking. Blackberries picked off a dusty hedgerow by the roadside clearly need to be washed, and so do currants if they are speckled with pieces of leaf and aphis. But we shouldn't ourselves dream of washing clean soft fruit straight out of the garden, or glistening blackberries picked early in the season from a hedge in the middle of a field.

Washing, when it is necessary, should be carried out as rapidly as possible, and in ice-cold water, so that the minimum amount of juice is lost.

In many of the fruit recipes we have given the methods for making desserts from frozen as well as from fresh fruit. Sometimes this is much the better method: mousses, soufflés and ices, for instance, tend to deteriorate in texture and flavour if they are kept in the freezer for a long time, whereas if they are freshly made from frozen fruit they are delicious.

PASTRY

Pastry freezes excellently, both cooked and uncooked, and it is one of the most useful items to keep in the freezer. Indeed freezing seems if anything to improve the flavour and texture.

It can be kept in the freezer in several different ways:

1. *Uncooked, in a ball or slab*: freeze in the quantities you most frequently use (see chart below). It will need between 1 and 3 hours, depending on the quantity, at room temperature before it can be rolled out.

2. *Blind flan-cases, cooked or uncooked*: these empty flan-cases are very fragile, and have to be treated with great care in the freezer.

3. *Filled pies or flans, covered or open*: these may be frozen cooked or uncooked, depending on the filling, and the best method will be indicated in each recipe.

Some general rules for cooking pastry dishes before and after freezing

1. Tarts with fruit fillings are not entirely satisfactory, since if the fruit produces a lot of juice the pastry may become soggy. To some extent this can be prevented by baking the pastry blind before you fill it with fruit. The taste of the tarts is not affected by the freezing; it is only the texture of the pastry that sometimes suffers. The exception is apple tart, which freezes perfectly, since the apples make no excess juice.

2. Always put pies and flans direct from the freezer into a hot oven. We have given the approximate cooking time in each recipe, but this will obviously vary a little according to the size of the dish.

3. Even pastry dishes which are to be eaten cold, such as fruit flans, benefit after freezing from $\frac{1}{2}$ hour in a hot oven, before they are left to cool. This crisps up the pastry and does the fillings no harm.

4. Always eat pastry dishes which have been in the freezer as soon as they are ready.

We refer in various recipes throughout the book to shortcrust and sweetened shortcrust pastry, and give suggested recipes below. (Bought frozen pastry is also excellent.) When the filling is sweet, either the sweetened or the unsweetened pastry may be used, unless specifically indicated otherwise.

SHORTCRUST PASTRY

1 lb. flour
pinch of salt
5 oz. lard

4 oz. shortening or margarine
4–5 tbs. cold water

Sift the flour and salt together in a basin, roughly dice the lard and shortening into it, and rub together with the fingertips until the mixture has the consistency of breadcrumbs. Sprinkle on the water and mix together with a knife until you can gather the dough together into a ball. Use as little water as possible.

SWEETENED SHORTCRUST PASTRY

1 lb. flour
2 oz. caster or icing sugar
½ lb. butter or margarine
1 egg

1 tbs. milk
1 tbs. vinegar.
pinch of salt

Sift the flour and salt into a bowl or on to a pastry board and add the sugar and the diced butter or margarine. Make a well in the centre, break the egg into it and add the milk and vinegar. Chop all well together with a palette knife until it is very fine, and finally briefly knead the pastry. When it is quite smooth leave to rest in the refrigerator for 1 hour before using, or freeze.

RICH SWEETENED SHORTCRUST PASTRY

1 lb. flour
4 oz. icing sugar

10 oz. butter
pinch of salt

Sift the flour, icing sugar and salt into a bowl or on to a pastry board. Dice the butter and rub it in with the tips of the fingers until the mixture is like very fine breadcrumbs. Mould it lightly into a ball and leave to rest in the refrigerator for ½ hour before using, or freeze. This pastry is very crumbly, and can be either rolled out in small quantities, or kneaded or patted into flan-tins. It will need rather longer than the others to thaw after freezing.

Amounts of shortcrust pastry needed to line flan-tins

For uncovered tarts:

> To line a 6-in. flan-case allow 4 oz. pastry
> To line a 7-in. flan-case allow 5 oz. pastry
> To line an 8-in. flan-case allow 6 oz. pastry
> To line a 10-in. flan-case allow 10 oz. pastry
> To line a 12-in. flan-case allow 1 lb. pastry

For covered tarts allow about half as much again.

BREAD

Bread is one of the most useful things to have in the freezer. And homemade bread is so infinitely superior to most shop varieties that once you have made your own you will never want anything else. The recipes given here are very easy to make, and the three kinds of bread are all quite different from one another. We have given alternative methods for the white and the wholemeal bread, but you can if you prefer make the brown bread according to the recipe for white bread, or vice versa – use whichever method you find easiest and most successful.

Dried yeast can be used instead of fresh yeast; generally half the quantity is needed, but the instructions on the packet or tin should be followed. However, use fresh yeast if you possibly can, as the bread tastes much better. It freezes well, so you can buy it in bigger quantities and divide it into 1 oz. or 2 oz. portions before freezing.

White Bread

2 oz. fresh yeast
1½ pt warm water
3 lb. unbleached strong white
    flour

2 tsp. salt
2 oz. lard

Dissolve the yeast in the warm water and leave for 10 minutes in a warm place to get frothy. Meanwhile mix the salt into the flour and rub in the fat. Work the yeast mixture into the flour to produce a firm dough which leaves the bowl clean. Place the ball of dough on to a floured surface and knead it for about 10 minutes, until it is firm and elastic and no longer sticky. Return to the bowl, cover with a clean cloth and leave in a warm place to rise (about 1 hour). When the dough has doubled in size knead it once more (it should be very springy this time) and leave for another ½ hour to rise. Divide into as many parts as you wish to make loaves, punch each ball of dough well so as to leave no pockets of air, shape into loaves and place in greased loaf-tins or on a greased baking sheet. Cover once more with a clean cloth and leave to rise for ½ hour, or until the dough begins to flatten slightly. Bake in a hot oven (450°F., gas 8) for 40 to 50 minutes, until the loaves are nicely browned and have shrunk away from the sides of the tins.

To freeze: leave to cool. Wrap and freeze.

To serve after freezing: leave to thaw at room temperature for 5 to 6 hours. If you have to use straight from the freezer place in a hot oven for about ½ hour and leave to cool.

Note: you can keep aside a little of the dough and make a pizza at the same time (see p. 227).

Wholemeal Bread

3 lb. 100% wholemeal flour	2 heaped tsp. barbados sugar
1 tbs. salt	1¾ pt tepid water
1 oz. yeast	a little strong unbleached
1 oz. lard	plain white flour

Put the wholemeal flour in a large mixing bowl and mix in the salt. Place in a warm oven for a few minutes. Meanwhile put the yeast in a small basin with the sugar, and cream them together until they are liquid (this process takes only a minute or two). Pour in a little of the tepid water and stir well together. Remove the mixing bowl from the oven and rub in the lard. Make a well in the centre of the flour, pour in the yeast mixture and stir it into the flour with your fingers or a wooden spoon. Gradually add the rest of the water until all the flour has been mixed into a fairly wet, sticky dough. Knead for 10 minutes, adding a little of the plain white flour from time to time as the dough becomes too sticky to knead easily.

Put the mixing bowl in a warm place for 1 hour for the dough to rise, covered with a cloth. In hot weather it is a good idea to put a piece of polythene – an old polythene bag will do – over the dough, beneath the cloth, to prevent the formation of a skin. Knead again for 1 minute and divide into 3 or 4 equal portions. Place in 3 large or 4 small bread-tins, well greased and warmed. Cover, and leave for a further 20 minutes to rise. Place in the middle of a hot oven (450°F., gas 8). After 30 minutes turn the heat down to 350°F., gas 4, and cook for a further 15 to 20 minutes.

To freeze: leave to cool. Wrap and freeze.

To serve after freezing: thaw at room temperature for 5 to 6 hours.

Note: this bread is excellent if it is made with virtually no kneading at all. When you add the water to the flour, simply mix it in firmly with your fingers until the dough comes away from the side of the basin and forms a neat ball. Put straight into the warmed and greased bread-tins, leave to rise for 1 hour, and bake as above. The loaves will not rise quite so much and the bread will be slightly stickier and heavier, but the taste is delicious.

Scofa Bread

The advantage of scofa bread is that it doesn't need yeast. This recipe is a modified version of the one given on the packets of scofa flour, and produces a lighter, tastier loaf.

3 lb. scofa flour	2 small tsp. baking powder
1 generous tsp. salt	$\frac{3}{4}$ pt cold milk (sour milk is
2 tbs. brown sugar	excellent)
2 oz. lard	$\frac{3}{4}$ pt cold water

Mix together the flour, salt and sugar and rub in the lard. Add the baking powder. Pour in the milk and the water and mix well. The mixture should not be stiff, so add a little more liquid if necessary, until the dough is fairly slack. Turn out on to a floured board, shape into a flattish round and cut it into 6 triangular shapes. Put these on to floured baking tins and place at once in the middle of a hot oven (425°F., gas 7). Bake until the loaves are light brown and crusty.

To freeze: leave to cool. Wrap and freeze.

To serve after freezing: thaw at room temperature for 4 to 5 hours.

ICE-CREAMS, WATER-ICES AND SORBETS

A constant supply of homemade ices – which are invariably better and usually cheaper than the bought variety – is one of the chief joys of owning a freezer.

General rules for ices

Ice-creams keep well in the freezer for about a month, after that they tend to become grainy, and the flavour may suffer.

Water-ices keep well for 2 to 3 weeks.

If an ice has been kept too long in the freezer and has lost its smooth texture, leave it at room temperature for about ½ hour for water-ices, or 1 hour for ice-creams, beat well in a blender or mixer and return to the freezer for 3 to 4 hours before serving.

Ices made with fruit will keep well for the periods indicated above, but they are at their best when freshly made. So during the soft-fruit season make only the ices you will eat immediately, and freeze as much fruit purée as you can. You can then make fresh-tasting ices throughout the winter months for eating straight away, as the sweetened fruit purées keep remarkably well in the freezer.

Ice-creams made only with cream and fruit or flavouring

should be taken out of the freezer 1 hour before serving and kept in the refrigerator, in order to soften a little. Egg-based ice-creams, water-ices and sorbets should be taken out of the freezer and kept at room temperature for 15 minutes before serving.

STAND-BYS TO KEEP IN
THE FREEZER

Bacon. This can often be bought cheaply in a piece and cut into 4-oz. chunks before freezing, for use in casseroles, etc.

Bread (see p. 29).

Breadcrumbs (fresh).

Bouquets garnis (see p. 116).

Butter.

Cream. This can be bought ready frozen or you can freeze ordinary dairy cream. Fresh double cream should have a little sugar mixed in before freezing, and should be stirred well or whipped before serving. Single cream is not satisfactory frozen.

Ice-cream.

Ice-cubes. If these are spread out on a baking tray and left in the freezer for 1 or 2 hours before packing in polythene bags, they will not stick together.

Lemons. For grating and juice.

Meringues.

Milk (in cartons).

Mushrooms in air-tight pannets.

Pancakes.

Pastry.

Cooked rice. Frozen in small quantities, this is useful for stuffing poultry and game, pimentoes, tomatoes, etc.

Stock.

Tomato sauce (see p. 231).

Vol-au-vent cases (uncooked).
One good cooked meal for unexpected guests.

The following do not freeze successfully:

Mayonnaise.
Eggs in the shell.
Hard-boiled eggs.
A few salad vegetables and some fruit (see pp. 24, 25).

SAFETY RULES

All food should be frozen while it is still absolutely fresh – never leave it lying about in the kitchen.

Cooked food should be allowed to cool and should then be frozen immediately.

All frozen food should be eaten or cooked as soon as possible after it comes out of the freezer.

If food needs to be thawed, put it in a cool, clean place. The refrigerator is best from the point of view of hygiene, but the thawing process can be so interminable that sometimes a cool larder is more practical.

Once meat and fish have thawed do not refreeze them unless they have been cooked in the meantime.

It is perfectly safe to freeze vegetables and fruit twice, but there is nothing to be said for doing so, since the flavour and texture both suffer.

USING THIS BOOK

The instructions and recipes in this book have been divided into three categories, [A], [B] and [C]:

[A] – Methods of freezing raw ingredients
[B] – Recipes for dishes which are cooked or prepared before freezing
[C] – Recipes for using frozen raw materials

The key letter is put at the left of each recipe. Sometimes a recipe can be made equally well from fresh materials and frozen, or from frozen raw materials for eating immediately: we have classified these recipes as '[B/C]'.

Since one of the most valuable ways of using a freezer is to work on the principle of 'make two – eat one – freeze one', we have wherever relevant given instructions both for immediate eating and for freezing. In some recipes one or two of the ingredients appear in bold italic; this means that they should be added just before serving, and so, if the dish is for the freezer, should be added *after* freezing.

January

PHEASANT

The season lasts from October to February, but the price generally drops considerably after Christmas, so we have included pheasant in January.

If you have some birds which you do not want to cook immediately, pluck and draw them, and freeze them wrapped separately in foil, polythene film or tissue.

[B/C]   *Roast Pheasant*

If you have a plump young pheasant the simplest, and one of the most delicious, ways to cook it is to roast it. There is little to choose in taste between a bird that has been frozen raw and then roasted and one which is roasted first and then frozen. So it is mostly a matter of convenience which you decide to do.

To roast: pluck and draw the pheasant and wipe it inside and out. If you are using a frozen bird, allow it to thaw thoroughly, preferably overnight in the refrigerator.

Cover the breast with slices of streaky bacon and roast in a moderate oven (350°F., gas 4) for 50 to 60 minutes. About 10 minutes before serving remove the bacon, sprinkle a little flour over the breast, baste it and return it to the oven. Baste once or twice more to give it a crisp brown skin.

To serve immediately: traditionally pheasant is served with game chips, fried breadcrumbs, bread sauce, redcurrant jelly and gravy. Braised chestnuts and glazed onions are also excellent (see pp. 279 and 194).

To freeze: allow to cool, scrape up all the juices which will have gelled, and spread them over the breast of the bird. Freeze wrapped in foil, polythene film or tissue.

To serve after freezing: allow to thaw at least 5 hours at room temperature or overnight in a refrigerator. Heat for 30 to 40 minutes in a moderate oven (350°F., gas 4) and serve as above.

[B/C] *Normandy Pheasant*

2 pheasants
4 oz. butter
1 onion
4 medium cooking apples
1 small glass calvados or
  brandy

¼ pt stock
½ pt single cream
salt and pepper

If you are using pheasants from the freezer, allow them to thaw before cooking.

Melt the butter in a flameproof casserole and brown the birds on all sides. Lift them out, and sauté the chopped onion and the peeled and chopped apples until they are slightly soft. Replace the pheasants on top, pour over the calvados or brandy and set it alight. Douse with the stock and cream. Season, cover the casserole and cook over a very low heat, or in a moderate oven (350°F., gas 4), for 40–50 minutes or until the birds are tender. Adjust the seasoning, and if the apples were very sour you may like to add a pinch of sugar.

The sauce should now be fairly smooth, but if you like you can lift out the pheasants and pass it through a sieve.

To serve immediately: carve the pheasants, replace in the casserole with the sauce, warm through and serve.

To freeze: allow to cool and freeze in foil or plastic containers.

To serve after freezing: Thaw in the refrigerator overnight or for at least 5 hours at room temperature. Heat gently in the casserole on top of the stove or in a low oven (325°F., gas 3) for about 40 minutes. If you have to use it straight from the freezer, allow at least 2½ hours in a low oven.

[B/C] *Pheasant à la Crème*

2 pheasants	a pinch of thyme and 1 bayleaf
1 oz. butter	2 tbs. brandy
1 tbs. olive oil	½ pt double cream
2 medium onions	salt and pepper
2 carrots	

If you are using pheasants from the freezer, allow them to thaw before cooking.

Melt the butter and oil in a flameproof casserole and brown the pheasants all over. Add the finely chopped onions and carrots, and the thyme and bayleaf. Cover the casserole and leave it on a very low heat for 20 minutes. Warm the brandy in a spoon, pour it over the pheasants and set it alight. Douse with the cream. Season, cover the casserole again and continue to simmer until the pheasants are tender – probably another 30 minutes. Test for seasoning, remove the bayleaf and serve.

To freeze : allow to cool and freeze in foil or plastic containers.

To serve after freezing : thaw in the refrigerator overnight or for at least 5 hours at room temperature. Heat gently in the casserole on top of the stove or in a low oven (325°F., gas 3) for about 40 minutes. If you have to use straight from the freezer, allow at least 2½ hours in a low oven.

[B/C] *Pheasant with Herbs*

This dish goes well with natural (brown) rice, which can be obtained from health-food shops and many large grocers.

2 pheasants	½ tsp. thyme
1 onion	⅜ pt white wine
2 oz. butter	2 tbs. cream
8 cloves garlic	1 tbs. chopped parsley
6 bay leaves	salt and pepper

If you are using frozen pheasants, allow them to thaw before cooking.

Cut the pheasants into serving pieces and make a stock with the carcasses and the onion. While this is simmering, season the pieces of pheasant and brown them gently in the butter in a flameproof casserole. Add the whole cloves of garlic, bay leaves, thyme, and wine. Cover the casserole and simmer until the pheasants are tender – about 30 minutes, but longer may be necessary if they are on the tough side. When they are done take them out (and for immediate eating put them on a serving dish and keep warm). Remove the garlic and bay leaves from the juice in the casserole and add ½ to ¾ pint of the stock, according to how much sauce you like. Add the cream, bring to the boil and stir until the sauce is smooth. Sprinkle on the parsley.

To serve immediately: test the sauce for seasoning, pour it over the pheasants and serve.

To freeze: allow to cool and freeze in foil or plastic containers, or see method 4 on p. 17.

To serve after freezing: tip the frozen pheasants into a flameproof casserole or heavy pan and warm through over a very gentle heat, stirring from time to time. Allow 30 to 40 minutes for this.

[B/C]   *Pheasant Casserole with Mushrooms*

2 pheasants	2 cloves garlic
2 tbs. olive oil	½ pt stock
2 oz. butter	1 lb. button mushrooms, fresh,
1 medium onion	or frozen raw or blanched

Stuffing

4 oz. cooked ham	2 tbs. brandy (optional)
4 tbs. cooked rice	1 egg
thyme and marjoram	salt and pepper

If you are using frozen pheasants allow them to thaw before cooking. Mushrooms can be used straight from the freezer.

Make the stuffing first. Chop the ham finely, add the rice

42

and the herbs, season, and mix with the brandy and enough egg to make the mixture soft but not mushy. Stuff the pheasants, truss them firmly, and brown them well in a flameproof casserole in the oil and half the butter, with the finely chopped onion and the garlic. Add the stock, cover the casserole and place in a slow oven (300°F., gas 2) until the birds are nearly cooked (about 2 hours). Meanwhile sauté the whole mushrooms in the rest of the butter. Season, and add to the casserole at the end of the cooking. The dish is now ready to serve.

To freeze: allow to cool and freeze in foil or plastic containers.

To serve after freezing: thaw in the refrigerator overnight or for at least 5 hours at room temperature. Heat gently in the casserole on top of the stove or in a low oven (325°F., gas 3) for about 40 minutes. If you have to use straight from the freezer, allow at least 2½ hours in a low oven.

If there is any left over, it is delicious cold – and the stuffing makes the pheasants go much further than they would otherwise do.

[B/C] *Pheasant Pâté*

This is a good way of using any leftover roast pheasant – adjust the other ingredients according to the amount of pheasant you are using. If you are making it from frozen roasted pheasant, do not freeze the pâté.

1 pheasant	1 large onion
1 lb. veal (pie veal will do)	2 cloves garlic
1 lb. chicken livers	2 tbs. brandy
4 oz. butter	salt, pepper, bayleaf

Roast the pheasant as described on p. 39, and put the veal into the oven with it for ½ hour. Gently sauté the chicken livers in 2 oz. of the butter. Strip the meat off the pheasant and mince it with the veal and the chicken livers.

Finely chop the onion and the garlic and add to the meat.

Blend in the cooking liquid from the chicken livers, the rest of the butter, softened, and the brandy. Season and mix well.

To serve immediately: put into pâté dishes and chill for a few hours before serving. Place a bayleaf on top of each pâté.

To freeze: freeze in foil or plastic containers or see methods 2 or 3 on p. 17.

To serve after freezing: allow to thaw for 5 to 6 hours at room temperature or overnight in the refrigerator.

JERUSALEM ARTICHOKES

[A] *To freeze blanched:* peel the artichokes and cut them into pieces roughly the same size. Blanch for 3 minutes. Drain, cool and freeze in polythene bags.

To freeze puréed: peel the artichokes and cut them into pieces roughly the same size. Cook them in a little salted water or stock until they are soft. Drain very thoroughly and pass through a blender or mouli. Allow to cool and freeze in waxed or plastic containers.

[C] *To serve after freezing blanched:* turn the frozen artichokes into a saucepan with a tablespoon or so of water – just enough to keep them from catching – and a knob of butter. Season, and cook very gently until they are soft.

Tomato purée made from fresh tomatoes (see p. 225) goes well with Jerusalem artichokes. Warm up a little – about $\frac{1}{4}$ pint to 1 lb. artichokes – and pour over just before serving.

To serve after freezing puréed: turn the frozen purée into a saucepan, add a knob of butter, and warm through over a very gentle heat, stirring from time to time. Add pepper, and more salt if necessary. You can also add a little cream or top of the milk, or some fresh tomato purée (see p. 225). Or add one or two fresh tomatoes, in the proportion of 1 medium tomato to $\frac{1}{2}$ pint purée. Skin the tomatoes, cut them up roughly, and stir them into the purée as it is getting hot.

[B/C]   *Artichoke Soup*

3 lb. artichokes   2 pts chicken stock
1 oz. butter   salt and pepper
1 onion

½ *pt milk*
a little cream and parsley for serving (optional)

If you are using frozen artichokes, there is no need to wait for
them to thaw.

Peel and cut the fresh artichokes into roughly equal pieces.
Melt the butter in a heavy saucepan, sweat the chopped onion
in it for a few minutes, add the artichokes and allow to cook for
another minute or two. Pour on the stock, season and simmer
gently until the artichokes are cooked. Pass through a blender,
mouli or sieve.

To serve immediately: return the soup to the stove and add
the milk. Test for seasoning. Serve hot, adding if you like a
spoonful of cream and a sprinkling of parsley to each
helping.

To freeze: allow to cool and freeze in plastic or waxed
containers.

To serve after freezing: tip the frozen soup into a saucepan, add
the milk, heat gently and serve as above.

See also Scallop and Artichoke Soup (p. 267).

[B/C]   *Braised Artichokes*

2 lb. artichokes   1 tbs. sugar
1 lb. button onions   salt and pepper
1 oz. butter

If you are using frozen artichokes, there is no need to wait for
them to thaw.

Peel and cut the fresh artichokes into roughly equal pieces.
Peel the onions. In a heavy saucepan or flameproof casserole

melt the butter, add the sugar and stir. Add the artichokes and onions, cover, and leave to braise over a very low heat for about 40 minutes, or until the artichokes and onions are tender and golden brown (frozen artichokes will not take quite so long). Stir occasionally to ensure even browning. Season with salt and plenty of freshly ground pepper. Serve.

To freeze: cool and freeze in waxed or plastic containers or polythene bags.

To serve after freezing: It is important that the artichokes should not become puréed in the reheating, so they should be allowed to thaw for about 4 hours at room temperature, and then heated in a moderate oven (350°F., gas 4) for $\frac{1}{2}$ hour. Do not heat them in a saucepan, as they might become mushy when stirred.

LEEKS

Leeks are a splendid and versatile vegetable, and are useful for incorporating in any number of recipes, so it is worth while having in your freezer as many bags of them as possible.

[A] *To freeze blanched:* trim off the coarse outer leaves and tops and wash thoroughly. This can be done by slitting the leeks down the top for 3 or 4 inches and running cold water through the leaves. Blanch for 3 or 4 minutes, according to size. Drain, cool and freeze in polythene bags.

Freeze some also ready cut into 1-inch slices, which will save trouble later on. In this case they will only need to be blanched for 2 minutes. Pack them in small quantities – $\frac{1}{2}$ lb. in each bag is probably quite enough.

[C] *To serve after freezing:* put the frozen leeks in a little boiling salted water. As they start to soften, break up the mass gently with a fork. As soon as they are soft, drain well and serve with a knob of butter, a spoonful of cream or a béchamel sauce.

[B/C]   *Vichyssoise*

This is well worth making in large quantities, as it can not only be eaten hot in the winter, but also makes a delicious cold soup for the summer, sprinkled with fresh chives.

2 lb. fresh leeks or 1½ lb. frozen sliced	2 medium potatoes
1 medium onion	2 pts chicken or veal stock
1 oz. butter	salt and pepper

½ pt single cream
chives

If you are using frozen leeks, there is no need to wait for them to thaw. Mince the onion and sweat it for 5 minutes in the butter. Add the sliced leeks and the peeled potatoes cut into small cubes. Stew gently in the butter for a further 5 minutes. Add the stock, bring to near boiling point, season, cover, and simmer for 20 minutes or until the leeks are cooked. Put through a blender, mouli or sieve.

To serve immediately:

   To serve hot – reheat gently, add the cream and test for seasoning.

   To serve cold – stir in the cream, chill, and serve with a sprinkling of chopped chives or chervil.

To freeze: cool and pack in plastic or waxed containers.

To serve after freezing:

   To serve hot – turn the frozen soup into a saucepan, reheat it gently and proceed as above.

   To serve cold – allow to thaw at room temperature or in a refrigerator. Stir in the cream when the soup has thawed. If necessary, chill again in the refrigerator and serve as above.

[B/C]   *Leek, Tomato and Potato Soup*

1 lb. fresh leeks or ¾ lb. frozen   1½ lb. potatoes
   sliced   1 tbs. sugar
2 oz. butter   2 pts water
1 lb. tomatoes   salt and pepper

3 tbs. cream or top of the milk
parsley

If you are using frozen vegetables, there is no need to wait for
them to thaw.

Cook the sliced leeks gently in the butter in a heavy saucepan.
Add the peeled tomatoes and cook for a few more minutes
before putting in the peeled and diced potatoes. Season, add the
sugar, and stir well. Add the water, and cook until the potatoes
are soft (about ½ hour). Put through a blender, mouli or sieve
and test for seasoning. You may want to add a little more sugar.

To serve immediately: bring to the boil again, stir in the cream
or top of the milk, and sprinkle a little finely chopped parsley
over each portion.

To freeze: cool and freeze in plastic or waxed containers.

To serve after freezing: turn the frozen soup into a saucepan,
cover, and cook gently until it boils. Add the cream or top of
the milk and parsley as above, and serve.

[C]   *Leek and Mutton Hotpot*

12 neck chops   3 oz. pearl barley
1½ lb. leeks frozen sliced   salt and pepper
2 carrots

Put the chops into a saucepan and just cover with cold water. If
you have taken the meat from the freezer, it is best to use it
immediately, so that the juices will go into the stock, but make
sure that the water does not reach boiling point before the
meat has completely thawed. Bring slowly to the boil and skim.

Cut the carrots into thin strips and add to the pan, together with the pearl barley. Season, and cook until the meat is tender (about ¾ hour). Cool, and take the fat off the top. Bring gently to the boil again, add the frozen leeks, and simmer until they are soft (15 to 20 minutes). Test for seasoning. The dish is now ready to serve.

If fresh leeks are used, about 2 lb. will be needed.

[B/C] *Leek Pie*

1 lb. fresh leeks or ¾ lb. frozen sliced	2 oz. butter
	2 egg yolks
10 oz. shortcrust pastry (see p. 28)	2 tbs. cream
	salt and pepper

If you are using frozen leeks there is no need to wait for them to thaw.

Flour an 8-inch flan-case and line it with the pastry, keeping aside enough for the top. If the pie is to be frozen, use a foil dish or see p. 18.

Cook the sliced leeks gently in the butter until they are soft. Add them to the beaten yolks and stir in the cream. Season.

To serve immediately: pour the mixture into the flan-case and cover with the rest of the pastry. Cook in a fairly hot oven (400°F., gas 6) until the pastry is done – about 45 minutes. Serve very hot.

To freeze: allow the mixture to cool and when it is quite cold pour it into the flan-case and cover with the rest of the pastry. If you have used a foil dish wrap well before freezing. Otherwise, see p. 18.

To serve after freezing: place the frozen pie in a hot oven (450°F., gas 8). After 30 minutes turn the oven down to 350°F., gas 4, and cook for a further 30 minutes, or until the pastry is lightly browned. Serve very hot.

Any that is left over will be excellent cold the next day.

[B/C] *Leek Quiche*

2 lb. fresh leeks or 1½ lb. frozen sliced

10 oz. shortcrust pastry (see p. 28)

4 oz. bacon, ham or salt pork, preferably bought in a piece

½ pt stock

4 eggs

¼ pt double cream

salt and pepper

If you are using frozen leeks there is no need to wait for them to thaw.

Butter one 10-inch or two 7-inch flan-tins. If you are freezing the quiches, use foil flan-cases or see methods 2 or 3 on p. 18. Line the tins with the pastry.

Dice the bacon, ham or pork and put it into a saucepan with the sliced leeks. Add the stock and simmer together for about 20 minutes. When the leeks are tender but not mushy drain them and reserve the liquid. Spread the leek and bacon mixture over the pastry cases.

Beat the eggs lightly in a basin, add the cream and season, but be careful not to oversalt in case the bacon is very salty. Beat in not more than ¼ pint of the reserved stock and pour this mixture over the leeks. Cook in a medium oven (375°F., gas 5) for 40 minutes.

To serve immediately: cook for a further 5 minutes, until the top is golden brown.

To freeze: allow to cool. If you have used a foil flan-case wrap it well before freezing. Otherwise, see p. 18.

To serve after freezing: place the frozen quiche in a hot oven (425°F., gas 7). After 20 minutes lower the temperature to 350°F., gas 4, and leave for a further 30 to 40 minutes, according to the size of the quiche, until it has heated right through. Place a piece of foil over the top if necessary, to prevent excessive browning.

[C]   *Poireaux en Hachis*

This is a useful dish which is quite filling enough to provide the main course for supper. It should be served with hot mashed potatoes.

1½ lb. leeks frozen sliced	2 egg yolks
2 oz. butter	1–2 tbs. milk
1 dsp. flour	salt, pepper and a shake of
¼ pt double cream	nutmeg

Cook the frozen leeks in a little salted water until they are tender, and drain them very thoroughly. Put the butter in a saucepan, and when it has melted add the leeks, the seasoning and the nutmeg. Sprinkle on the flour and stir well over a gentle heat until the leeks are very hot. Add the cream, and continue to stir over the heat for 2 to 3 minutes. Mix the yolks with the milk and add them to the saucepan. Test for seasoning, put on to a very hot dish, and surround the leeks with a border of mashed potatoes.

If you make this dish with fresh leeks, you will need 2 lb.

[C]   *Leeks à la Provençale*

This dish is served cold as a salad or hors d'oeuvre.

1½ lb. leeks frozen sliced	2 oz. black olives
2 tsp. olive oil	1 lemon (juice and rind)
½ lb. tomatoes	salt and pepper

Heat the oil in a shallow flameproof dish and add the frozen leeks. Cook them gently for about 10 minutes, breaking them up with a fork, until they have quite separated. Add the peeled and chopped tomatoes, the stoned olives, and the juice and finely grated peel of the lemon, and cook for a further 10 minutes, or until the leeks are soft but not mushy. Season to taste, allow to cool and serve.

If you make this dish with fresh leeks you will need 2 lb.

SEVILLE ORANGES

These are available in the shops for only a very short period, so if you do not have time to make marmalade immediately, or if you particularly like the taste of freshly made marmalade, freeze them and make the marmalade at your convenience.

[A] *To freeze:* freeze whole in polythene bags.

[C] *For use after freezing:* most people have their favourite method for making marmalade, and frozen citrus fruit can be used in any recipe. If you normally cut up the fruit before cooking, allow it to half-thaw for 2 to 3 hours, by which time it will be ready to slice or shred but will not be too squashy.

We give one recipe which is particularly easy to make from frozen fruit, as the fruit does not need to be thawed at all but can be used straight from the freezer and is only sliced after it has simmered for some time. We give it as a three-fruit marmalade, but it can be made with any combination of citrus fruits or with Seville oranges alone.

[C]   *Three Fruits Marmalade*

2 lb. Seville oranges ⎫
3 sweet oranges   ⎬ or 3 lb. fruit in all
2 lemons   ⎭
6 pts water
6 lb. sugar

Put the frozen fruit, whole, into a preserving pan with the water and simmer, uncovered, for 2 to 2½ hours, or until the fruit is soft. Take the fruit out one by one, starting with the lemons which will probably be soft first, then the sweet oranges and lastly the

Seville oranges, and slice or shred each one, putting the fruit in a basin and returning the pips to the pan so that they can continue to simmer with the remaining fruit. When all the fruit has been cut up leave the pips to simmer for a further 10 minutes and then either remove them with a slotted spoon or strain the liquid. Return the fruit and the liquid to the pan, simmer for another 10 minutes, add the sugar and bring to boiling point. Stir well until all the sugar has dissolved, and boil fast until the marmalade begins to set. This may take anything between 10 minutes and $\frac{1}{2}$ hour.

Yield: about 10 lb.

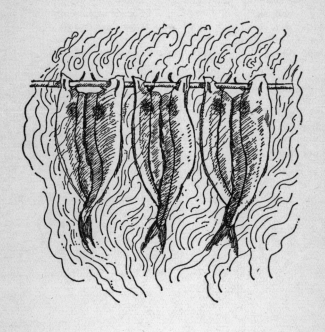

SMOKED HADDOCK

This is the time of the year for young haddocks (or Finnans, as they are called in Scotland). Like most fish, haddock are not worth freezing in their natural state unless they are straight from the sea, but smoked haddock is particularly succulent now. Stored in the freezer in a creamy sauce, as in the recipe given below, it can be used later to make impromptu supper dishes. It is especially good combined with eggs.

[B]   *Smoked Haddock in Cream Sauce*

2 lb. smoked haddock	2 oz. butter
1 pt milk	2 oz. flour
1 onion	pepper

parsley

Place the haddock in a large saucepan, skin side up to prevent it from sticking, cover with the milk and add the onion cut in quarters. Bring to the boil, cover closely and remove from the heat. Leave for ½ hour, by which time the fish should be cooked and cool enough to handle. Lift it out and flake it, carefully removing first the skin and any bones.

Make a sauce with the butter, the flour and the strained milk in which the fish was cooked. When the sauce has thickened add the fish.

To serve immediately : test for seasoning – it is very unlikely to need any salt – and add some finely chopped parsley. Serve with rice.

To freeze : cool and freeze in plastic or waxed containers. It is useful to divide the mixture into 4 equal quantities for making any of the recipes given below.

To serve after freezing: tip the frozen haddock into a saucepan, heat gently and proceed as for immediate eating.

[C]   *Smoked Haddock Soufflé*

½ pt smoked haddock in cream sauce (¼ of the quantity given on p. 57)
1 oz. butter
1 oz. flour
¼ pt milk
1 oz. grated cheese
2 egg yolks
4 egg whites
pepper

Make a white sauce with the butter, flour and milk, stir in the frozen haddock and warm through thoroughly. Stir in the grated cheese and then the egg yolks. Add the pepper and test for seasoning, adding a little salt if necessary. Whip the egg whites until they are stiff, fold them into the haddock mixture, pour it into a buttered soufflé dish and cook in a moderate oven (375°F., gas 5) for 35 to 40 minutes. The top should be well risen and browned and the inside still quite creamy. Serve at once.

[C]   *Omelette Arnold Bennett*

2 eggs per person
1 tbs. smoked haddock in cream sauce per person (see p. 57)
salt and pepper

Tip the frozen haddock into a saucepan and heat gently. Make an omelette in the usual way, adding a good tablespoon of the warmed haddock mixture to the lightly beaten eggs. You may find this omelette too bulky to fold over, in which case you can finish it off under a hot grill. Or put a tablespoon of the haddock into the centre of the omelette just as it is beginning to set, fold over and serve.

[B/C] *Smoked Haddock Mousse*

1 lb smoked haddock in
  cream sauce (half the
  quantity given on p. 57)
½ oz. gelatine
⅛ pt water

¼ pt mayonnaise
2 hard-boiled eggs
⅛ pt double cream
salt and pepper

2 hard boiled eggs
parsley (optional)
½ pt aspic jelly

This mousse should not be frozen if it is made from frozen creamed haddock.

Turn the creamed haddock into a large bowl. If you are using the mixture from the freezer, allow it to thaw. Melt the gelatine in the water, heat gently, and when all the gelatine has dissolved stir into the haddock. Add the mayonnaise and 2 hard-boiled eggs, finely chopped or mashed. Season. Lightly whip the cream and fold it into the mixture.

For immediate eating: turn the mixture into a soufflé dish and leave to set. Slice the remaining eggs and arrange them on the top. A few tiny sprigs of parsley can be added to make the mousse look pretty. Make up ½ pint aspic jelly, and when it is cold pour over enough to cover the eggs. Leave for a couple of hours for the aspic to set.

To freeze: see methods 2, 3 or 4 on p. 17.

To serve after freezing: return the frozen mousse to the soufflé dish and allow to thaw for 3 to 4 hours. Then complete as for immediate eating.

[B] *Arbroath Smokies*

These are young haddocks left whole and hot-smoked to a dark tarry colour. Like the Finnan haddock, they are at their freshest and best at this time of the year.

The quantity given below is enough for a starter for 6, or a supper dish for 2.

2 Arbroath smokies	**1 oz. grated cheese**
2 onions	**½ pt double cream**
½ lb. tomatoes	**pepper**

Flake the flesh of the smokies and set aside. Grate or finely chop the onions and put half into a small casserole. For freezing, use a foil dish or see method 2 on p. 17. Pile on the fish, add the remaining onions and season well with freshly ground black pepper. Cover with a single layer of sliced tomatoes, sprinkle the grated cheese over these and pour in the cream. Place in a medium oven (375°F., gas 5) for 20 minutes.

To serve immediately: leave in the oven for a further 10 minutes, until the top is lightly browned.

To freeze: allow to cool. If you have used a foil dish, wrap well and freeze. Otherwise see p. 17.

To serve after freezing: place the frozen smokies in a hot oven (425°F., gas 7) for 20 minutes, lower the oven to 350°F., gas 4, and continue to cook for a further 30 to 40 minutes, until the dish is hot right through.

WINTER WARMERS

[B]   *Bean Soup*

This typical Italian soup is a meal in itself for cold weather. It should really be made from burlotti beans (see recipe for cassoulet, p. 61), which give it a delicious flavour and a rich brown colour. However, if these are unobtainable, you can also make it with haricot beans, relying on the parsley to provide the colour. These quantities will serve 8 to 10 people.

1 lb. burlotti or haricot beans
3 pts water
1 medium onion
1 medium potato

1 clove garlic
1 tbs. olive oil
approx. 2 oz. spaghetti
salt and pepper

chopped parsley
olive oil

Soak the beans overnight. Drain off the water, put the beans in a large saucepan with 4 pints of cold water, cover, and cook them until they are soft, which will take 1½ to 2 hours. Meanwhile slice the onion, cut the peeled potato into small dice, chop the garlic finely and sauté all together gently in the olive oil in a large pan until they are tender. When the beans are ready, purée half of them with the water in which they were cooked. Then add the rest of the beans and the purée to the onion and potato and bring to the boil. Break up the spaghetti roughly and add; season, and cook for another 20 minutes.

To serve immediately: just before serving, add plenty of chopped parsley and test for seasoning. The Italian custom is to hand round olive oil, so that everyone can pour a spoonful into his serving and mix it in, which gives the soup its characteristic taste and consistency. But the olive oil must be a rich one, best of all the lovely green-tinged variety.

To freeze: allow to cool and freeze in waxed or plastic containers.

To serve after freezing: tip the frozen soup into a saucepan and bring gently to the boil, stirring now and then. Serve with chopped parsley and olive oil, as above.

[B/C]   *Cassoulet*

This splendid and succulent dish freezes excellently. It is warming for the cold winter months, and is useful for making ahead of time for a party. The whole of the cooking can be done beforehand, and on the day all that is necessary is to heat the dish up.

The quantities given below are sufficient for 10 to 12 people, and a very large casserole, holding about 7 pints, will be needed. Special earthenware casseroles for making cassoulet can be bought, and as they are not expensive they are worth investing in, since they are useful for many other purposes.

Cassoulet can be made in several different ways, one probably as good as another. The important point is to see that there are enough, but not too many, beans: too few will mean that the cassoulet lacks body and flavour, too many that it is stodgy. Also, make sure that it doesn't dry up during the prolonged cooking: if it does, add water or stock.

The following recipe can be varied by substituting pork for some of the lamb. Or instead of the shoulder a cheaper joint of lamb can be used, such as middle neck. In the classic recipes preserved goose is used, but for most people this is too expensive and too difficult to obtain, and it is not necessary. The garlic sausage, however, is essential. Instead of haricot beans the small Italian brown-flecked beans known as burlotti are excellent.

2 lb. white haricot beans (not butter beans)	2 onions
	2 tbs. oil or dripping
a small piece (about 6 oz.) of fat bacon or salt pork	3 cloves garlic
	$\frac{1}{2}$ lb. tomatoes
$\frac{1}{2}$ shoulder of lamb (about 2 lb.)	bouquet garni
	$\frac{1}{2}$ lb. fresh breadcrumbs
1 lb. garlic sausage in one piece	salt and pepper

If you are using frozen lamb it should be allowed to thaw before cooking. Tomatoes can be used straight from the freezer.

Put the beans into a large saucepan and fill it with as much cold water as it will hold. Cover, bring to the boil, simmer for 5 minutes, then take off the stove and leave with the lid on for about 45 minutes.

In the meantime remove the rind as thinly as possible from the bacon or pork. Cut the rind into small squares. Slice the onions. Heat the oil or dripping in a large frying-pan and fry the onions, the garlic, the pieces of rind, the bacon or pork, and the whole piece of lamb for a few minutes.

After the beans have soaked for 45 minutes, drain them, and put them back in the saucepan with 3 pints of cold water. Bring to the boil and then pour them, with their cooking liquid, into the cassoulet casserole. Add the contents of the frying pan, as well as the skinned tomatoes, the whole garlic sausage and the bouquet garni. Season well. Finally sprinkle the crumbs on top.

Cook in a very low oven (250°F., gas 1). The pan should be uncovered, and cooking should be long and slow, taking at least 6 hours. Best of all is to give the cassoulet two or three successive cookings of about 3 hours, each time pressing down the layer of crust which forms on the top, and adding more water if necessary.

To serve immediately: when you are ready for the cassoulet (rather than the other way round), take out the lamb and the sausage. The piece of bacon or pork will probably have disintegrated. Bone the lamb and cut the meat and the sausage into convenient pieces for eating. Put back into the casserole, test for seasoning, warm through again, and serve.

To freeze: allow to cool and freeze in plastic containers or very strong polythene bags. It is better to freeze the cassoulet in more than one container, since otherwise the bulk is so great that it takes an unnecessarily long time to thaw.

To serve after freezing: take the cassoulet out of the freezer well before you want to eat it – the day before is not too long – and thaw at room temperature. Turn it into the cassoulet casserole and heat up very gently, uncovered, in a slowish oven (325°F., gas 3) for at least 2 hours or on top of the stove on an asbestos mat. Take out the meat, bone it and cut it into convenient pieces, cut up the sausage, put all the meat back into the casserole, and finish warming through before serving.

Any that is left over will be excellent warmed up next day; but if you make this dish for freezing it is important not to cut up the meat and sausage until just before serving, as otherwise the cassoulet loses its character and the beans and meat become too much amalgamated.

[B]   *Pork and Sauerkraut Goulash*

A warming, filling and inexpensive dish, which is easy to make in large quantities and freezes excellently. It should be served with freshly boiled potatoes or with chunks of black bread and chilled white wine or cider. The quantities given here will serve 10 to 12 people.

3 lb. shoulder or belly of pork	1 lb. peeled tomatoes
3 lb. sauerkraut	1 oz. flour
1 tbs. oil	1 tbs. water
1 lb. onions	¼ pt (1 carton) sour cream
2 cloves garlic	salt and pepper
approx. 1 tbs. paprika	
approx. 1 tbs. caraway seeds (optional)	

Heat the oil in a large flameproof casserole and sauté the roughly chopped onions and garlic until they are soft. Add the meat cut into dice and fry all together until golden brown. Add the paprika – it is impossible to give precise quantities for this as the strength varies so much – and the chopped caraway seeds and stir well (chopping the caraway seeds brings out the flavour). Add the drained sauerkraut and the roughly chopped tomatoes, season and stir. Cover and simmer for at least 1 hour, adding a little water if necessary to prevent it from catching. The dish is ready to serve when the sauerkraut is tender, but you can go on cooking it almost indefinitely, until you are ready to eat it. Just before serving mix the flour, water and sour cream in a cup, pour over the goulash and cook for 5 minutes more, stirring well.

To serve immediately: test for seasoning, adding a little more paprika if it is not strong enough, and serve.

To freeze: allow to cool and freeze in plastic containers or polythene bags, or see method 4 on p. 17.

To serve after freezing: tip the frozen goulash into a flame-proof casserole and heat through well, adding a little more water if necessary to prevent it from catching. Allow at least an hour for this. Test for seasoning, adding a little more paprika if necessary, and serve.

VEAL

[B] *Veal Goulash*

The veal for this dish can be cut from the shoulder or breast, or bought from many butchers already cut off the bone and sold as pie veal. The advantage of buying it on the bone is that you can then make wonderful jellied veal stock from the bones, for use in this and many other recipes. You can also use braising beef but the result will be less delicate. (See also p. 218 for beef goulash.) The paprika speck can be bought from many delicatessen shops. If it is not available, use streaky bacon.

Goulash may be served with rice, noodles or potatoes, but in Austria and Hungary it is traditionally served with little dumplings called nockerln (see below).

2 lb. boned veal	bayleaf, pinch of oregano and
4 oz. paprika speck or streaky	thyme
bacon	1 green pimento (optional)
2 onions	½ lb. mushrooms, fresh, or
1 clove garlic	frozen raw or blanched
approx. 1 teaspoon paprika	(optional)
2 tbs. flour	¼ pt (1 carton) sour cream
½ pt stock	salt and pepper

If the pimentoes and the mushrooms are frozen, there is no need to wait for them to thaw.

Cut the speck or bacon into small cubes and fry them gently in a flameproof casserole. Add the sliced onions and garlic and the meat cut into small cubes, and sauté all until golden brown. Sprinkle on the paprika. It is difficult to give exact quantities for paprika, as it varies so much in strength – the fresher it is, the hotter it will be. Add the flour and cook gently for another

2 minutes, stirring well all the time. Add the stock, herbs and seasoning, continue to stir while it is coming to the boil and then cover and simmer very slowly, or place in a low oven (300°F., gas 2) for about 1½ hours, until the meat is tender. Half-an-hour before the end of the cooking time you may add the chopped green pimento and the chopped or sliced mushrooms. Just before serving, stir in the sour cream and test for seasoning. The dish is now ready to serve.

To freeze: allow to cool and freeze in foil or plastic containers, or see method 4 on p. 17.

To serve after freezing: return the frozen goulash to the flame-proof casserole and warm over a low heat, allowing 45 minutes to 1 hour. You may need to add a little more stock.

Nockerln (Dumplings)

8 oz. flour	½ pt milk
2 oz. dried breadcrumbs	1 oz. butter
1 egg	salt

Mix the flour and breadcrumbs, beat in the egg and make a stiff batter with the milk. Beat this well for a few moments with a wooden spoon.

Heat a large panful of salted water, and when it is boiling drop in teaspoonfuls of the batter one by one, about 8 or 10 at a time, depending on the size of your pan. Leave them to boil for about 10 minutes, by which time all the dumplings should have risen to the surface. Take them out of the water with a slotted spoon, and repeat this operation until all the batter has been used up. Rinse the dumplings briefly under a cold tap, and heat them in a frying pan with a little butter.

These dumplings make an excellent simple supper dish for children. After you have boiled and rinsed them roll the dumplings in breadcrumbs, fry them golden brown in butter and serve them with scrambled eggs or tomato sauce. Creamed tomatoes (see p. 230) go well with this.

[B/C]   *Blanquette of Veal*

2–3 lb. shoulder or breast of veal, preferably in a piece
2 slices of lemon
1 onion
1 carrot
bouquet garni
3 oz. butter
3 oz. flour

½ lb. button onions, fresh, or frozen in white sauce
¼ lb. button mushrooms, fresh, or frozen blanched
2 egg yolks
½ pt single cream
salt and pepper

Buy the veal on the bone, and in one piece if possible. Take the meat off the bone, cut it into bite-sized cubes and put them into a large bowl, cover with cold water, add one slice of lemon and leave overnight to draw out the blood. Drain, put the meat in a large saucepan together with the bone, cover with cold water and bring to the boil slowly. Drain off the water once more, rinse the pan, cover the meat and bone again with cold water and bring to the boil. Add another slice of lemon, the roughly quartered onion and carrot, the bouquet garni and the seasoning, and leave to simmer for about 1½ hours, until the meat is tender. Strain and set aside the cooking liquid, and take off any further meat from the bone.

Melt the butter in a clean saucepan, add the flour and cook, stirring, for 5 minutes. Slowly add up to 2 pints of the cooking liquid (if there is more, freeze it separately and use for veal stock on other occasions) and simmer slowly until it begins to thicken. If you are using frozen onions and mushrooms add them to the sauce and allow them to heat through gently. If you are using fresh onions blanch them for 10 minutes, and blanch fresh mushrooms for 5 minutes, before adding them to the sauce.

Beat the cream into the egg yolks and add to the sauce. Stir over a very low heat, and be careful not to allow to boil. Check for seasoning and add also a squeeze of lemon juice if necessary. Return the meat to the sauce.

For immediate eating: heat all through together, without allowing to boil, and serve with rice.

To freeze: cool, and freeze in foil or plastic containers or see method 4 on p. 17.

To serve after freezing: tip the frozen blanquette into a saucepan and heat through gently. Allow at least 45 minutes for this, as it must be done very slowly and on no account be allowed to boil. Serve with rice.

CITRUS FRUITS

Oranges, lemons and grapefruit freeze well – whole, segmented or as juice – and it is useful to store some in the freezer.

We do not recommend freezing the more delicately flavoured citrus fruits, such as tangerines and satsumas, since freezing seems to alter and spoil their taste.

[A] *To freeze whole:* freeze in polythene bags, either separately or together.

To freeze as juice: freeze in waxed cartons, sweetened or unsweetened.

To freeze in segments: freeze in waxed or plastic containers, sweetened or unsweetened.

[C] *To use after freezing:* the fruit will take several hours to thaw, according to variety and size. If you wish to grate it you should do so while the fruit is still frozen, when it will grate very finely and easily. Once thawed, the fruit should be used without delay.

[B/C]   *Chicken with Lemon*

4-lb. roasting chicken | 1 clove garlic
2 carrots | small bunch of parsley
4 shallots or 2 small onions | ¼ tsp. saffron
2 tbs. olive oil | salt and pepper
1 oz. butter

Sauce

4 oz. mushrooms, fresh, or frozen raw or blanched	2 egg yolks
½ lemon (juice and rind). Use a little more juice if you like the lemon taste to be strong	¼ pt double cream
	1½ oz. butter
	2 tbs. flour
	salt and pepper

Frozen chicken must be allowed to thaw before cooking. Mushrooms should be left for about 15 minutes until they are soft enough to quarter.

Coarsely chop the onions and carrots, and gently cook them in the olive oil and butter in a flameproof casserole. When the onions are soft, place the chicken on top. Add the crushed garlic, the parsley and the saffron. Season, and add about 1 pint of water (it should half-cover the chicken). Bring to the boil, cover, and simmer gently till the chicken is tender (1 to 1½ hours).

While the chicken is cooking, start to make the sauce. Cut the mushrooms into quarters. Peel the lemon thinly, and cut the peel into matchsticks. Mix together in a bowl the mushrooms, lemon peel, lemon juice, beaten yolks and cream.

When the chicken is ready, take it out of the casserole, and if you are going to eat it immediately cut it into serving pieces, and keep warm while you finish off the sauce.

Melt the butter in a saucepan, add the flour and stir until smooth. Strain the juice in which the chicken was cooked and gradually add this to the butter and flour roux over a gentle heat, stirring well, until the sauce is quite smooth. Then add the contents of the bowl, season, and continue to stir until the sauce thickens, but do not allow to boil. The sauce can be made in a double saucepan if you prefer.

To serve immediately: put the pieces of chicken on a large warmed dish, pour the sauce over and serve.

To freeze: allow to cool before cutting the chicken into serving pieces. Freeze in a plastic container with the sauce or see method 4 on p. 17.

To serve after freezing: replace in the casserole and allow to thaw at room temperature for about 10 hours or double that time in a refrigerator. Warm through very gently on top of the stove, stirring frequently to prevent the sauce from separating. Do not leave over heat for longer than you need, or the sauce will lose its creamy texture and become thin and runny. Do not attempt to heat this dish from the frozen state, both because the sauce would need prolonged attention to prevent it from separating, and also because the long period of reheating would take away from the fresh taste of the lemon and cream sauce.

[B] *Lemon Meringue Pie*

This cannot be finally prepared before it is frozen unless you intend to eat it fairly soon, since the meringue topping does not freeze satisfactorily for any length of time. However, the lemon mixture can be made and poured into the pastry case and the pie frozen at this stage, ready to be finished off when it comes out of the freezer.

2 lemons (juice and rind)	7 oz. sugar
6 oz. shortcrust pastry (see p. 28)	½ pt water
	2 egg yolks
2 oz. cornflour	

2 egg whites
¼ tsp. cream of tartar
2 oz. caster sugar

Butter an 8-inch flan-tin and line it with the pastry. If you intend to freeze the pie, use a foil flan-case or see methods 2 or 3 on page 18. Bake blind in a hot oven (425°F., gas 7) for about 15 minutes. Cool.

Make a sauce with the cornflour, the sugar and the water, and stir over a gentle heat for 2 or 3 minutes while it thickens. Add the juice and grated lemon rind and cook for another minute or two. Beat the egg yolks and gradually add the hot mixture to them, stirring all the time to ensure a smooth consistency. Return to the saucepan and bring almost to the boil, continuing to stir. Do not allow to boil. Remove from the heat and allow to cool before pouring into the flan-case.

For immediate eating: beat the egg whites until they stand in peaks. Add the cream of tartar and beat again. Then add the caster sugar very gradually, beating all the time. Spread over the top of the lemon mixture, being careful to see that the meringue adheres to the sides, to prevent shrinkage in cooking. Put in a fairly slow oven (325°F., gas 3) for about 20 minutes, until the top is nicely browned. Serve warm or cold.

To freeze: if you have used a foil case, wrap and freeze. Otherwise see p. 18. You can if you like freeze the unwhipped egg whites separately – labelling them carefully so that they will be identifiable in six months' time!

To serve after freezing: allow the pie (and the whites, if you are using frozen ones) to thaw for a couple of hours, and then add the meringue topping and bake as described above.

Note: for short-term freezing – not more than 2 or 3 days – complete the pie by spreading the meringue over the lemon mixture and put in the freezer. When the meringue has frozen (it will not become completely hard) wrap or cover lightly. When you come to eat it, put it straight from the freezer into a hot oven (425°F., gas 7) for 20 minutes. Then turn the oven down to 325°F., gas 3, and cook for a further 20 minutes.

[B] *Rich Lemon Curd Tart*

2 lemons (the juice of 2 and the rind of 1)
4 oz. sugar
2 oz. ground almonds
10 oz. sweetened shortcrust pastry (see p. 28)
4 oz. butter, preferably un-salted
4 egg yolks
¼ pt double cream

Line one buttered 10-inch flan-case or two 7-inch cases with the pastry. If the tart is for the freezer use foil flan-cases or see methods 2 or 3 on p. 18.

Beat together the egg yolks and sugar, add the ground almonds, the softened butter, the cream, and the juice of both lemons and grated rind of one. Continue to beat until the mixture is smooth and creamy. Pour this filling into the pastry cases and bake in a fairly slow oven (325°F., gas 3) for 40 minutes, or until the top is golden brown. Serve warm or cold.

To freeze: cool. If you have used a foil case, wrap and freeze. Otherwise, see p. 18.

To serve after freezing: place the frozen tart in a hot oven (425°F., gas 7) for ½ hour. Serve warm or cold.

[B]   *Lemon Mousse (1)*

This sweet is very refreshing at the end of a rich meal.

2 lemons (juice and rind)   **6 oz. caster sugar**
4 eggs   **slightly under ½ oz. gelatine**

Separate the eggs, and whisk the yolks with the sugar until they are light and fluffy. Grate in the lemon rind. Heat the lemon juice and the gelatine gently together until the gelatine has completely dissolved. Pour this liquid very slowly into the egg mixture, continuing to whisk. Taste for sweetness, and if necessary add a little more caster sugar, stirring well to dissolve it. Fold in the whites, beaten until they are stiff but not dry. Once you have started to add the gelatine it is important to work fast, otherwise the mousse may begin to set.

To serve immediately: pour into a dish and leave to set in the refrigerator for 1 or 2 hours.

To freeze: see methods 2, 3 or 4 on p. 17.

To serve after freezing: allow to thaw at room temperature for 2 to 4 hours.

[B]   *Lemon Mousse (2)*

This is a richer version of the previous recipe.

2 lemons (juice and rind)   **½ oz. gelatine**
4 eggs   **½ pt double cream**
4–6 oz. caster sugar

Make as for the previous recipe until you have beaten the gelatine into the yolks. Lightly whip the cream and fold it into the mixture. Complete as for the previous recipe.

[B] *Lemon Honeycomb Mould*

2 lemons (juice and rind)	3 oz. sugar
3 eggs	½ oz. gelatine
1 pt milk or ½ pt milk and ½ pt single cream	

Make a custard by combining the egg yolks, the milk and cream
and the sugar, and stirring them over a low heat or in the top of
a double boiler until they thicken to a creamy consistency.
Sprinkle in the gelatine and stir well to make sure it has dissolved. Set aside to cool. Stir the grated peel and juice of the
lemons into the cooled custard. Do not do this too soon or the
mixture will curdle. Whip the egg whites until they are stiff
and fold them into the custard.

To serve immediately: rinse out a 2-pint mould or soufflé dish
with cold water, pour in the custard and chill. Turn out when it
has set. It should be in three layers – the top a clear lemon jelly,
the middle a creamy milk jelly and the bottom a fluffy lemon
mousse.

To freeze: pour into a foil or plastic mould, allow to cool,
cover and freeze. Or see method 4 on p. 17.

To serve after freezing: allow to thaw at room temperature for
3 to 4 hours or overnight in the refrigerator. Turn out
before serving.

[B] *Lemon Curd*

Although lemon curd keeps well in the store cupboard for
some time, the advantage of freezing it is that it may be kept
indefinitely, and tastes and looks as good as ever when it
comes out of the freezer.

3 lemons (juice and rind)	approx. 12 oz. caster sugar
2 oz. butter	3 eggs

Put the butter, lemon juice and grated rind and sugar in a
heavy saucepan and melt slowly. (There should be about

¼ pint lemon juice.) Do not allow to boil. Beat the eggs just enough to amalgamate the yolks and whites. When the sugar has completely dissolved add the mixture to the eggs very slowly, beating all the time. Test for sweetness. Return to the saucepan and cook over a low heat, stirring constantly. The mixture will at first become more runny, and then will start to thicken. When it does so – and being very careful not to let it reach boiling point – take off the stove and leave to cool.

To freeze: when the lemon curd is cold, freeze in yogurt or small cream cartons. These quantities will make about 1½ lb.

To serve after freezing: thaw at room temperature for 3 to 4 hours.

[B]   *Lemon Mimosa Cake*

3 eggs   3 lemons
the weight of the eggs in: approx. 8 oz. caster sugar (for
  butter   the icing)
  caster sugar
  flour

angelica and crystallized mimosa balls for decorating (optional)

Cream the butter and sugar till they are light and fluffy. Add the grated rind of the lemons. Whip the eggs and add alternately with the sieved flour, beating well. Line with greased paper a shallow baking tin about 10 inches square, and spread in the mixture. Put in the middle of a medium oven (350°F., gas 4). After 20 minutes turn the heat down to 300°F., gas 2. The cake should be done in about 40 minutes altogether, but towards the end of the cooking time test by putting a skewer in the middle: if it comes out clean, the cake is ready.

Meanwhile, make the icing from about 8 oz. caster sugar dissolved in the juice of two of the lemons. This is spread on the cake when it cools, and the process is easier if the icing is allowed to stand for an hour or two to set a little. Stir from time to time. Add more sugar if necessary, but it is important that the icing should be slightly tart, as otherwise the cake will be sickly.

When the cake has cooled, stand it on a large board or dish and spoon the icing over it in small quantities. If it runs over the side (as it probably will), scoop it up and put it back on again. This will take time, but eventually it should be possible to spread all the icing on. Leave for 2 or 3 hours to harden.

To serve immediately: cut the cake into rectangles, and decorate each slice with angelica and little crystallized mimosa balls, arranged to look like miniature sprays of mimosa.

To freeze: stand on a piece of greaseproof paper and put in the freezer, uncovered, for 24 hours. Wrap in foil or a polythene bag, and replace in the freezer.

To serve after freezing: allow to thaw for 4 or 5 hours and decorate as above.

[B]
Lemonade

Lemonade may seem an odd thing to put in the freezer. But in fact there is a lot to be said for doing so, since it can be made easily and cheaply in large quantities, and if it is stored in the freezer there is no risk that it will start to ferment, which may happen under ordinary storage conditions. So make it in this concentrated form, and freeze in waxed cartons until you need it. Drink diluted with water.

5 oranges	2 oz. tartaric acid
5 lemons	5 lb. sugar
1 oz. citric acid	3 pts boiling water
1 oz. Epsom salts	

Squeeze the juice out of the fruit and cut up the rinds roughly. Put both into a large bowl, together with the pips and pulp, and add all the other ingredients. Stir well until the boiling water has dissolved the sugar. Cover and allow to cool. When it is quite cold give it another good stir and strain, squeezing out as much juice as you can from the rinds. Freeze in waxed cartons.

[B⅓]   *Orange Ice-Cream*

6 oranges   2 eggs and 2 extra yolks
2 lemons   ⅔ pt double cream
8 oz. icing sugar

(If ⅔ pt cream seems a bit extravagant you can use ½ pt, but the ice-cream won't have quite the same smooth richness.)

Mix the sieved icing sugar with the juice of the oranges and lemons. Beat the whole eggs and the yolks, and add. Pour into the top of a double saucepan and heat gently, stirring all the time, until the mixture starts to thicken. Cool, and fold into the whipped cream. Freeze in waxed or plastic containers.

To serve after freezing: remove from the freezer 15 minutes before serving.

[B]   *Rich Orange or Lemon Ice-Cream*

2 oranges or 2 lemons   ½ pt double cream
6 egg yolks   2 tbs. Grand Marnier (optional,
½ lb. caster sugar   for orange ice-cream only)

Whisk the egg yolks with the sugar until they are thick and white. Gradually beat in the grated rind and juice of the oranges or lemons. For orange ice add the Grand Marnier. Beat the cream until it is thick but not stiff, and fold it into the mixture. Pour into waxed or plastic containers and freeze.

To serve: remove from the freezer 10 to 15 minutes before serving.

[B]   *Orange Water-Ice*

7 juicy oranges (smooth-   ¾ pt water
   skinned Spanish navel   ½ lb. sugar
   oranges are better than large 2 tbs. Grand Marnier or
   Jaffas)   Orange Curaçao (optional)
1 lemon

Make a syrup by boiling the water and sugar hard for 10 minutes with the finely pared peel of the lemon and of 1 orange. Strain and allow to cool.

Meanwhile cut the tops off the remaining 6 oranges and scoop out the flesh from both tops and bottoms, being very careful not to break or injure the shells, but leaving the insides as clean as possible. This is best done with a teaspoon or a grapefruit knife. Extract as much juice from the pulp as you can by pushing it through a nylon sieve. If you do not want to serve the ices in the orange shells – and, though this is the prettiest way, it takes much longer to do – you can simply squeeze the oranges in the usual way. Add the juice of the peeled orange and of the lemon, and the liqueur, and mix with the cooled syrup. Pour into ice-trays and freeze for 1 or 2 hours, until the mixture has reached a mushy state.

Turn the frozen mixture into a bowl or blender and beat well. Then either freeze in waxed or plastic containers, or spoon the mixture into the orange cups, allowing it to come a little over the tops of the cups. Press on the lids and freeze again, keeping the oranges in an upright position in a tin or tray, for about 1 hour. If they are sticky wipe them with a clean cloth or kitchen paper before packing them in polythene bags and storing them in the freezer.

To serve: remove from the freezer 10 to 15 minutes before serving.

[B]   *Lemon Water-Ice*

¼ pt lemon juice (juice of   ¾ pt water
   between 3 to 6 lemons   ½ lb. sugar
   depending on size)

Boil the sugar and water for 5 minutes, and then make in exactly the same way as the orange water-ice, but do not add any liqueur, as this would spoil the refreshingly tart flavour of these ices. The yield will be less than for the orange water-ice, as there is less fruit juice, but there will be more than you can fit into the lemon shells.

[B]   *Grapefruit Water-Ice*

2 grapefruit   ½ lb. sugar
¾ pt water

Make in exactly the same way as for orange water-ice, but do
not add any rind to the sugar and water when you are making
the syrup. Instead, add the finely grated rinds of both grapefruit to the juice; this will add a great deal to the unusual and
refreshing flavour of this ice. Freeze in waxed or plastic
containers.

Orange, Lemon or Grapefruit Sorbet

Make these as for water-ices, but fold in 2 stiffly beaten egg
whites before returning the ices to the freezer for the second
time.

[B]   *Glacé Orange, Lemon and Grapefruit Peel*

This is a good way of using up the peel from oranges, lemons
and grapefruit. The glacé peel can be put into cakes or puddings, or handed round after dinner.

The peel of 2 grapefruit, 2   1¼ lb. caster sugar
  lemons and 4 oranges (or   ¼ cup honey
  any combination which
  produces roughly the same
  amount of peel)

Cut the peel into thin slices, being careful to see that the
orange peel in particular is cut thinly, since it softens in cooking
less readily than the grapefruit and lemon peel. Put in a large
saucepan with 2½ pints cold water, bring to the boil and boil for
10 minutes. Drain. Repeat this process once more, using fresh
water. After you have drained the peel for the second time, put

in the saucepan ¾ lb. sugar, the honey and ¾ pint water. Bring to the boil, boil for 1 minute, and then add the peel. Boil vigorously for 10 minutes, stirring all the time and making sure that it does not catch on the bottom. Drain, and put the peel in a bowl. Sprinkle over the rest of the sugar, and shake so that it is absorbed by the fruit. Place on greaseproof paper to dry out.

To freeze: freeze in small quantities in waxed cartons or polythene bags.

To serve after freezing: thaw at room temperature from 1 to 3 hours.

March

PIGEONS

Pigeons should be plentiful this month. They are a cheap source of meat; if you choose plump birds they are very tender; and they can be cooked in many different ways.

To freeze: pluck and draw the birds, wipe them well with a dry cloth or kitchen paper, and wrap them individually in foil, polythene film or moisture-vapour-proof tissue. Put several together in a polythene bag and freeze.

[B/C]   *Pigeons à la Crème*

4 pigeons	½ pt white wine
2 oz. butter	1 tbs. brandy (optional)
1 tbs. oil	a squeeze of lemon juice
4 rashers bacon	salt and pepper

½ *pt single cream*
2 *egg yolks*

If you are using frozen pigeons for this recipe, allow them to thaw.

Melt the butter and the oil in a large flameproof casserole and brown the pigeons on all sides. Then place them breast-side up, cover each one with a rasher of bacon to help keep the meat moist, pour on the wine, add the brandy, the squeeze of lemon juice, and the salt and pepper. Cover and simmer over a gentle heat for 30 to 40 minutes, until the pigeons are tender.

To serve immediately: lift the pigeons out of the casserole and keep them warm while you are finishing the sauce. Strain the liquid in the casserole. Whisk together the egg yolks and the cream and stir them into the liquid. Continue to cook over a gentle heat until the sauce thickens, but do not allow it to boil. Test for seasoning. Return the pigeons to the casserole, heat through and serve. This dish is particularly good served with a purée of artichokes (see p. 44).

To freeze: cool and freeze in foil or plastic containers.

To serve after freezing: allow to thaw for at least 4 to 5 hours at room temperature. Replace in the casserole, heat through gently on top of the stove and make the sauce as for immediate eating.

[B/C] *Pigeons in Tomato Sauce*

4 pigeons
2 oz. bacon fat
1 clove garlic
½ lb. mushrooms, fresh, or frozen raw or blanched
1 onion

bouquet garni
2 lb. tomatoes
¼ pt water
1 tbs. brown sugar
salt and pepper

If you are using frozen pigeons allow them to thaw. Tomatoes and mushrooms can be used straight from the freezer.

Melt the bacon fat in a flameproof casserole, add the finely chopped garlic and gently brown the pigeons. Chop the mushrooms and put them in the casserole, together with the chopped onion and the bouquet garni. Add the peeled and chopped tomatoes and the water. Season and add the sugar. Bring to the boil, cover the casserole, and cook in a medium oven (350°F., gas 4) for 1½ hours. Test for seasoning and serve.

To freeze: cool and freeze in foil or plastic containers.

To serve after freezing: thaw for at least 4 to 5 hours at room temperature. Heat through gently on top of the stove for about ½ hour or in a medium oven (350°F., gas 4) for at least 45 minutes.

[B/C] *Casserole of Pigeons and Mushrooms*

4 pigeons
2 oz. bacon fat
2 tsp. flour
½ pt water
½ pt white wine
bouquet garni

½ lb. pickling onions, fresh, or frozen blanched
½ lb. mushrooms, fresh, or frozen raw or blanched
2 oz. butter
salt and pepper

If you are using frozen pigeons for this recipe, allow them to thaw. Onions can be used straight from the freezer, but mushrooms should be left for ½ hour until they are soft enough to slice.

Melt the bacon fat in a flameproof casserole and gently brown the pigeons on all sides. Remove them, sprinkle in the flour, and stir for a minute or two to brown it. Add the water and the wine and the bouquet garni. Season. Boil for a few minutes, replace the pigeons, cover the casserole and continue to cook gently. Meanwhile brown the onions in the butter in a separate pan, add the sliced mushrooms, and gently sauté them together. Add to the casserole, and continue cooking until the pigeons are tender (about 40 minutes).

Take the pigeons out of the casserole and for immediate eating keep them warm. Remove the bouquet garni. If the sauce is too thin, thicken it with a beurre manié made with 1 tbs. flour and ½ oz. butter, pour over the pigeons, test for seasoning and serve.

To freeze: cool and freeze in foil or plastic containers.

To serve after freezing: thaw for at least 4 to 5 hours at room temperature. Heat through gently on top of the stove for about ½ hour, or in a medium oven (350°F., gas 4) for at least 45 minutes.

[B/C]   *Pigeons in Red Cabbage*

4 pigeons (they may be elder-
    ly for this recipe as they will
    be cooked very slowly)
2 oz. butter
4 rashers streaky bacon
1 medium red cabbage⎫
4 onions   ⎪ or 2–2½ lb. frozen
1 apple   ⎬ red cabbage
¼ pt red wine   ⎪ (see p. 272)
2 tbs. brown sugar   ⎭
6 juniper berries
juice of ½ lemon
salt and pepper

If you are using frozen pigeons for this recipe, take them out of the freezer at least 3 to 4 hours before cooking, so that they are at any rate partially thawed. Frozen red cabbage can be used straight from the freezer (see below).

Melt the butter and the chopped bacon in a flameproof casserole and brown the pigeons on all sides. Remove them from the casserole and brown in it the chopped onions and the chopped, peeled apple. Finely slice the red cabbage and add it to the casserole, together with the other ingredients, stir, and heat through. If you are using frozen red cabbage put it in the casserole with a little water, the juniper berries and the lemon juice, and heat slowly. Season.

As soon as the cabbage is hot place the pigeons on top, cover, and leave over a very low heat for 2½ to 3 hours. Check from time to time that the cabbage is not catching on the bottom of the pan and add a little more liquid if necessary (water, stock or wine).

To serve immediately: when the cabbage is cooked test it for seasoning. Lift out the pigeons, cut them in half, replace them on the bed of cabbage and serve.

To freeze: cool and freeze the pigeons and cabbage together in foil or plastic containers, or see method 4 on p. 17.

To serve after freezing: thaw for at least 4 to 5 hours at room temperature and heat through gently on top of the stove. You may need to add a little water, stock or wine if the dish appears too dry.

WATERCRESS

[B] *Watercress Soup*

4 bunches watercress	4 potatoes
2 oz. butter	2 pts stock
4 onions	salt and pepper

1 pt milk
a little cream for serving

Wash the watercress well, and pick off any of the stalks that are too thick or hairy.

Melt the butter in a large pan, add the roughly chopped onions and potatoes and sweat them gently for about 5 minutes. Pour on the stock, add half the watercress and the seasoning, and simmer for about 20 minutes, or until the potatoes are cooked. Pass through a mouli or a blender until the soup is smooth. Then either blend again briefly with the remaining watercress, or chop the cress roughly and add, so that you have a pale green soup with large flecks of dark green, fresh-tasting cress.

To serve immediately: return to the stove and add the milk, check for seasoning, and heat through. Pour into bowls and add a swirl of cream to each helping.

To freeze: allow to cool and freeze in waxed or plastic containers.

To serve after freezing: tip the frozen soup into a saucepan, add the milk and heat through gently – this will take at least 15 minutes, and should not be hurried. Serve as above with cream.

BROCCOLI, SPROUTING BROCCOLI AND CURLY KALE

These are all very good vegetables to freeze, since they retain excellent colour, flavour and texture and are in fact indistinguishable from fresh.

[A]   BROCCOLI, WHITE AND PURPLE

To freeze blanched: break the heads into flowerlets of roughly equal size. Wash thoroughly. Blanch for 2 minutes. Drain, cool and freeze in polythene bags.

[A]   BROCCOLI, WHITE AND PURPLE, SPROUTING

To freeze blanched: cut the shoots into roughly equal lengths. Wash thoroughly. Blanch for 2 minutes. Drain, cool and freeze in polythene bags.

[A]   CURLY KALE

To freeze blanched: cut the shoots into roughly equal lengths. Wash thoroughly. Blanch for 2 minutes. Drain, cool and freeze in polythene bags.

[C] *To serve broccoli and kale after freezing:* melt some butter in a heavy saucepan. Tip the frozen vegetables into the saucepan and heat very gently, stirring with a fork from time to time to break up the mass. Season lightly, but be careful not to add too much salt. The broccoli will be cooked in a few minutes.

It is also possible, of course, to cook these vegetables in a little salted water, but they keep their flavour and shape better if only butter is used, or at most a couple of tablespoons of water.

April

LAMB

Spring and lambs go together, so we are giving most of our lamb recipes this month. But in fact there is no one month that is best for buying a lamb for the freezer, and most families are in any case likely to get through several in a year.

April is the month when English spring lambs begin to appear in the shops. English lamb is probably the best in the world, but it is also the most expensive. When young and fresh it should be eaten and enjoyed as a treat, and unless you have a particularly cheap source of supply it is probably not worth freezing it then. Better to wait till the winter, when the price has dropped considerably, so that it is only a little dearer than the imported.

New Zealand lamb is considerably cheaper than English lamb for most of the year, and as it arrives frozen there is every reason to buy a whole carcass at a time for the freezer, and benefit from the substantial saving involved.

The new season's lambs from New Zealand arrive in this country in November or December, but many wholesalers have a stockpile of imported lambs, so the new ones may not appear in the shops until January or February. New Zealand lamb is therefore likely to be at its cheapest in the spring, when English lamb is at its most expensive.

To summarize: the best plan seems to be to buy a New Zealand lamb for the freezer in the late spring, and an English lamb in the winter. Apart from there being little difference in the price by that time, English lambs will then be rather bigger than the imported ones, so that their joints will be larger, though the meat may be a little coarser.

If you buy several lambs in the course of a year, and if you do your own butchering or can arrange to have the carcass carved up according to your special wishes (see notes on bulk buying of meat on p. 20), it is worth ringing the changes, sometimes having the loin and best end of neck cut up into chops, sometimes leaving them in a piece for roasting; sometimes having a whole saddle of lamb for a special dinner, and occasionally making up a crown of lamb. And take any bones which are left after butchering – boiled with plenty of seasoning, and especially with a lot of oregano, they make an excellent stock or basis for winter soups.

We give some recipes for using the breast and neck, which are the cheapest cuts and which people sometimes shy away from because they do not know how to make them into appetising dishes. Legs and shoulders are most often roasted, but we give two alternative recipes which involve boiling them. These are particularly economical since the meat does not shrink when boiled, and they are also less usual and very tasty.

The average lamb weighs between 30 and 40 lb., and takes up between 1 and 1½ cubic feet of freezer space.

[B/C]   *Scotch Broth*

2 New Zealand breasts of   2 onions
   lamb (unboned)   2 oz. pearl barley
2 carrots (and a little of any salt and pepper
   other root vegetable you
   may happen to have around)

parsley

Put the breasts of lamb in a large saucepan, cover with cold water and bring slowly to the boil. If you have taken the meat from the freezer, it is best to use it immediately, so that the juices will go into the stock, but make sure that the water does not reach boiling point before the meat has completely thawed. Skim if necessary, and add the chopped vegetables and the pearl barley. Season, and simmer gently for about 2 hours, until the meat is cooked. Remove the meat and taste the soup for seasoning.

To serve immediately: serve with a sprinkling of chopped parsley.

To freeze: cool and freeze in waxed or plastic containers.

To serve after freezing: tip the frozen broth into a saucepan and heat. Serve as above.

Note: The meat may be taken off the bone, and each small piece dipped in egg seasoned with plenty of salt, pepper and thyme or oregano, rolled in breadcrumbs and fried in butter or grilled.

[C] ## *Roast Breast of Lamb*

Although breast is perhaps the least prized cut, the meat is tender and tasty. If you are using New Zealand lamb, each breast will feed 2 to 3 people. English lamb bought later in the season is generally bigger, and one breast should be enough for 4.

2 breasts of lamb (boned)	**French mustard, salt, pepper and chopped herbs (thyme, oregano or rosemary)**

If the meat is frozen it should be allowed to thaw before roasting.

Score the skin of the meat well and spread it thickly with French mustard, salt – coarse sea salt if possible – coarsely ground black pepper and herbs. Roast in a medium oven (375°F., gas 5) for about 1 hour.

[B/C] ## *Stuffed Roast Breast of Lamb*

This is a very economical but enjoyable family supper dish. These quantities will serve 4 to 6 people (see previous recipe).

2 boned breasts of lamb	**¼ lb. fresh breadcrumbs**
1 onion	**1 egg**
parsley and marjoram	**salt, pepper and mustard**
a piece of lemon peel	

If the meat is frozen it should be allowed to thaw before preparing.

Make a fine hash of the onion, the parsley and marjoram (at least one good tablespoon of each), and the strip of lemon peel. Combine this with the breadcrumbs, season, and bind it with the egg.

Lay out the breasts of lamb on a flat board, spread the inside surface with a little mustard and some salt and pepper, and spread the stuffing evenly over each one. Roll them up, tie with some string or thread, dot with a little butter and roast for about 1 hour in a hot oven (425°F., gas 7). The dish is now ready to serve.

To freeze: cool and freeze wrapped in foil, polythene or moisture-vapour-proof tissue.

To serve after freezing: thaw at room temperature for at least 4 to 5 hours, and reheat in a moderate oven (350°F., gas 4) for about 1 hour. If the dish seems to be dry, add a little stock.

[C] *Neck of Lamb Boulangère*

This also makes an inexpensive but very satisfying family supper dish. Serve it with a green salad.

scrag end of neck chops – 1 or 2 per person	1 clove garlic
1 potato per person	parsley
½ pt lamb or beef stock for every 2 lb. potatoes	salt and pepper

The meat can be used straight from the freezer, but it will be more tender if it has been allowed to thaw at least partially.

Peel the potatoes, cut them into ¼-inch slices and lay them on the bottom of a large roasting tin. Sprinkle with salt and pepper. Rub both sides of each chop with a cut clove of garlic and with salt and pepper and place them on top of the potatoes. Add the stock. Cook in a medium oven (375°F., gas 5) for 1 to 1½ hours, or until the meat and potatoes are cooked. Sprinkle with plenty of finely chopped parsley and serve.

[C] *Irish Stew*

2–3 lb. neck of lamb chops	¾ pt stock
2½ lb. potatoes	salt and pepper
2 lb. onions	

Frozen lamb chops do not need to be thawed before cooking.

Peel the potatoes and the onions and cut them into ½-inch slices. In a flameproof casserole put a layer of potatoes, then a layer of onions, and place half the lamb chops on top. Season generously and repeat the operation. Finish with a layer of potatoes. Pour on the stock, bring the stew gently to the boil, then cover and simmer very slowly for 2 hours. Test for seasoning and serve very hot.

[B/C] *Italian Lamb Stew*

2–3 lb. neck of lamb chops	1 small tin of concentrated
1 oz. butter	tomato purée
1 tbs. oil	1 tsp. each of oregano, thyme
1 lb. onions	and rosemary
1 clove garlic	salt and pepper and one lump
½ pt red wine	of sugar

parsley

Frozen chops should be allowed to thaw partially – about 3 hours should be enough.

Melt the butter and oil in a flameproof casserole. Slice the onions and brown them gently with the garlic for a few moments, then add the lamb chops and brown them on both sides. Pour on the red wine and allow it to boil fiercely for a few minutes until it has reduced by almost half. Add the tomato purée, the herbs and the seasoning and some water if necessary, enough for the meat to be just covered by liquid. Cover the casserole and leave it to simmer for about 2 hours, until the meat is tender.

To serve immediately: test for seasoning, sprinkle with plenty of parsley and serve.

To freeze: lift out the chops and strip the meat off the bones. Chill the sauce, and when it is cold remove the fat. Combine the meat with the sauce and freeze in plastic or foil containers.

To serve after freezing: Tip the frozen stew into a saucepan and heat through very slowly. Allow at least 30 minutes for this. Sprinkle with parsley before serving.

[C]   *Devilled Best End of Neck*

An agreeable variation on plain roast best end of neck, which makes this relatively economical cut interesting enough to serve at a dinner party. Allow about 2 chops per person.

2 large best ends of neck, whole
1 large clove of garlic
4 tbs. French mustard
1 large onion
parsley, tarragon, marjoram
small piece of finely pared lemon peel

4 oz. fresh white breadcrumbs
black peppercorns very coarsely crushed
Worcestershire sauce
1 oz. butter

If the meat is frozen it should be allowed to thaw at least partially before cooking.

Rub the meat well with the cut clove of garlic and spread the mustard liberally on both sides. Chop the onion, herbs and lemon peel finely, mix them with the breadcrumbs, spread over the outside of the meat and pat on firmly. Sprinkle on a little Worcestershire sauce and plenty of coarsely crushed peppercorns, dot with butter and cook in a hot oven (450°F., gas 8) for 45 minutes to an hour. The meat should be crisp on the outside and still pink on the inside. Serve with a fresh green salad.

You could also cook a saddle of lamb in the same way, but the roasting time will of course be somewhat longer.

[B/C] *Blanquette of Lamb*

1 shoulder of lamb	2 oz. butter
1 onion stuck with 2 or 3 cloves	2 oz. flour
oregano and thyme	¼ pt double cream
½ lb. small onions, fresh, or frozen in white sauce	a squeeze of lemon juice
½ lb. button mushrooms, fresh, or frozen blanched	salt and pepper

If you are using frozen onions or mushrooms, they do not need to thaw before they are added to this dish.

Place the shoulder of lamb in a large saucepan, add the onion stuck with cloves, the herbs and the seasoning, cover with cold water and bring it very slowly to the boil. If you have taken the meat from the freezer, it is best to use it immediately so that the juices will go into the stock, but make sure that the water does not reach boiling point before the meat has completely thawed. Leave it to simmer, covered, for 1 to 1½ hours, according to the size of the shoulder. When the meat is just done (it should still be pink inside, but if you prick it with a fork the liquid that comes out should be colourless) lift it out and allow to cool. When it has cooled, carve the meat into slices or cubes, leaving aside any pieces of fat. Skim the fat off the broth and remove the onion.

Peel the small onions (if you are using fresh ones) and cook them in the broth for 10 to 15 minutes, when they should be tender but not mushy. Sauté the whole mushrooms briefly in 1 oz. of the butter.

Make a beurre manié with the remaining butter and the flour. Slowly dissolve this in the broth and cook gently, stirring all the time, until the sauce begins to thicken. If you are using onions frozen in white sauce, add them now. Stir in the double cream. Add the meat, the mushrooms with the cooking juices, and the squeeze of lemon juice, and test for seasoning.

To serve immediately: Heat through gently and serve. This dish is particularly good served with noodles.

To freeze: cool, and freeze in foil or plastic containers, or see method 4 on p. 17.

To serve after freezing: tip the frozen blanquette into a saucepan and heat through very gently – do not allow to boil. Serve as above.

[B/C]   *Boiled Lamb in Caper Sauce*

1 leg or shoulder of lamb	2 oz. flour
1 onion	1 tbs. capers (or more)
1 carrot	2 tbs. cream
bouquet garni	salt and pepper
2 oz. butter	

Place the leg or shoulder in a large saucepan, cover it with cold water and bring it very slowly to the boil. If the lamb is from the freezer, it is best to use it immediately, so that the juices will go into the stock, but do not let the water boil before the lamb has completely thawed. Skim the water very carefully, add the onion and carrot roughly chopped, the bouquet garni and seasoning, and simmer very slowly until the meat is just done (anything between 1 and 2 hours, depending on the size of the joint). Remove the meat and for immediate eating transfer it to a serving dish and keep it warm while making the sauce.

Melt the butter in a heavy saucepan, add the flour and cook very gently for 2 minutes, stirring all the time. Gradually add $\frac{3}{4}$ pint of the strained lamb broth, stir until smooth, add the capers and the cream and test for seasoning. If you like a very sharp taste, you could also add a little of the caper vinegar.

To serve immediately: carve the meat at table and hand the sauce separately.

To freeze: allow the meat to cool and carve it into thick slices. Freeze with the sauce in foil or plastic containers, or see method 4 on p. 17.

To serve after freezing: tip the frozen mass into a saucepan and heat very slowly. Allow at least 40 minutes for this. You may wish to add some more capers and caper vinegar at this stage as the capers seem to lose some of their sharpness in freezing.

Strain the remaining broth into a clean saucepan, add the lamb bone and a tablespoon of dried oregano, and boil briskly until it is reduced by half. Strain, cool and freeze for later use as a basis for soups.

SPINACH

Blanching spinach is a long job, for only a little can be processed at a time. It is much simpler, and just as good, to cook it before freezing.

[A] *To freeze cooked:* strip the leaves off the stalks, wash them thoroughly, and put them in a large, heavy saucepan without any added water. Sprinkle over some salt and cook until tender. The time taken will vary according to how young and fresh the spinach is: if it is really young, and straight out of the garden, it shouldn't take more than 7 to 10 minutes, but 10 to 15 minutes may be necessary if it is older and not so fresh.

When it is cooked, drain very well, allow to cool, and then squeeze out the moisture very thoroughly with your hands. Chop roughly. Freeze in small quantities in polythene bags.

It is useful to weigh the contents of each bag and write the weight on the label, as this is a helpful guide later on when you come to use the spinach in recipes.

[C] *To serve after freezing:* put the frozen spinach in a heavy saucepan. Add a knob of butter and some top of the milk. Heat very gently, stirring from time to time. You may find that the spinach has become rather dry in the freezing, and needs more butter and top of the milk than would normally be necessary. Test for seasoning and serve. Or, to make the spinach go further, you can fold it into a cheese sauce. Eaten with a baked potato, and an egg, this makes a very good supper dish.

SPINACH STALKS

One of the most useful varieties of spinach to grow is Swiss chard – the type with big leaves and a thick white stalk – because both stalks and leaves can be used.

[A] *To freeze blanched:* when you have stripped off the leaves take the best and largest of the stalks, trim them so that they are roughly the same length, and blanch for 2 minutes. Drain, cool and freeze in polythene bags.

[C] *To serve after freezing:* cook the frozen stalks for a few minutes in a little salted water. When they are soft, drain them, and serve with melted butter poured over them.

[B/C]   *Spinach Soup*

1 lb. fresh spinach or 6 oz.	½ oz. cornflour
frozen (cooked)	1 pt chicken or veal stock
1 oz. butter	salt and pepper

1 pt milk
1–2 tbs. cream or top of the milk

Cook the spinach as described on p. 99. If you are using frozen spinach, there is no need to wait for it to thaw.

Make a roux with the butter and cornflour and add the stock, stirring all the time. When it boils, add the spinach, and simmer for a few minutes. If the spinach is frozen, break up the mass with a knife as the soup is cooking. Season, and put the soup through a blender or a fine mouli.

To serve immediately: add the milk. Cook for a further 10 minutes and remove any scum. Test for seasoning, stir in the cream and serve.

To freeze: cool and freeze in waxed or plastic containers.

To serve after freezing: turn the frozen soup into a saucepan, add the milk and heat gently, stirring from time to time. Test for seasoning and add the cream or top of the milk before serving.

[B/C] *Sole Florentine*

This dish, which can be made with almost any white fish –
Dover or lemon sole, plaice, haddock, cod – is an excellent way
of using frozen spinach, though it can also be made of fresh
spinach and frozen. The quantities given here are enough for
4 people.

8 fillets of sole or plaice (skinned), or about 1½ lb. filleted
haddock or cod
1½ lb. fresh spinach or 8 oz.
frozen (cooked)
1 medium onion
¼ pt white wine

2 or 3 tbs. top of the milk
2½ oz. butter
1½ oz. flour
½ pt milk
2 tbs. cream
1 oz. grated cheese
salt and pepper

1 oz. grated cheese

Place the fish in a casserole; if you are using sole or plaice, fold
each fillet into three. Season, and add the onion, roughly cut up.
Pour over the wine, cover with a piece of buttered foil or
greaseproof paper and the casserole lid, and cook in a moderate
oven (350°F., gas 4) for about 20 minutes, until the fish is
cooked and has lost its translucent appearance. Lift it out of the
casserole, and keep it warm if you are going to eat the dish
immediately. Strain the liquid in which the fish was cooked into
a small saucepan, and boil hard until about half of it has
evaporated.

If you are using fresh spinach, cook it as described on p. 99.
If you are using frozen spinach there is no need to wait for it
to thaw. Put the cooked spinach in a saucepan with the top of
the milk and 1 oz. of butter and warm gently. If you are
using frozen spinach a little more butter and milk will be
necessary.

Make a béchamel sauce with 1½ oz. butter, the flour and
the milk, and add the liquid in which the fish was cooked.
Stir in the cream and the cheese and season. Put a thin layer of
the sauce at the bottom of an ovenproof dish. For freezing, use

a foil dish or see method 2 on p. 17. Cover with the spinach and arrange the fish on top of this. Pour over the remainder of the sauce.

To serve immediately: sprinkle on the grated cheese, warm through in a moderate oven (350°F., gas 4) for about 15 minutes, and serve.

To freeze: allow to cool. If you have used a foil dish, wrap well and freeze. Otherwise see p. 17.

To serve after freezing: remove from the freezer, sprinkle over the cheese and place in a hot oven (450°F., gas 8) for 20 minutes. Turn the oven down to 350°F., gas 4, and cook for a further 40 to 45 minutes.

[B/C]   *Spinach Pancakes*

This is an excellent dish to keep as a stand-by for unexpected visitors, as the pancakes can be put straight from the freezer into a hot oven, and freezing seems to improve their taste and texture.

Batter

½ pt milk   4 eggs
½ pt water   salt and pepper
8 oz. flour

Filling

1–1½ lb. fresh spinach, or 8 oz.   2 oz. mushrooms
   frozen (cooked)   2 oz. grated cheese
3–4 tbs. top of the milk   1 tbs. cream (optional)
2–3 oz. butter

Sauce

1½ oz. butter   1 pt milk
1½ oz. flour   salt and pepper

2 oz. grated cheese

Make the batter with the milk, water, flour and eggs, and season well. Allow to stand for at least an hour.

Meanwhile prepare the filling. If you are using fresh spinach, cook as described on p. 99. If you are using frozen spinach, there is no need to wait for it to thaw.

Put the spinach in a saucepan with the top of the milk and 1 oz. butter (for frozen spinach you may need a little more of both). Warm through gently and chop roughly.

Sauté the mushrooms for a few minutes in the rest of the butter and then put them through a coarse mouli or briefly in the blender. Do not purée them. Mix together the spinach, the mushrooms, the grated cheese and the cream.

Make a béchamel sauce with the butter, flour and milk. Stir this into the spinach mixture, test for seasoning and keep warm if the pancakes are to be eaten immediately.

Give the batter another beat before you start to make the pancakes. These should be quite small – if you use a frying-pan which is 5 inches in diameter, this quantity will make about 30. Spread a small quantity of the spinach filling on each pancake and roll them up.

To serve immediately: arrange the pancakes on a shallow oven-proof dish, sprinkle the grated cheese on top, and warm through in a moderate oven (350°F., gas 4) for about 20 minutes.

To freeze: when the pancakes are cold, arrange them side by side on large pieces of foil in the quantities you would normally need for a meal – two of them make a fairly substantial starter. Wrap securely before freezing.

To serve after freezing: transfer the pancakes from the foil to a shallow oven-proof dish. Sprinkle the grated cheese on top and put them at once in the upper part of a hot oven (450°F., gas 8) for about 30 minutes. They are better reheated in this way than if they are allowed to thaw first.

[C] *Spinach Soufflé*

This soufflé is enough as a starter for 3 to 4 people.

3 oz. frozen spinach (cooked)	2 tbs. double cream
approx. 1 oz. butter	3 oz. grated cheese
2–3 tbs. top of the milk	salt and pepper
3 eggs and 1 extra white	

Tip the frozen spinach into a saucepan with about half the butter and the top of the milk and warm through gently until it has thawed. Put through a blender or a mouli. Beat the yolks and stir them into the purée. Add the grated cheese and the lightly whipped cream and season. Finally fold in the stiffly beaten whites. Pour into a 2-pint buttered soufflé dish and dot with the rest of the butter. Cook in the centre of a moderate oven (350°F., gas 4) for about 35 minutes. Serve immediately.

If fresh spinach is used, about 8 oz. will be needed.

[C] *Florentine Eggs*

12 oz. frozen spinach (cooked)	2 tbs. flour
6 eggs	1 pt milk
4 oz. butter	2 oz. grated cheese
approx. 3 tbs. top of the milk	salt, pepper, nutmeg

Put the frozen spinach into a saucepan with 2 oz. of the butter and the top of the milk and warm it gently. Make a sauce with the rest of the butter, the flour and the milk, season, and when the sauce has thickened pour about half into another saucepan and keep warm. Add the spinach to the sauce remaining in the pan and stir well together. Test for seasoning, and turn it into a heated shallow ovenproof dish. Keep warm.

Poach the eggs, which should be slightly underdone when you take them out of the water. Arrange them on top of the spinach, and pour over them the remainder of the sauce, to which about half the cheese and a couple of shakes of nutmeg have been added. Sprinkle the remaining cheese on top, and brown quickly under the grill.

If you make this dish with fresh spinach, you will need 1½ to 2 lb.

[C]   *Spinach with Rice*

8 oz. frozen spinach (cooked)   ¾ pt milk
8 oz. risotto rice, preferably   ¼ pt single cream
   Italian   3 oz. grated cheese
2 oz. butter   salt, pepper, nutmeg
1½ tbs. flour

Put the rice on to cook and meanwhile make a sauce with the butter, flour and milk. Add the frozen spinach and simmer gently for 10 to 15 minutes, chopping the spinach roughly as it thaws. Add the cream, the grated cheese, the seasoning and two or three shakes of nutmeg.

When the rice is ready drain it well, put it in a casserole, place a piece of foil loosely on top and allow it to dry off in a low oven for a few minutes. See that the sauce is very hot, pour it over the rice, and serve immediately.

If you make this dish with fresh spinach, you will need about 1 lb.

RHUBARB

Rhubarb is one of the best of all fruits to freeze, and the flavour and colour are preserved perfectly when it is frozen without sugar.

[A] *To freeze:* wash the stalks or wipe them with a damp cloth, cut them into convenient lengths for cooking later on and freeze in polythene bags.

[C] *To serve after freezing:* put the frozen rhubarb in a stainless steel or enamel saucepan, with 1 tablespoon of water to prevent it from sticking and sugar in the proportion of 4 to 6 oz. to 1 lb. rhubarb. Leave on the gentlest possible heat until the rhubarb is cooked. This can also be done in a double saucepan or a covered casserole in a moderate oven.

[B/C]   *Rhubarb Crumble*

1 lb. rhubarb	**6 oz. flour**
4 oz. sugar	**4 oz. sugar**
grated rind of 1 orange (optional)	**2 oz. butter**

[B] *To make with fresh rhubarb*

Cut the rhubarb into small pieces and place it in a casserole. If you are freezing the crumble use a foil piedish or see method 2 on p. 17.

* Sprinkle on the sugar and the grated orange rind and stir in well.

Make the crumble top by mixing the flour with the sugar and then rubbing in the butter. Spread this mixture over the top of the rhubarb and pat it down firmly.

To serve immediately : place in a medium oven (375°F., gas 5) and cook for about one hour, until the crumble is golden brown.

To freeze : make sure the crumble is very firmly patted down. If you have used a foil dish wrap well before freezing. Otherwise see p. 17.

To serve after freezing : place the frozen crumble in a hot oven (425°F., gas 7) for ½ hour. Turn the oven down to 375°F., gas 5, and cook for a further hour.

[C] *To make with frozen rhubarb*

This pudding is excellent made with frozen rhubarb for eating straight away – but not, of course, for freezing, since it would spoil the rhubarb to freeze it twice. Place the rhubarb in a piedish, add 1 to 2 tablespoons of water, and proceed as from * above.

[C] *Skegness Pudding*

This pudding can be made equally well with frozen plums or blackberries, either on their own or combined with apple

1–1½ lb. frozen rhubarb	3 oz. margarine
6–8 oz. sugar	1 egg
6 oz. self-raising flour	a little milk

Allow the rhubarb to thaw for 3 to 4 hours. Place it in an oven-proof dish with all but 1 oz. of the sugar. Rub the flour into the margarine and add the remaining 1 oz. sugar, the beaten egg and a very little milk – enough to make a stiff, cake-like mixture. Spread this on top of the rhubarb. Bake in a moderate oven (350°F., gas 4) for about 45 minutes, until the top is golden brown and crusty.

[C] *Foamy Rhubarb Tart*

1 tart serves 4–6 people.

1 lb. frozen rhubarb	2 eggs
6 oz. sweetened shortcrust pastry (see p. 28)	2 tbs. cream or sour cream
6 oz. sugar	grated rind of ½ lemon

Place the frozen rhubarb in a bowl with 4 oz. of the sugar and leave for 4–5 hours to draw out the juice.

Line a buttered 8-inch flan-tin with the shortcrust pastry and bake blind for 10 minutes in a hot oven (425°F., gas 7). Take the rhubarb out of the bowl with a slotted spoon, so that most of the juice remains in the bowl, and spread it on the pastry case. Sprinkle on the rest of the sugar and bake for 30–40 minutes in a medium oven (375°F., gas 5) until the rhubarb is tender.

Beat the egg yolks into the rhubarb juice and add the grated lemon rind and the cream. Fold in the stiffly beaten egg whites, pour over the tart, and return it to the oven until it has set – about 25 minutes.

Serve hot or cold.

[B/C]   *Rhubarb Mould*

This is blander than most rhubarb dishes, and is often more popular with children.

2 lb. rhubarb   **2 oz. cornflour**
approx. 1 lb. sugar

If you are using fresh rhubarb, cut it into small pieces, place them in a bowl, sprinkle on the sugar and leave for at least 2 hours to draw out the juice. If you are using frozen rhubarb, leave with the sugar on for at least 5 hours.

Turn the rhubarb and juice into a saucepan, add enough water to cover, bring to the boil and simmer, covered, until the rhubarb is very tender. Mix the cornflour to a smooth paste with 2 tbs. water. Pour into the rhubarb and boil for 5 minutes, stirring all the time, until the mixture thickens and loses any cloudiness. Test for sweetness.

To serve immediately: rinse out a bowl or mould with cold water. Pour in the rhubarb mixture and chill. Turn out when it has set, sprinkle a little sugar on top, and serve with cream.

To freeze: pour into a foil or plastic mould, allow to cool, cover and freeze. Or see method 4 on p. 17.

To serve after freezing: allow to thaw at room temperature for 5 to 6 hours or overnight in the refrigerator. Turn out, sprinkle a little sugar on top and serve with cream.

May

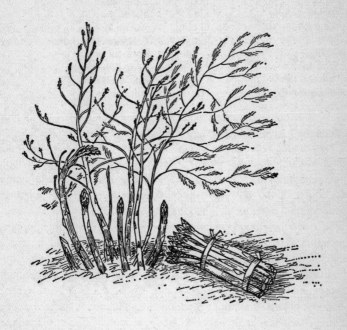

[B] *Crab Bisque*

A fitting use for an elderly crab, more likely to be encountered towards the end of the season.

Although as soups go this is expensive, you can make about 3½ pints of soup with one large crab, which will provide a rich beginning for at least two dinner parties for 6.

1 large whole cooked crab	1 oz. butter
2 onions	1 oz. flour
2 carrots	2 egg yolks
1 tbs. gin (optional)	½ pt single cream
½ lemon	salt and pepper
parsley, fennel, bayleaf	

a dash of Pernod (optional)

Wash the crab thoroughly, crack it open and take out all the meat, discarding the inedible lungs (or 'dead man's fingers' as they are sometimes called). Put the shells in a large saucepan, add the roughly chopped onions and carrots, place on a high flame for a few moments and then pour on the gin, leaving it to evaporate for one minute over the flame. This may be omitted, but it makes a perceptible difference to the luxurious taste of the soup. Add enough cold water to cover the shells amply (about 4 pints), bring to the boil, skim, add the lemon juice and peel and the herbs and simmer for about 1 hour.

Set aside the meat from the claws and pass the rest of the meat through a blender with a little of the stock, or put through a mouli. Strain the remaining stock, blend in the crab purée, and add the flaked meat from the claws.

Make a beurre manié by working the flour into the butter. Drop this into the soup and stir while it dissolves and the soup thickens. Whisk the egg yolks briefly with the cream and add this to the soup, continuing to stir over a low heat. Do not allow the soup to boil once the eggs have been added. Season and serve – for special occasions with a dash of Pernod in each bowl.

To freeze: cool and freeze in waxed or plastic containers.

To serve after freezing: tip the frozen soup into a saucepan, and reheat very gently. On no account allow it to boil, as this will curdle the eggs.

[B]   *Crabmeat in Sauce*

Like most fish dishes, this is only worth freezing if you have some really fresh crabs. Served on croûtons it makes an unusual and delicious first course for a dinner party or a light supper dish; or it may be used as a filling for vol-au-vents.

8 oz. crabmeat	½ tsp. French mustard
1 oz. butter	2 tbs. cream
1 oz. flour	squeeze of lemon juice
½ pt milk	salt and pepper
1 tbs. sherry or brandy	

Flake the crabmeat. Make a sauce with the butter, the flour and the milk, and cook until it is thick and smooth. Add the crabmeat, the sherry or brandy, the mustard, the cream and a squeeze of lemon juice, and season to taste.

To serve immediately: heat very gently without allowing the mixture to boil, and serve in either of the ways suggested above.

To freeze: cool, and freeze in plastic or waxed containers.

To serve after freezing: tip the frozen mass into a saucepan and reheat gently, stirring frequently. You may need to add another tablespoonful of cream if the mixture seems a little dry. Serve as above.

[B] *Crab Quiche*

6 oz. crabmeat
10 oz. shortcrust pastry (see p. 28)
2 whole eggs
4 egg yolks

1 tsp. French mustard
1 oz. grated cheddar or gruyère cheese (optional)
½ pt single cream
salt and pepper

Line one 10-inch or two 7-inch buttered flan-tins with the pastry. If you are freezing the quiches use foil flan-cases or see methods 2 or 3 on p. 18.

Beat the whole eggs and the yolks lightly with a fork, until they are well amalgamated but not frothy. Add the mustard and the cheese and season well. Gradually beat in the cream, stir in the crabmeat and pour this mixture into the pastry cases. Bake in a moderate oven (375°F., gas 5) for 35 to 40 minutes.

To serve immediately: cook for a further 5 minutes, or until the top is golden brown.

To freeze: allow to cool. If you have used a foil case wrap well before freezing. Otherwise see p. 18.

To serve after freezing: place the frozen quiche in a hot oven (425°F., gas 7). After 20 minutes lower the temperature to 350°F., gas 4, and leave for a further 30 to 40 minutes, according to the size of the quiche, until it has heated right through. Place a piece of foil over the top, if necessary, to prevent excessive browning.

ASPARAGUS

The season for asparagus is short and it is a luxury food whether you buy it or grow it. So enjoy it fresh while you can and don't bother to freeze it unless you have a glut, especially as frozen blanched it tends to become stringy and rather tasteless.

However, for anyone who does have some to spare, here are two recipes to be made in conjunction with each other which do freeze well.

[B]   ASPARAGUS TART

2 lb. asparagus (preferably the   6 eggs
  thin, green English variety)   ¼ pt single cream
10 oz. shortcrust pastry (see   1 oz. grated cheese
  p. 28)   salt, pepper and sugar

Line one 10-inch or two 7-inch buttered flan-tins with the shortcrust pastry. If you are freezing the tarts, use foil flan-cases or see methods 2 or 3 on p. 18.

Trim the asparagus and boil in salted water to which you have added 1 lump of sugar to take away any bitterness. When it is cooked lift it carefully out of the saucepan and reserve the water. Cut off all the tender part of the stalks and arrange these in the pastry cases. Keep the rest of the stalks and water for making asparagus soup (see p. 115). Beat the eggs lightly with the cream, add the cheese and the salt and pepper and pour over the asparagus. Bake in a medium oven (375°F., gas 5) for 40 minutes.

To serve immediately: cook for a further 5 minutes, until the top is golden brown.

To freeze: allow to cool. If you have used a foil case wrap well before freezing. Otherwise see p. 18.

To serve after freezing: place the frozen tart in a hot oven (425°F., gas 7) for 20 minutes. Turn the oven down to 350°F., gas 4, and cook for another 30 to 40 minutes, according to the size of the tart, until it has heated right through. Place a piece of foil over the top if necessary to prevent excessive browning.

[B] *Asparagus Soup*

This quantity is enough for 4 people.

remains of the asparagus stalks (see asparagus tart)	1 oz. flour
1 pt asparagus water	2 egg yolks
1 oz. butter	⅛ pt single cream

Melt the butter in a saucepan, add the flour and cook gently for 5 minutes, stirring all the time. Gradually add ¾ pint of the asparagus water and stir until it is smooth. Put the remains of the asparagus stalks into a blender with the remaining ¼ pint of the asparagus water, and blend for a few minutes. (If you haven't a blender, use a mouli for this.) Pass through a sieve and add to the soup.

Combine the egg yolks with the cream and add them to the soup. Reheat the soup gently, but do not allow it to boil. Season and serve.

To freeze: cool, and pour into waxed or plastic containers.

To serve after freezing: tip the frozen soup into a saucepan and reheat very gently. On no account allow it to boil, as this will curdle the eggs.

(You can of course make this soup much more extravagantly by using the whole asparagus. In this case chop the tips into ½-inch lengths and add them to the soup at the end.)

HERBS

Perennial herbs are at their best and freshest in May, so now is the time to freeze them. It is well worth freezing any which you use in large quantities or in a great many dishes. Mint, parsley, chives, basil and tarragon, for instance, are a boon to have in the freezer, and bouquets garnis are worth their weight in gold.

Which other herbs you freeze is largely a matter of convenience and taste and it is worth experimenting to find what best suits you. In our view it is not worth going to the bother of freezing herbs that are used in very small quantities, for the dried varieties which can be bought nowadays are in general very good indeed.

Herbs have an extremely strong odour once they are in the freezer, and will contaminate other foods unless they are stored in airtight containers. This applies particularly to mint; even the smallest quantity, insufficiently wrapped, can make the whole freezer smell. So store them in screw-topped jars – coffee or honey jars are excellent.

The taste and strength of herbs frozen raw sometimes alters unpredictably, but when they are used in dishes which are cooked before freezing they do not seem to change at all.

Freeze the herbs in either of the following ways:

[A] 1. Prepare a really large number of bouquets garnis with two or three sprigs of parsley and a sprig each of marjoram and thyme and a bay leaf. Tie them in small bunches, and pack loosely in an airtight jar. Later you can take them out one by one as you need them.

2. Parsley, mint, tarragon and any other herbs which you will use separately and in larger quantities, can be packed into individual airtight jars. Use straight from the freezer, crumbling out as much as you need.

[B] *Parsley Soup*

a large bunch of fresh parsley
  (approx. 4 oz.)
2 onions
2 potatoes

2 oz. butter
2 pt chicken stock
salt and pepper

cream for serving (optional)

Cut the parsley tops off the stalks and set aside. Sweat the chopped onions and potatoes in the butter for 5 minutes, then add the chicken stock and the parsley stalks and cook for 10 minutes or until the potato is soft. Remove the stalks and pass the soup through a blender together with the parsley tops, until the parsley is quite fine. If you do not have a blender, pass the soup through a mouli or nylon sieve and then add the very finely chopped parsley. Season.

To serve immediately: this soup is equally good served hot or cold, and it may be improved by the last minute addition of a small amount of cream to each serving.

To serve hot – reheat gently, test for seasoning and serve.

To serve cold – chill, test for seasoning and serve.

To freeze: cool and pack in waxed or plastic containers.

To serve after freezing:

To serve hot – tip the frozen soup into a saucepan, reheat it gently and proceed as above.

To serve cold – allow to thaw at room temperature or in the refrigerator. Serve while still very cold.

Meat with Herbs

Meat is excellent roasted with herbs, which give a deliciously subtle flavour and also improve the taste very much when the meat is cold. If you are roasting a joint of beef, such as topside, flank or brisket, take off the string and the fat in which the butcher has rolled it, and cover the meat lavishly with salt, pepper and several tablespoonsful of chopped fresh or frozen herbs – parsley, rosemary, marjoram, thyme, and anything else you may have. Replace the fat and the string, and roast in the ordinary way. Any of the meat left over can be frozen and eaten cold later on.

A leg or shoulder of lamb can be scored very deeply – almost to the bone – in half-a-dozen places, and sprigs of rosemary tucked into the cuts. Pour over 3 or 4 tablespoons of olive oil and roast. The rosemary, as well as giving the meat a pleasantly piquant taste, becomes crisp in the cooking, and some or all of it can be served up with the meat. After you have had the joint hot, remove the rosemary, carve the meat into slices, and freeze. If you put a piece of moisture-vapour-proof tissue between each slice the meat will thaw more quickly and be easier to serve. (It is better to carve it first – otherwise the bone will take up so much room.)

Another method is to insert chopped herbs, mixed with a little butter, into the cuts in the shoulder or leg – rather like herb bread – before pot-roasting the joint. Put some olive oil or dripping into a flameproof casserole, rub salt on the meat, and brown it well all over. Add about ½ pint of white wine and cook gently – about 1½ to 2 hours for a medium joint – until the meat is tender. Then take the meat out, skim the fat off the juice remaining in the casserole and use the rest of the liquid for making gravy.

For an economical but excellent meal, try roast breast of lamb stuffed with herbs (see p. 93), or brisket (see p. 242).

[B/C]   *Chicken with Tarragon*

1 roasting chicken (about 4 lb.)	1 onion
	1 carrot
6 or 7 sprigs of tarragon	1 tbs. flour
2 tbs. butter	2 tbs. sherry (optional)
2 tbs. olive oil	salt and pepper

Frozen chicken must be allowed to thaw before roasting.

Put 3 sprigs of tarragon inside the chicken, together with 1 tablespoon of the butter and a little salt and pepper. Truss. Melt the oil and the rest of the butter in a flameproof casserole, and use some of this to brush over the chicken. Gently cook the sliced onion and carrot and the remaining sprigs of tarragon for a few minutes, keeping aside a little tarragon for serving with the gravy. Add the chicken to the casserole and brown it thoroughly all over. Season, baste the chicken well with the butter and oil in the casserole, and cover with a piece of foil and the casserole lid. Put the casserole in the middle of a medium oven (350°F., gas 4) for 1 to 1½ hours, according to the tenderness of the chicken. Baste once or twice. Meanwhile make a stock with the giblets.

When the chicken is tender, take it out of the casserole, and for immediate eating keep it warm while you make the sauce. Strain the liquid in which the chicken was cooked and remove the fat. Put 1 tablespoon of this fat back into the casserole, add the flour and mix well, scraping up any coagulated juices. Make the cooking liquid up to 1 pint with the chicken stock and add gradually, stirring until the sauce is smooth and has thickened. Add the sherry and test for seasoning. Strain, add the reserved tarragon leaves, chopped, and hand this sauce round with the chicken.

To freeze: allow to cool and freeze, either whole or jointed, in a polythene bag or plastic container. The chicken and the sauce can be frozen either together or separately, whichever is the least trouble.

To serve after freezing: If the chicken has been frozen whole, allow it to thaw for about 8 hours at room temperature, or overnight in the refrigerator. Put into a flameproof casserole with the sauce, and warm through in a moderate oven or over a very low heat for 1 to 1¼ hours. You may need to add a little more stock. If it has been frozen jointed, there is no need to wait for it to thaw. Warm over a low heat for 45 minutes to 1 hour, adding a little more stock if necessary.

[C]   *Herb Butter*

Since herbs sometimes alter in strength and flavour when they are frozen, it is best to make herb butter from your stock of frozen herbs as and when you want it; the results are then excellent. The proportions of herbs given below are approximate. This quantity of butter is enough for a medium-sized French loaf.

4 oz. butter	2 crushed cloves garlic
1 tbs. chopped chives	½ tsp. finely grated lemon peel
2 tsp. chopped parsley	(optional)
½ tsp. chopped marjoram	salt and pepper

Soften the butter, and mix well with the herbs, the garlic, and the lemon peel if you are using it. Season.

To make herb bread: cut a medium-sized French loaf into 1 to 1½ inch slices almost down to the bottom crust, and spread the herb butter on one side of each of the slices. Wrap the loaf in foil and put it in a hot oven for about 15 minutes. Take it out of the foil and separate the slices before serving.

                        Mint Ices

If you like the taste of mint and grow your own (and if you have the freezer space), it is well worth making a quantity of these ices now, when the mint is young and tender. With their delicate green colour and unexpected taste, they make a most refreshing end to a rich dinner.

[B]   MINT ICE-CREAM

The quantities given are enough for 6 servings, but multiply them indefinitely. The proportion of cream does not have to be exact, so add as much as you can spare.

1 handful of mint leaves
stripped off the stems
4 oz. sugar
¼ pt water

juice of 1 lemon
¼ pt double cream, or less, if
you want a slightly less rich
ice-cream

Bring the water and sugar to the boil, stirring until all the sugar has dissolved. Boil for 3 minutes and allow to cool.

Meanwhile wash the mint leaves and place them in a blender, pour over the syrup and blend thoroughly. Strain through a nylon sieve, pressing as much of the mint through as possible, add the strained lemon juice, pour it into an ice-tray and freeze for about 1 hour, until it is 'soft frozen'. Then put it back into the blender, blend well, and fold into the lightly whipped cream. Pour into plastic containers with very well fitting lids, so that they are absolutely airtight, and freeze.

To serve: remove from the freezer 1 hour before serving and leave in the refrigerator.

[B]   MINT SORBET

1 handful of mint leaves,
stripped off the stalks
¼ pt water

4 oz. sugar
juice of 1 lemon
2 egg whites

Make in the same way as mint ice-cream, substituting the stiffly beaten egg whites for the whipped cream.

To serve: remove from the freezer 10 to 15 minutes before serving.

June

BROAD BEANS

Broad beans, tender and straight out of the garden, are particularly good for freezing.

[A] *To freeze blanched:* shell the beans and blanch them for 2 minutes. Drain, cool as quickly as possible, and freeze in polythene bags.

[C] *To serve after freezing:* tip the frozen beans into a saucepan containing about 1 inch of salted boiling water and cook gently till they are soft, breaking up the mass carefully with a fork once or twice. Be careful not to overcook the beans, which can easily happen if they are very young. Drain and serve with plenty of butter, or stir in a little cream (about 2 tablespoons to ½ lb. of beans) and some chopped parsley. Or make some béchamel sauce and stir in lots of finely chopped parsley, so that the sauce is quite green, and pour this over the beans.

[B/C] *Lamb with Broad Beans and Lemon Sauce*

If you are making this dish for the freezer, you must use fresh broad beans. For eating straight away it is excellent made with frozen beans.

1 shoulder or leg of lamb	2 yolks of eggs
2 lb. broad beans, or 1 lb. frozen	¼ pt single cream
1 clove garlic	juice of 1 lemon
¼ pt chicken or lamb stock	salt and pepper

If the lamb is frozen it should be allowed to thaw before roasting.

Rub the meat all over with the cut surface of the garlic, and with salt and pepper. Put it in a roasting tin, placing the remains of the garlic underneath. Roast in a medium oven

(375°F., gas 5) for about 1 hour, depending on the size of the joint. The meat should be pink but not raw at the centre, a little less cooked than you will ultimately like to eat it, as it will be reheated in the sauce. Take it out of the oven and pour off the fat. Remove the garlic.

Meanwhile boil the broad beans in some salted water until they are just tender. Drain, but do not throw away the water.

Carve the meat into thick slices, being careful to preserve all the juice. Set it aside, put the roasting pan with the meat juices on a very low heat, add the chicken stock and the egg yolks beaten up with the cream. Stir constantly on a low heat until the sauce thickens but do not allow it to boil. Gradually add the lemon juice and as much of the bean water as the sauce will take without becoming too thin. Check for seasoning.

To serve immediately: return the meat to the pan and allow it to heat through, still being very careful not to allow it to boil. Add the beans and serve.

To freeze: allow the meat, the beans and the sauce to cool, and freeze all together in a foil or plastic container.

To serve after freezing: allow to thaw for at least 5 to 6 hours, reheat, adding a little more stock if necessary, and serve. This dish must not be used straight from the freezer as the long period of heating would overcook the beans and make them tough and dry.

APRICOTS

Apricots can be frozen in sugar or syrup, as a purée, or cooked. They should be dipped briefly into a lemon juice solution as soon as they have been halved for stoning, so that they do not become discoloured. Ripe fruit should be chosen for freezing.

[A] *With sugar:* wash, halve and stone the fruit, and dip it for a few seconds in a solution of water and lemon juice, using the juice of $\frac{1}{2}$ lemon to 1 pint water. Mix the fruit with sugar in the proportion of 4 oz. sugar to 1 lb. fruit (weighed before stoning). Freeze in polythene bags.

In syrup: wash, halve and stone the fruit, and dip it in the lemon solution. Put the fruit in waxed or plastic containers, and cover with cold syrup made in the proportion of 7 oz. sugar to 1 pint water. Put a piece of crumpled foil over the top of the fruit, under the cover, to keep it below the syrup.

Cooked: this is a useful way of freezing fruit which is not quite ripe. Wash, halve and stone the apricots. Put them at once into a saucepan with syrup made in the proportion of 7 oz. sugar to 1 pint of water. A generous $\frac{1}{4}$ pint of syrup should be sufficient for 1 lb. apricots. Cook gently until the fruit is soft. Cool, and freeze in waxed or plastic containers.

Purée: wash, halve and stone the fruit. Purée in a blender with sugar in the proportion of 4 oz. sugar to 1 lb. fruit (weighed before stoning). To prevent discolouration, add about 1 teaspoon lemon juice for every 1 lb. fruit. The purée is still likely to darken a little, but the taste should not be affected. Put through a nylon sieve and freeze in waxed or plastic containers.

[B/C]   *Apricot Tart*

One tart serves 4 to 6 people.

1 lb. apricots, fresh, or frozen with sugar	4 oz. sugar
	$\frac{1}{2}$ oz. butter
6 oz. sweetened shortcrust pastry (see p. 28)	

[B] *To make with fresh apricots*

Line a buttered 8-inch flan-tin with the pastry. If the tart is for the freezer use a foil flan-case or see methods 2 or 3 on p. 18. Bake blind for 10 minutes in a hot oven (425°F., gas 7).

Sprinkle half the sugar on the pastry case, halve the apricots and stone them, and place them domed side up on the pastry, as close together as possible. Sprinkle on the rest of the sugar, and dot each half-fruit with a small knob of butter. Put in a moderate oven (375°F., gas 5) and bake for 30 minutes or until the fruit is cooked, by which time the pastry should be a rich golden brown and a thick syrup will have formed.

To serve immediately: serve hot or cold.

To freeze: allow to cool. If you have used a foil flan-case wrap and freeze. Otherwise see p. 18.

To serve after freezing: place the frozen tart in a hot oven (425°F., gas 7) for ½ hour. Serve hot or cold.

[C] *To make from frozen apricots*

Make as above, using the fruit as soon as it has thawed enough to separate, and omitting the sugar from the list of ingredients. Do not freeze the tart if it has been made with frozen fruit.

[B/C] *Frozen Apricot Mousse*

[B] *To make with fresh apricots*

1 lb. apricots	3 eggs
6 oz. caster sugar	¼ pt double cream
1 tsp. lemon juice	

Make a purée with the apricots, 4 oz. of the sugar and the lemon juice by the method described on p. 127.

* Whip the eggs with the remaining 2 oz. sugar until they are thick and almost white. Gradually add the purée and fold in the lightly whipped cream. Test for sweetness.

To serve immediately: pour into a dish and freeze for 3 to 4 hours. This mousse should be served still almost frozen, so take it out of the freezer 10 to 15 minutes before serving.

To freeze: see methods 2, 3 or 4 on p. 17.

To serve after freezing: remove from the freezer 10 to 15 minutes before serving.

[C] *To make from frozen apricot purée*

½ pt apricot purée   2 oz. caster sugar
3 eggs   ¼ pt double cream

Allow the purée to thaw to a mushy state, and then proceed as from * above.

[B/C]   *Apricot Ice-Cream*

[B] *To make with fresh apricots*

1 lb. apricots   1 tsp. lemon juice
6 oz. sugar   ½ pt double cream

Make a purée with the apricots, the sugar and the lemon juice by the method described on p. 127.

   * Whip the cream lightly and fold into the apricot purée. Pour into an ice-tray or a basin and freeze for 1 to 2 hours or until the mixture has reached a mushy state. Take out of the freezer, beat well, pour into waxed or plastic containers and replace in the freezer.

   To serve: remove from the freezer 1 hour before serving, and leave in the refrigerator.

[C] *To make from frozen apricot purée*

½ pt apricot purée   ½ pt double cream
2 oz. caster sugar

Allow the purée to thaw to a mushy state and complete the recipe as from * above.

CHERRIES

Cherries can be frozen with sugar, in syrup or cooked. Ripe, sound fruit, either red or black, should be chosen. If the stones are removed before freezing, the cherries are easier to use in recipes afterwards. Also, if they are frozen with the stones in, they may acquire an almond-like flavour.

[A] *With sugar:* remove the stalks, wash the fruit and take out the stones. To 1 lb. fruit (weighed before stoning) allow 4 oz. sugar. Mix the fruit and sugar together before freezing in polythene bags.

In syrup: remove the stalks, wash the fruit and take out the stones. Put the fruit in waxed or plastic containers. Cover with cold syrup made in the proportion of 9 oz. sugar to 1 pint water. Put a piece of crumpled foil over the top of the fruit, under the cover, to keep it below the syrup.

Cooked: this is a particularly good method of freezing cherries. Remove the stalks, wash the fruit and take out the stones. Cook the cherries gently in syrup made with 9 oz. sugar to 1 pint water. About ½ pint syrup should be sufficient for 1 lb. fruit (weighed before stoning). When the fruit is soft (after about ¼ hour), allow to cool and pour into waxed or plastic containers.

[B] *Cherry Pie*

1 lb. cherries
10 oz. sweetened shortcrust pastry (see p. 28)
2 oz. ground almonds or ground walnuts
3–4 oz. sugar

Line a floured 8-inch flan-tin with two thirds of the pastry. If the pie is for the freezer use a foil flan-case or see p. 18. Sprinkle the nuts on the pastry and arrange the stoned cherries on top. Sprinkle on the sugar and cover with the rest of the pastry. Seal well.

To serve immediately: cook in a medium oven (375°F., gas 5) for about 50 minutes. Serve cold.

To freeze: if you have used a foil flan-case wrap and freeze. Otherwise, see p. 18.

To serve after freezing: put the frozen tart into a hot oven

(425°F., gas 7) for 30 minutes. Then turn the oven down to 375°F., gas 5, and cook for a further 45 minutes (1¼ hours in all).

[B]   *Frangipan Cake*

3½ lb. cherries, morello or firm black ones	4 oz. butter
	4 oz. sugar
12 oz. sweetened shortcrust pastry (see p. 28)	2 eggs
	2 oz. flour
4 oz. cake or biscuit crumbs	6 oz. ground almonds

For the glaze

4 tbs. apricot jam or marmalade	2 tbs. water

For the icing

4 oz. icing sugar	juice of ½ lemon
2 tbs. water	

Line two buttered 8-inch flan-tins with the pastry and bake them blind for 10 minutes in a hot oven (425°F., gas 7). When they have cooled a little sprinkle the biscuit crumbs over the pastry cases and arrange the stoned cherries on top.

Cream the butter and sugar and add the eggs, the flour and the ground almonds. Spread this mixture over the cherries and bake in a medium oven (375°F., gas 5) for 40 minutes. When the tops are a pale golden brown take the flans out of the oven, allow them to cool for a few minutes and transfer them to a wire tray.

To serve immediately: make the glaze by boiling the jam or marmalade with the water for a few minutes until it thickens, strain through a nylon sieve, and paint the cakes with two coats of the glaze, allowing the first to dry before you apply the second.

When the glaze has dried put the icing sugar, the water and the lemon juice in a saucepan and boil gently, stirring continuously, for about 2 minutes. Allow to cool for a few minutes and paint two coats on the cakes, allowing the first to dry a little before applying the second. When the icing has set the cakes are ready to serve.

To freeze: allow to cool and wrap well before freezing.

To serve after freezing: place the frozen tart in a hot oven (425°F., gas 7) for ½ hour. Then finish off with the glaze and the icing as for immediate eating.

Note: you can also freeze the cake after it has been glazed and iced, but you will then not be able to put it into the oven to crisp up the pastry.

[B/C]   *Cherry Ice-Cream*

[B] *To make from fresh cherries*

½ lb. cherries (6 oz. after stoning)	¼ lb. sugar
	¼ pt single cream
¼ pt water	¼ pt double cream

Stone the cherries. Make a syrup with the water and sugar and stew the cherries gently until they are soft.

* Cool, and put through a blender or mouli. If you use a blender do not purée the fruit too much, as the ice-cream is more interesting if there are bits of cherry in it. This quantity should make about ½ pint purée. Pour it into an ice-tray or a basin, cover, and put in the freezer until it starts to set. Take it out, beat well or put it back into the blender for a minute or two, and fold in the lightly whipped cream. Pour into a waxed or plastic container and replace in the freezer.

To serve after freezing: take out of the freezer about 1 hour before serving and leave in the refrigerator.

[C] *To make from frozen cherries*

For this recipe it is easiest to use ½ lb. cherries frozen in syrup; the proportion of liquid to cherries then works out about right. Stew the cherries gently in their syrup until they are soft, and complete the recipe as from * above.

[C]   *Hot Cherry Sauce and Ice-Cream*

This is a quick and easy dessert for unexpected guests. The quantities given below will provide enough sauce for 8 to 10 people.

1 pt cherries, frozen cooked or   2 tbs. kirsch
   in syrup   vanilla ice-cream
¼ pt brandy

Turn the frozen cherries into a saucepan and warm gently. If they have been frozen uncooked, continue to simmer them until they are soft. Strain off the syrup, and continue to warm the cherries until they are very hot right through. Pour the brandy over them and set it on fire. When the flames have died down, add the kirsch. Serve at once, poured over the individual helpings of ice-cream.

GOOSEBERRIES

Gooseberries can be frozen in almost any form – with sugar, in syrup, as a purée or cooked. The methods you choose will depend on what you need them for later on.

[A] *With sugar:* top and tail the fruit and wash and dry it. To 1 lb. fruit allow 4 oz. sugar. Mix the fruit and the sugar together before freezing in polythene bags.

In syrup: top and tail the fruit. Wash it and put in waxed or plastic containers. Cover with cold syrup made in the proportion of 9 oz. sugar to 1 pint of water. Put a piece of crumpled foil over the top, under the cover, to keep the fruit below the syrup.

Cooked: gooseberries frozen in this way are excellent served as a compôte, and are particularly tender. Top and tail the fruit and wash it. It can be cooked either in the oven or stewed. For the oven method, put it in an oven-proof dish, sprinkle on sugar in the proportion of 4 oz. sugar to 1 lb. fruit, cover, and cook in a moderate oven (350°F., gas 4) for about ½ hour, until the fruit is soft but still unbroken. To stew it, cook the gooseberries in syrup made with 9 oz. sugar to 1 pint water. About ½ pint syrup should be sufficient for 1 lb. gooseberries. Cook very gently until the fruit is soft. Cool and freeze in waxed or plastic containers. Tastes in sweetness vary so greatly that it is impossible to be exact about the amount of sugar, so sample before the fruit cools, and add more sugar if necessary.

Purée: wash the fruit, but do not bother to top and tail it. Add sugar in the proportion of 4 oz. sugar to 1 lb. gooseberries and 2 or 3 tablespoons of water – just enough to stop the fruit from catching – and simmer gently: when it is soft, pass through a nylon sieve. Cool and freeze in waxed or plastic containers.

[B/C]   *Gooseberry Tart*

One tart serves 4 to 6 people.

1 lb. gooseberries, fresh, or frozen with sugar	2 egg yolks
	3 oz. sugar
6 oz. sweetened shortcrust pastry (see p. 28)	¼ pt single cream

[B] *To make with fresh gooseberries*

Line a buttered 8-inch flan-tin with the pastry or, if the tart is for the freezer, use a foil flan-case or see methods 2 or 3 on p. 18. Bake the tart blind for 10 minutes in a hot oven (425°F., gas 7).

Top and tail the gooseberries. Pack them into the pastry case as closely as possible – if you stand them on end you can get more into the space.

Beat the egg yolks lightly with the sugar and the cream and pour this over the gooseberries. Return to the oven and bake for a further 30 to 40 minutes at a moderate heat (375°F., gas 5) until the eggs and cream have set. Serve hot or cold.

To freeze: if you have used a foil flan-case, allow to cool, wrap and freeze. Otherwise see p. 18.

To serve after freezing: place the frozen tart in a hot oven (425°F., gas 7) for ½ hour. Serve hot or cold.

[C] *To make from gooseberries frozen with sugar*

Make as above, omitting the sugar from the list of ingredients. Place the frozen gooseberries in the flan-case with any sugar that adheres to them, and beat up the rest of the sugar with the egg yolks and cream. The cooking will take about 10 minutes longer. Do not freeze the tart if it has been made with frozen fruit.

[B/C] ## *Gooseberry Mousse*

[B] *To make from fresh gooseberries*

1 lb. gooseberries	a squeeze of **lemon juice**
4–6 oz. sugar	2 egg whites
½ oz. gelatine	¼ pt double cream

Do not bother to top and tail the gooseberries. Put them in a saucepan with the sugar and 2 tablespoons of water and simmer them gently for about 15 minutes, or until they are soft. Pass them through a nylon sieve.

* Soak the gelatine in 2 tbs. water. Stir this into the hot purée immediately, so that the heat of the fruit will completely dissolve it. Add the lemon juice, test for sweetness, and stir in a little more caster sugar if necessary. Allow to cool.

Whisk the egg whites till they are stiff but not dry and fold them into the gooseberry mixture. Beat the cream lightly and fold this in also.

To serve immediately: pour into a dish, chill and serve.

To freeze: see methods 2, 3 or 4 on p. 17.

To serve after freezing: allow to thaw at room temperature for 5 to 6 hours, or overnight in the refrigerator.

[C] *To make from frozen gooseberries*

½ pt. gooseberry purée	½ oz. gelatine
or	a squeeze of lemon juice
1 lb gooseberries frozen with	2 egg whites
sugar	¼ pt double cream

Heat the frozen purée gently. If you are using frozen goose-berries cook them gently with 2 tablespoons of water and pass them through a nylon sieve. Stir the sugar into the purée and complete the recipe as from * above.

[B/C]   *Gooseberry Fool*

2 lb. gooseberries	2 egg yolks
¼ pt water	2 tsp. custard powder
½ lb. sugar	½ pt milk

½ pt double cream

[B] *To make from fresh gooseberries*

Do not bother to top and tail the gooseberries. Make a syrup with the water and sugar and stew the gooseberries gently until they are soft. Rub them through a nylon sieve and leave them to get cold. This quantity should yield about 1 pint of purée.

* Make a custard with the egg yolks, the custard powder and the milk, and leave this also to get cold. It is best to make this custard in a double saucepan so that there is no risk that it will curdle. Mix the gooseberry purée and the custard together and test for sweetness. If it is not quite sweet enough, stir in a little caster sugar.

To serve immediately: fold in the lightly whipped cream and chill before serving.

To freeze: freeze in a waxed or plastic container.

To serve after freezing: allow to thaw for 4 to 5 hours. Stir well, and fold in the lightly whipped cream.

136

[C] *To make from frozen gooseberries*

Gooseberries frozen by any method can be used for fool – it is simply a question of adjusting the quantities of the other ingredients to the amount of purée you have. Easiest of all, of course, is to use sweetened purée, in which case you can simply complete the fool by proceeding from * above. Otherwise the sugar or water may need to be omitted, or the quantity altered. But gooseberry fool is such an adaptable dish that exact proportions are not important, so long as the texture is smooth, there is enough cream, and, most important of all, the taste of gooseberry is strong enough.

[B/C]   *Gooseberry Ice-Cream*

[B] *To make from fresh gooseberries*

1 lb. gooseberries   **½ pt double cream**
6 oz. sugar

Make a purée with the gooseberries as given on p. 134, but using 6 oz. sugar instead of 4 oz. Allow to cool. Whip the cream lightly until it has thickened and fold it into the purée. Turn into a basin or ice-tray and freeze for 1 to 2 hours until the mixture has reached a mushy state. Take out of the freezer, beat well, pour into waxed or plastic containers and replace in the freezer.

To serve: remove from the freezer 1 hour before serving and leave in the refrigerator.

[C] *To make from frozen gooseberry purée*

½ pt frozen gooseberry purée   ½ pt double cream
2 oz. caster sugar

Allow the purée to thaw to a mushy state. Whip the cream lightly with the sugar, and fold into the purée. Freeze and serve as above.

PEACHES

[A] Peaches are particularly delicious frozen. The methods of freezing are the same as for apricots (see p. 126), but they should be peeled before freezing. If the skins do not come off easily, pour boiling water over the peaches, leave them for 15 seconds or more, according to how ripe they are, and plunge them immediately into cold water. They are even more apt to discolour than apricots, so they should be prepared for freezing as quickly as possible.

There is no need to sieve peach purée.

[B/C]   *Peach Tart*

This is made in exactly the same way as apricot tart (see p. 127), and is if anything more delicious. Use the small yellow peaches – you will need 5 or 6, according to size. The peaches should be peeled before they are put in the pastry case.

[B/C]   *Peach and Raspberry Compôte*

6 peaches
approx. 4 oz. sugar
½ pt water
½ lb. raspberries

Alpine strawberries (not essential, but even a few of them make a great difference to the taste)

2 tbs. kirsch or brandy
a few almonds
whipped cream

[B] *To make from fresh fruit*

Skin the peaches (see above) but leave them whole. Make a syrup with the sugar and water, and poach the peaches gently until they are soft. Leave them in the syrup until they are cold. Then stone them, and cut each half-peach into three or four pieces. Add the raspberries and the strawberries.

To serve immediately: skin the almonds and cut them into slices. Add to the compôte. Pour on the kirsch or brandy, and leave for two or three hours. Chill slightly, and serve with lightly whipped cream.

To freeze: pour into a waxed or plastic container.

To serve after freezing: thaw the fruit in the unopened container. Then put it in a bowl, add the almonds and kirsch or brandy, leave it for about ½ hour, and serve with whipped cream.

[C] *To make from frozen fruit*

Since peaches and raspberries both freeze excellently, this is a good dessert to make from frozen fruit. Use frozen cooked peaches, and raspberries frozen in sugar. Or make it with ripe peaches frozen in syrup, as the syrup will provide the juice. Thaw the fruit in the unopened containers before mixing them in a bowl. Add the almonds and brandy or kirsch, and leave for about ½ hour before serving.

[B/C] *Peach Crème Brûlée*

This is a simple but unusual way of serving peaches. It can be varied by the addition of small seedless grapes, Alpine strawberries or raspberries.

6 large peaches
    or
4 peaches and ½ lb. any soft
    fruit
2–4 oz. soft brown sugar

caster sugar
¼ pt double cream (or more)

[B] *To make with fresh fruit*

Peel and slice the peaches, and add any other fruit you are using. Mix all together, sugar to taste, and place in a soufflé or other heat-proof dish, or, if you are going to freeze it, in a foil pie-dish. Whip the cream until it is stiff, sweeten it very slightly and spread it over the top of the fruit.

To serve immediately: chill in the coldest part of the refrigerator for several hours. Then sprinkle the brown sugar over the cream, spreading it quite thickly: the exact amount of sugar and cream will therefore vary with the shape of the container you have used. Place this for a few minutes under a very hot grill, until the sugar has melted. Or use a salamander. Return to the refrigerator for about half-an-hour before serving – the sugar will form a delicious hard brown crust over the cream.

To freeze: wrap the foil dish well before freezing.

To serve after freezing: remove the dish from the freezer 4 to 6 hours before you are going to serve it. Sprinkle on the brown sugar immediately, and place under the grill as above. Then leave to thaw for 4 hours at room temperature or for 6 hours in the refrigerator.

[C] *To make with fruit frozen with sugar*

Allow the fruit to thaw for 1½ to 2 hours, or until it is soft enough to spread out in the heat-proof dish. Whip the cream until it is stiff, sweeten it very slightly, spoon it over the fruit and flatten the top. Chill in the refrigerator for ½ hour. Sprinkle on the brown sugar, caramelize it as for immediate eating, and leave for 2 to 3 hours at room temperature, to allow the fruit to finish thawing.

[B] *Spiced Peaches*

These are particularly good as an alternative to chutney with cold ham, pork, duck or pheasant.

2 lb. peaches	1 tsp. ground cloves
1 lb. sugar	½ tsp. ground nutmeg
2 tsp. each ground cinnamon, allspice and coriander seeds	bare ½ pt cider or wine vinegar, or a combination of the two

Peel the peaches and halve and stone them. Mix the sugar, the spices and the cider or vinegar in a large saucepan. Place on a low heat until the sugar has dissolved, and then bring slowly to simmering point. Add the peaches and simmer gently for about 5 minutes. Lift the fruit out with a slotted spoon, and continue to boil the syrup for about 10 more minutes, until it thickens. Strain it over the peaches and allow to cool.

To freeze: freeze in small quantities in waxed or plastic containers.

To serve after freezing: allow to thaw for 3 to 4 hours before serving.

STRAWBERRIES

The best way of freezing strawberries is to purée them, and mousses and ice-creams made with the frozen purée have the miraculous taste and fragrance of the freshly picked fruit.

Frozen whole, they are the least satisfactory of the soft fruits, since they tend to become mushy and tasteless when they thaw. The best method of freezing them whole is in syrup; the disadvantage is that, though they taste delicious, there is so much juice that they can only be used as a compôte or for adding to fruit salad. So it is also useful to have a few packets frozen in sugar, even though the taste and texture may not be as good.

The thawing of strawberries is very important – see general note on fruit (p. 25).

[A] Purée: hull the strawberries and purée in a blender with sugar in the proportions given below. Freeze in waxed or plastic containers.

Strawberry purée can be used as a base for mousses and ices, but different quantities of sugar are needed. So it is easier to make two lots of purée, one rather sweeter than the other.

For *strawberry mousse* (see below), blend the fruit in the proportion of 10 oz. sugar to 2 lb. strawberries. Freeze this quantity in one container, ready for making the mousse.

For *water-ices, sorbets and ice-cream*, blend the fruit in the proportion of 3 oz. sugar to 1 lb. strawberries and freeze in waxed or plastic containers.

WITH SUGAR: hull the fruit and leave whole or slice. To 1 lb. fruit allow 3 to 4 oz. sugar. Mix the fruit and sugar gently together before freezing in polythene bags.

IN SYRUP: hull the fruit and leave whole or slice. Put into waxed or plastic containers and cover with cold syrup made in the proportion of 7 oz. sugar to 1 pint of water. Put a piece of crumpled foil over the fruit, under the cover, to keep it below the syrup.

[B/C] *Strawberry Mousse*

[B] *To make from fresh strawberries*

2 lb. strawberries	juice of 2 lemons
4 tbs. cold water	3 egg whites
1 oz. gelatine	½ pt double cream
10 oz. caster sugar	

Tie a collar of double thickness of greaseproof paper round one 2-pint soufflé dish, or two 1-pint dishes, so that it rises about 1½ inches above the top of the rim. It is essential to tie the paper very tightly, or else the soufflé mixture will leak away between the paper and the rim. If the dish is to be frozen, see methods 2, 3 or 4 on p. 17.

Purée the strawberries, but if the mousse is to be eaten straight away keep back a few for decoration.

* Put the water into a small saucepan, sprinkle in the gelatine, and leave for 5 minutes. Add the sugar and lemon juice, and stir over a low heat until the sugar and gelatine have dissolved. Do not allow to boil. Take off the heat, add to the

strawberry purée, test for sweetness, and if necessary stir in a little more caster sugar. Leave the mixture until it is cold and starts to thicken.

Whisk the whites until they stand in peaks (but be careful not to overbeat), beat the cream lightly, and fold both into the purée. Pour into the prepared soufflé dish.

To serve immediately: put in the refrigerator or a cool place until the mousse is firm. (This will take several hours.) Run a knife carefully round the top of the mousse and remove the paper collar. Serve decorated with the strawberries which you have kept on one side, sliced thinly.

To freeze: place a piece of foil over the top of the mousse and put it in the freezer for 24 hours. Then remove it from the dish (see p. 17), wrap securely, and replace in the freezer.

To serve after freezing: replace the frozen mousse in the original dish. Thaw at room temperature for 6 to 8 hours. Decorate with whipped cream.

[C] *To make from frozen strawberries*

This is an excellent dish to make from frozen strawberry purée (see p. 142), since it turns out light and fresh-tasting.

1¾ pt sweetened purée, made from 2 lb. fruit and 10 oz. sugar	1 oz. gelatine
	juice of 2 lemons
	3 egg whites
4 tbs. cold water	½ pt double cream

Allow the purée to thaw, and then complete the recipe as from * above, omitting the sugar. Decorate with whipped cream.

[B/C] *Strawberry Ice-Cream*

This is lighter than most ice-creams – more like a cross between an ice-cream and a water-ice. The exact proportion of cream to fruit is therefore not important, so add whatever cream you can spare.

[B] *To make with fresh strawberries*

1 lb strawberries
5 oz. sugar
⅛ pt water
1 tbs. lemon juice

1 tbs. orange juice
½ pt single cream or ¼ pt
    double cream

Purée the strawberries and pass them through a nylon sieve.

* Boil the water with the sugar gently for 3 minutes, leave to cool and stir into the strawberry purée together with the lemon and orange juice. If you are using single cream pour it into the mixture; if you are using double cream whip it very lightly and fold it in. Test for sweetness and add a little more caster sugar if necessary. Pour into a basin or ice-tray and freeze for 1 to 2 hours, or until the mixture has reached a mushy state. Take out of the freezer, beat well, pour into waxed or plastic containers and replace in the freezer.

To serve: remove from the freezer 1 hour before serving and leave in the refrigerator.

[C] *To make from frozen strawberry purée*

¾ pt strawberry purée made
    from 1 lb. fruit and 3 oz.
    sugar (see p. 142)
2 oz. sugar
⅛ pt water

1 tbs. lemon juice
1 tbs. orange juice
½ pt single cream or ¼ pt double
    cream

Allow the strawberry purée to thaw to a mushy state and then proceed as from * above.

[B/C]   *Strawberry Water-Ice*

[B] *To make with fresh strawberries*

¾ lb. strawberries
5 oz. sugar

½ pt water

Purée the strawberries. Boil the water and sugar for 5 minutes and leave to cool.

* Stir the cold syrup into the strawberry purée, pour into a basin or ice-tray and freeze for 1 to 2 hours, or until the mixture has reached a mushy state. Take out of the freezer and beat well. Freeze in waxed or plastic containers.

To serve: remove from the freezer 10 to 15 minutes before serving.

[C] *To make from frozen strawberries*

½ pt strawberry purée made   3 oz. sugar
  from 1 lb. fruit and 3 oz.   ½ pt water
  sugar (see p. 142)

Allow the purée to thaw to a mushy state.

Make a syrup with the water and the 3 oz. sugar and proceed as from * above.

July

SALMON

No fish freezes more successfully than salmon, or is better worth preserving in this way. It is a luxury food and yet it can be used economically; it is extremely nutritious and also very versatile. In July salmon should be plentiful and relatively cheap, and it is well worth freezing even when bought from a fishmonger, provided it is very fresh. But do not keep it in the freezer for more than 3 to 4 months – after this it seems to become rather unappetizing.

Look out particularly also for the young salmon or grilse, which are generally cheaper than the full-grown fish and combine the firmness of flesh of salmon with some of the delicacy of flavour of salmon trout. Salmon trout itself seems to lose its flavour when it is frozen.

Salmon may be frozen equally successfully raw or cooked, and it is merely a matter of personal convenience which method you choose. Freeze it whole or cut into portions, marking the weight on each label.

To freeze raw: clean and gut the fish and wrap it tightly in foil, polythene or moisture-vapour-proof tissue.

To freeze cooked: salmon may be poached gently in a court-bouillon or wrapped in foil and baked in the oven, and it is the latter method which we have found the most successful. Clean and gut the salmon. Oil it all over to prevent it from sticking to the foil, and then wrap it in a double or treble layer of foil, so that there is no risk of the juices escaping.

Bake in a low oven (300°F., gas 2), allowing about 20 minutes to the pound. Test to see if it is cooked by unwrapping carefully and slipping a knife a little way down the central spine – if the flesh comes away easily from the bone the fish is cooked. Remove it from the oven and pour off the juice, which will be an excellent concentrated fish stock, to be used in soups, sauces or mousses.

Allow to cool, and freeze well wrapped in fresh foil, polythene or moisture-vapour-proof tissue.

[C] *To cook after freezing raw:* allow to thaw slowly, preferably in the refrigerator, without unwrapping, so that the juices are not lost. Allow at least 24 hours' thawing time for a whole salmon. Then cook as for fresh salmon.

[B/C]   *Koulibiac*

This Russian dish is excellent for using up any left-over cooked salmon, or for making a little salmon go a long way. The quantities given are for 6 people, but they can be multiplied indefinitely. A really big koulibiac makes a splendid centrepiece for a buffet party.

1 lb. cooked salmon
½ lb. puff pastry
1 large onion
3 oz. butter
½ lb. mushrooms, fresh, or
  frozen raw or blanched

½ lb. long grain rice, cooked
2 hard-boiled eggs
salt, pepper and a little lemon
  juice

Sauce

½ pt single cream
½ pt fish stock (see p. 149)
1 tbs. chopped herbs – ideally a combination of parsley, chives and
* fennel – and a little finely grated lemon peel*

If you are using frozen cooked salmon, do not freeze the koulibiac. Allow the salmon to thaw for 2 to 3 hours so that you can flake it. Mushrooms can be used straight from the freezer.

Sauté the finely chopped onion in 1 ounce of the butter, and when it is transparent add the roughly chopped mushrooms, and cook for a further 5 minutes. Mix with the boiled rice and season liberally with salt, pepper and lemon juice.

Roll out the pastry thinly into a rectangle. (If you are making a larger koulibiac, see below.) Place on a buttered baking tray. If the koulibiac is intended for the freezer, line the baking tray with a sheet of foil. Spread half the rice mixture down the centre of the rectangle, flake the salmon over this and cover it with the sliced hard-boiled eggs. Spread the rest of the rice on top, and dot it with the remaining butter. Fold up the sides of the pastry towards the top and pinch the sides and ends together, sealing them with a little water if necessary.

If you are making a large koulibiac, you will probably find it easier to roll out the pastry into two equal rectangles. Spread the rice and fish mixture over the whole of one rectangle, leaving a 1-inch margin all round, then place the second rectangle over the top and seal all edges as before. For this larger koulibiac, increase the cooking times given below.

To serve immediately: brush the top of the koulibiac with milk or egg yolk, place it in a hot oven (425°F., gas 7) for ½ hour and then turn the oven down to 350°F., gas 4, and continue to cook for a further 20 minutes, or until the pastry is golden brown. Serve hot with the cream sauce.

To make the sauce: Boil the cream for a few minutes to reduce and thicken it, and then add the stock and the herbs. Serve separately, or if it is too difficult to eke it out for a large party, cut a few triangular holes in the pastry at the top, and pour in the sauce just before serving.

To freeze: the koulibiac may be frozen cooked or uncooked, and the two methods are equally successful.

Uncooked: freeze the uncooked koulibiac for 24 hours on the baking tray, and when it is rigid wrap it in a further layer of foil and store in the freezer.

Cooked: cook the koulibiac as for immediate eating, cool, and wrap and freeze as above.

To serve after freezing:

Frozen uncooked: put the frozen koulibiac into a hot oven (425°F., gas 7) for ½ hour. Turn the oven down to 350°F., gas 4, and continue to cook for a further 45 to 50 minutes, or until the pastry is golden brown.

Frozen cooked: put the frozen koulibiac in a hot oven (425°F., gas 7) for ½ hour. Turn the oven down to 350°F., gas 4, and leave for another 20 minutes. Place a piece of foil over the top for the last 20 minutes if necessary to prevent the top from getting too browned.

Serve with the sauce as for immediate eating.

[B/C]   *Salmon Tart*

1 lb. cooked salmon	½ oz. butter
10 oz. shortcrust pastry (see p. 28)	5 eggs
	½ pt single cream
1 large onion	salt and pepper

If you are using frozen cooked salmon allow it to thaw for 2 to 3 hours so that you can flake it, but do not then refreeze the tart.

Line one 10-inch or two 7-inch buttered flan-tins with the pastry. If you are freezing the tarts, use foil flan-cases or see methods 2 or 3 on p. 18.

Sauté the chopped onion in the butter. Flake the salmon into the flan-cases, spread the sautéed onion on top, beat the eggs with the cream, the salt and the pepper, and pour this mixture into the flans. Cook in a moderate oven (375°F., gas 5) for 40 minutes.

To serve immediately: cook for a further 5 minutes until the top is a rich golden colour. Serve hot or cold.

To freeze: allow to cool. If you have used a foil flan-case, wrap and freeze. Otherwise see p. 18.

To serve after freezing: place the frozen tart in a hot oven (425°F., gas 7) for 20 minutes, then turn the oven down to 350°F., gas 5, and leave for another 20 to 30 minutes, according to the size of the tart, until it has heated right through. Place a piece of foil over the top, if necessary, to prevent excessive browning. If you want to serve the tart cold, place it in a hot oven for 30 minutes only.

[C]   *Baked Salmon Loaf*

The quantities given are enough for 4.

8 oz. cooked salmon	⅜ pt milk
2 eggs	¾ oz. butter
2 oz. fresh breadcrumbs	¾ oz. flour
1 tbs. chopped parsley	½ pt milk
1 tbs. minced onion	¼ pt mayonnaise
1 tbs. butter	salt and pepper

for the sauce (optional)

Allow the salmon to thaw until it is soft enough to flake.

Butter a soufflé dish. Beat the eggs well and add the salmon, the breadcrumbs, the parsley and the minced onion. Heat the butter and the milk together and stir them into the mixture. Season, pour into the soufflé dish and cook in a medium oven (375°F., gas 5) for about 40 minutes, until the loaf is firm. Serve on its own, or with a béchamel sauce made in the usual way, with the mayonnaise stirred in until the sauce is smooth and hot.

[C]   *Salmon Soufflé*

This dish makes a good starter for 6, but if you use more salmon – anything up to 1 lb. – it will provide a substantial meal for 5 or 6 people.

½ lb. cooked salmon	2 oz. flour
2 oz. finely grated cheese –	½ pt milk
parmesan, gruyère or	4 eggs
cheddar	salt and pepper
2 oz. butter	

Allow the salmon to thaw for at least 3 hours before preparing this dish. Butter a 2-pint soufflé dish and sprinkle a little of the grated cheese round the sides. If you are using more than ½ lb. salmon line the bottom of the soufflé dish with the extra fish, flaked.

Make a sauce with the butter, flour and milk and stir in the

½ lb. salmon and the rest of the grated cheese. Remove from the heat and add the egg yolks one by one, beating them in well. Season to taste. Whip the egg whites stiffly, fold them into the sauce, and pour into the prepared soufflé dish. Cook in the centre of a moderate oven (375°F., gas 5) for 35 to 40 minutes, by which time the top should have risen and be golden brown, and the inside should still be creamy. Serve at once.

[B/C] *Salmon Mousse*

This is a good way to use up a small amount of cooked salmon, but if you are using frozen cooked salmon do not freeze the mousse. The quantities given will make an ample starter for 6, but they can be multiplied to make a substantial course for a cold meal or a buffet supper.

8 oz. cooked salmon
3 shallots or a dozen spring onions
½ oz. butter
¼ oz. gelatine
⅛ pt white wine

½ pt fish stock (preferably the stock in which the salmon was cooked, or best of all the juice from a salmon cooked in foil, see p. 149)
½ pt whipping cream or double and single cream mixed
salt and pepper

If you are using frozen cooked salmon, allow it to thaw for 3 to 4 hours.

Chop the shallots or onions and sweat very gently in the butter until they are soft but not coloured. Dissolve the gelatine in the white wine and add the stock and the wine and gelatine mixture to the onions. Heat until the gelatine has completely dissolved. Pour the mixture into a blender together with the salmon and blend at high speed for a few minutes. Season. Whip the cream very lightly so that it doubles in bulk without becoming stiff and fold in the salmon mixture when it has cooled.

To serve immediately: pour into a ring or fish-mould or a

soufflé dish. Chill in the refrigerator for about 2 hours or until the mousse has set. Turn out and serve.

To freeze: see methods 2, 3 or 4 on p. 17.

To serve after freezing: allow to thaw at room temperature for 6 to 7 hours.

CARROTS

Although carrots can be bought at any time reasonably cheaply, or, if you have a garden, can be stored through the winter, the advantage of freezing them is that with very little trouble you can have baby carrots all the year round.

They freeze well either blanched or cooked. Blanching them is useful if they are to be added to stews and casseroles, while cooking them is much better if they are to be eaten as a vegetable in their own right; they are quite delicious if they are cooked with a little butter and sugar before being frozen.

They can also be frozen unblanched, but the taste is inferior when they are eaten later on; and blanching is so quickly done that there is no point in not carrying out this process before freezing.

Choose young, tender carrots, and wash and scrape or scrub them. Leave them whole if they are small, or else cut them lengthwise or into rings.

[A] *To freeze blanched:* blanch for 3 minutes. Drain, cool and freeze in polythene bags.

To freeze cooked: for each 1 lb. carrots you will need a knob of butter, 1 tablespoon of water, 1 teaspoon of sugar and a little salt. Simmer all the ingredients gently together for about 10 minutes. It is important not to cook the carrots too long at this stage, as they will go on cooking after they have been taken off the heat. Turn into a large basin with the cooking liquid, allow to cool, and freeze the carrots and the liquid together in polythene bags.

[C] *To serve after freezing blanched:* if the carrots are to be used in stews or casseroles, they can be added to the dish straight out of the freezer. If they are to be served as a vegetable on their own, tip them, still frozen, into a heavy saucepan with a knob of butter, 2 or 3 tablespoons water to keep them from catching, a little salt, and a sprinkling of sugar. Cook very gently for about 30 minutes, or until they are soft, separating them carefully with a fork as they thaw. Test for seasoning and serve.

To serve after freezing cooked: tip the frozen carrots into a saucepan and heat through gently, separating them with a fork as they thaw. Add more butter if necessary. Test for seasoning and serve.

[B/C]   *Navarin of Lamb Printanier*

1 leg or shoulder of lamb
1 lb. baby carrots, fresh, or
    frozen blanched
1 oz. butter
1 tbs. oil
½ lb. small onions
1 oz. flour
1 pt stock

1 clove garlic
a sprig of rosemary
1 lb. baby turnips, fresh, or
    frozen blanched
1 lb. small new potatoes (omit
    when cooking for the
    freezer)
salt and pepper

1 lb. fresh broad beans or peas or ½ lb. frozen blanched

If the lamb is frozen it should be allowed to thaw at least partially before cooking. Frozen vegetables do not need to be thawed before they are added.

Heat the butter and oil in a heavy saucepan or flame-proof casserole. Sauté the onions until they are a light golden brown. Take them out and sear the meat on all sides. Remove the meat, sprinkle the flour into the pan and cook it gently for a few minutes, stirring all the time. Add the stock gradually and continue stirring until the sauce is smooth. Put back the meat and add the crushed clove of garlic, salt, pepper and rosemary. Cover and leave to simmer.

When the meat has cooked for an hour add the root

vegetables. If you are cooking for the freezer only, omit the potatoes, as they have a tendency to break up when reheated. Continue to simmer for another 40 minutes.

To serve immediately: add the beans or peas. If these are frozen, stir them in well. When they are cooked test for seasoning and serve.

To freeze: carve the meat into thick slices. Cool, and freeze together with the vegetables and sauce in plastic containers, or see method 4 on p. 17.

To serve after freezing: tip the frozen navarin into a saucepan or flameproof casserole and heat gently until it has thawed. Add the peas or beans and continue to cook for another 30 minutes, until they are ready. Test for seasoning and serve.

[B/C] *Kidney and Sausage Casserole with Carrots and Peas*

This is an appetising dish for either winter or summer, and is a useful way of stretching a small amount of meat.

6 lambs' kidneys	1½ tbs. flour
½ lb. chipolata sausages	¾ pt stock
1 lb. small young carrots, fresh, or frozen blanched	2 tbs. red wine or sherry
2 oz. butter or 2 tbs. olive oil	2 tsp. concentrated tomato purée
6 small onions or ½ lb. pickling onions	2 bay leaves
½ lb. mushrooms, fresh, or frozen raw or blanched	salt and pepper

1½ lb. fresh peas or 12 oz. frozen blanched

If the kidneys are frozen they should be allowed to thaw, but the sausages, the carrots and the peas can be used straight from the freezer. Frozen mushrooms should be left for about ½ hour until they are soft enough to slice.

Skin the kidneys, cut them in half and take out the core. Sauté them with the sausages in the butter or oil in a flameproof casserole until they are lightly browned. The sausages, in particular, should be well coloured. Add the onions and the sliced mushrooms, reduce the heat and cook slowly for 5 minutes or until they are soft. Stir in the flour and continue to cook gently, stirring, until it is browned. Add the stock, red wine, tomato purée, bay leaves and carrots. Season, cover the casserole with a well-fitting lid, and put it in a medium oven (350°F., gas 5) for 1 hour.

To serve immediately: add the peas and cook for ½ hour longer. If you are using frozen peas, stir them in well. When they are cooked test for seasoning and serve.

To freeze: cool and freeze in a plastic container or see method 4 on p. 17.

To serve after freezing: heat the frozen casserole gently for about 30 minutes, until it has thawed. Add the peas and continue to cook for another 30 minutes, until they are ready. Test for seasoning and serve.

[B/C] *Glazed Carrots*

2 lb. carrots, fresh, or frozen blanched	4 oz. butter
	2 tbs. sugar
approx. ½ pt stock	salt

chopped parsley for decoration (optional)

If you are using frozen carrots there is no need to wait for them to thaw. Leave fresh carrots whole if they are quite small. Otherwise cut them into rings or slices.

Put the carrots in a saucepan with the other ingredients and simmer for about 40 minutes, until they are soft and the cooking liquid has evaporated. Frozen carrots won't take quite so long.

It is impossible to be exact about the quantity of stock that will be required. If there is too much it doesn't evaporate and the carrots won't glaze, while if there is too little they won't become soft. So keep an eye on them for the last ¼ hour or so, and if necessary either add a little more stock or take the lid off the pan and turn up the heat to allow the liquid to evaporate more rapidly.

To serve immediately: test for seasoning and serve very hot, with chopped parsley sprinkled over.

To freeze: take off the heat while there is still a little liquid in the pan. Cool, and freeze with the liquid in a polythene bag.

To serve after freezing: tip the frozen carrots into a saucepan and warm through until they are hot, separating them carefully with a fork. Serve as above.

[B/C] ## *Carrots with Mushrooms*

2 lb. carrots, fresh, or frozen blanched	½ lb. mushrooms, fresh, or frozen sautéed
2 tbs. oil	salt and pepper
2 onions	

If you are using frozen carrots and mushrooms there is no need to wait for them to thaw.

Melt the oil in a large saucepan, sauté the finely chopped onions and then add the carrots. Leave fresh carrots whole if they are quite small; otherwise cut them into rings. Season, cover and cook over a low heat for 30 minutes. Then add the sliced mushrooms and continue to simmer, covered, until the carrots are cooked. Frozen blanched carrots will not take as long as fresh ones. Check seasoning and serve.

To freeze: cool and freeze in polythene bags.

To serve after freezing: tip the frozen vegetables into a saucepan and heat gently, breaking up the mass with a fork from time to time.

COURGETTES

Courgettes can be frozen unblanched, but if they are likely to be in the freezer for more than 2 to 3 months it is better to blanch them first.

[A] *To freeze raw:* trim each end and wipe with a damp cloth. Blanch for 2 minutes. Freeze in polythene bags.

[C] *To serve after freezing:* allow the courgettes to thaw just enough to make it possible to cut them into ½-inch slices. Sauté them in olive oil or butter, or a mixture of the two, sprinkled with salt and pepper and two or three pinches of mixed herbs, until they are tender and nicely browned on both sides. This will take about 20 minutes.

[C]   *Courgette Soufflé*

The quantities given below are enough as a starter for about 4 people. If you want to double the quantity, make two separate soufflés, as they cook better than one large one.

1 lb. courgettes	1 oz. grated cheese (cheddar
1 oz. butter	will do, but gruyère or
2 tbs. flour	parmesan is better
¼ pt milk	2 whole eggs
	2 extra whites
	salt and pepper

Cut the courgettes into ½-inch slices while they are still as frozen as possible and cook them gently in a tablespoon of water until they are tender. Strain off the liquid very thoroughly and put the courgettes through a blender or a mouli.

Make a sauce with the butter, the flour and the milk, and when it is smooth add the courgette purée. Cook for another minute or two. Add the cheese and the well-beaten egg yolks and season well. Allow the mixture to cool and then fold in the whites, which should be beaten well but not allowed to become grainy.

Pour into a well-buttered 2-pint soufflé dish, stand in a baking tin containing an inch or so of water, and cook in the middle of a medium oven (350°F., gas 4) for about 40 minutes, until the soufflé has set. It will never become as firm as a cheese soufflé, but it has a pleasantly creamy texture and a delicate taste.

[B/C]   *Courgettes Provençales*

The preparatory cooking for this dish is rather time-consuming. But as it makes an unusual vegetable, and can also be served as an hors-d'oeuvre, it is well worth making a large quantity when you have a lot of courgettes.

1½ lb. courgettes	¾ lb. onions
1 tbs. flour	1 lb. tomatoes
2 tbs. olive oil	salt and pepper

¼ pt stock
2 oz. grated cheese
1 tsp. chopped basil (optional)

If you are using frozen vegetables, allow them to thaw until they are just soft enough to slice. The courgettes will take 15 to 20 minutes and the tomatoes about 1 hour.

Cut the courgettes into ½-inch slices, dip the slices into the flour, and sauté them in the olive oil until they are golden brown. Frozen courgettes may need an extra spoonful of oil. Take them out of the pan and gently sauté the sliced onions until they are quite tender.

Meanwhile skin and slice the tomatoes. Put a layer of courgettes in a casserole, then of onion and then of tomato, and continue until the vegetables are used up. If the dish is to be frozen, use a foil container or see method 2 on p. 17. Season each layer.

To serve immediately : pour over the stock, and sprinkle on the basil and finally the grated cheese. Cook in a medium oven (375°F., gas 5) for about ¾ hour. The dish is now ready to serve.

To freeze : allow to cool. If you have used a foil dish, wrap and freeze. Otherwise see p. 17.

To serve after freezing : heat the frozen courgettes in a medium oven (375°F., gas 5) for ½ hour and then pour over the stock and sprinkle on the basil and the cheese. Continue to cook for another hour.

[B/C] *Courgettes au Gratin*

This recipe is useful if you have forgotten to pick all your baby courgettes in time and they have grown into marrows, as it can be made equally well with either.

approx. 1½ lb. courgettes or   2 oz. butter
  marrows   salt and pepper

2 oz. grated cheese

If you are using frozen courgettes, allow them to thaw for 15 to 20 minutes until they are just soft enough to cut.

Halve the courgettes lengthwise. If you are using marrows, peel off the skins, cut them lengthwise, take out all the pith and pips, and cut them into 1-inch slices.

Season the vegetables – being specially generous with the pepper – and sauté them gently on both sides in the butter until they are golden brown and tender.

To serve immediately: place the courgettes side by side in a shallow ovenproof dish, sprinkle the grated cheese on top, and warm through in a medium oven (375°F., gas 5) for about 20 minutes.

To freeze: allow the courgettes to cool, place them side by side in a foil dish or on a large piece of foil, and wrap securely before freezing.

To serve after freezing: unless you have used a foil dish, transfer the courgettes to an oven-proof dish, sprinkle over the grated cheese, and put them, while still frozen, in a medium oven (375°F., gas 5) for 45 minutes or until they are piping hot.

CUCUMBER

The high water-content of cucumbers makes them unsuitable for freezing raw, but it is quite simple to extract most of the moisture, and they can then be cooked and frozen very successfully. The simplest way of extracting the moisture is as follows.

Peel the cucumber, cut it in quarters lengthwise, discard the core, and then cut it into cubes. Place these in a bowl and sprinkle them with plenty of salt, a few drops of wine vinegar and a pinch of sugar. (The salt will extract the juices, and the vinegar and sugar help to retain the flavour.) Leave it for at least ½ hour, longer if possible, and then drain off the considerable amount of liquid that will have accumulated. It is wisest to be a little careful with the salt in whatever dish you then make, but most of the salt will probably have been drained away with the liquid.

The cucumber can now be used for any of the following recipes.

[B]   *Cream of Cucumber Soup*

2 cucumbers	1 oz. flour
1 onion	2 egg yolks
1½ pts chicken or veal stock	2 tbs. cream
1 oz. butter	salt and pepper

Prepare the cucumber as described above. Simmer the drained cubes together with the chopped onion in the stock for about 20 minutes. When the vegetables are soft, put them through a blender or a mouli.

Melt the butter in a saucepan, add the flour and cook for several minutes over a gentle heat, stirring all the time. Add the cucumber liquid, season and simmer for a further 3 minutes.

Take the soup off the heat, blend the egg yolks with the cream, and add this to the soup. Heat it gently until the soup thickens a little, but do not allow it to boil.

To serve immediately: serve hot or chilled, with a little chopped mint or some fine sticks of fresh cucumber.

To freeze: cool, and freeze in waxed or plastic containers.

To serve after freezing:

To serve hot – if possible, allow the soup to thaw at room temperature. Reheat very gently, and on no account allow it to boil.

To serve cold – allow to thaw at room temperature for 5 to 6 hours.

[B]   *Baked Cucumber*

Baked cucumber has a very distinctive taste – quite different from that of raw cucumber – though it retains some of the crispness of the fresh vegetable. It makes an excellent accompaniment to egg or fish dishes, and also combines particularly well with mushrooms.

2 cucumbers	2 oz. butter
1 tbs. chopped parsley, chives or basil, or a combination of these	salt and pepper

Prepare the cucumber as described on p. 163. Put the drained pieces in an oven-proof dish. Sprinkle with the herbs and dot with the butter. Season. Place the dish in a hot oven (425°F., gas 7) for ½ hour, turning the cucumber occasionally so that the pieces become evenly coated with the butter. At the end of this time the cucumber should taste cooked, but should still be quite crisp.

To serve immediately: serve hot, either alone or folded into mushrooms in cream sauce (see p. 216).

To freeze: cool, and freeze in waxed or plastic containers or in a polythene bag.

To serve after freezing: tip the frozen cucumber into a saucepan and heat gently. Serve as above.

[B]   *Cucumber Ragout*

This is excellent served hot with meat or with a strongly
flavoured fish, such as mackerel. It can also be eaten cold as an
accompaniment to cold meat, especially if it is topped with a
little yogurt.

1 cucumber	½ lb. new carrots
1 Spanish onion	1 green pimento
1 tbs. olive oil	salt and pepper

Prepare the cucumber according to the method given on p. 163.
Fry the finely sliced onion in the oil for a few minutes. Add the
drained cucumber, the carrots cut into thin slivers, and the
pimento cut into rings (make sure that all the seeds have been
removed). Season and cook gently for about 20 minutes, or
until the vegetables have become transparent. Serve hot or cold.

To freeze: cool, and freeze in waxed or plastic containers or a
polythene bag.

To serve after freezing

To serve hot – tip the frozen vegetables into a saucepan and
heat very gently.

To serve cold – allow to thaw at room temperature for 4 to
5 hours.

FRENCH BEANS

French beans are best frozen blanched, but they do not retain
their superlative taste as well as many other vegetables. So it
pays to give them rather special treatment afterwards.

[A] *To freeze blanched:* trim the ends off the beans and wash
them. Blanch for 2 minutes, drain, cool and freeze in polythene
bags.

[C] *To serve after freezing*: separate the frozen mass of beans as much as possible before you cook them. Any of the three following methods of cooking them helps to preserve their taste and colour.

1. Cook the frozen beans in a little boiling salted water until they are tender, which shouldn't take more than about 5 minutes if they were really fresh and young when they were frozen. Drain them, put a good knob of butter in the saucepan and gently reheat the beans in this for a few minutes, shaking the pan so that they become coated with the butter.

2. Put some olive oil into a saucepan – about 3 tablespoons for 1 lb. beans – add a little pepper and salt and sauté the frozen beans until they are tender. This will take 10 to 15 minutes.

3. Cook the beans in water as above, drain them, and while they are still hot mix them with French dressing. Chill before serving.

[B/C]   *Minestrone*

Minestrone is one of those comfortable soups which can be made in all sorts of ways. The quantities of vegetables given are approximate – vary both amounts and varieties according to your taste and what you have available. For freezing, it is best to omit the cabbage until the minestrone comes to be eaten. These quantities will serve 8 to 10 people.

½ lb. French or runner beans, fresh, or frozen blanched	4 rashers bacon
½ lb. haricot beans	2 tbs. olive oil
2 onions	½ lb. tomatoes
3 carrots	1–2 tbs. concentrated tomato purée
1 potato	approx. 3 pts water
4 celery stalks	salt, pepper and sugar
2 leeks	

approx. ½ lb. shredded cabbage
pasta (optional)
grated parmesan

If any of the vegetables are frozen, add them to the soup as soon as they have thawed enough to slice.

Leave the haricot beans to soak overnight. Chop the onions, carrots, potato, celery stalks and leeks fairly finely, and cut the bacon into dice. Cook them all briskly in the olive oil for 5 to 10 minutes and then add the drained haricot beans, the tomatoes skinned and roughly chopped, the green beans cut into small pieces and the tomato purée. Pour on about 3 pints of boiling water, add salt and pepper and sugar to taste, and simmer gently for about 2 hours, or until the haricot beans are quite soft.

To serve immediately: add the shredded cabbage after the minestrone has cooked for about an hour. The haricot beans give the minestrone body, but if you also like pasta in it break some into small pieces and add it about 10 minutes before the end of the cooking time. Test for seasoning and serve with grated parmesan.

To freeze: allow to cool and freeze in plastic containers.

To serve after freezing: tip the frozen soup into a saucepan and bring gently to the boil. Serve as above.

[C]   *Salade Niçoise with French Beans*

1 lb. French beans	1 tin tuna fish
French dressing	3 hard-boiled eggs
1 lb. tomatoes	approx. 10 anchovy fillets
1 cos lettuce	approx. ¼ lb. black olives

Cook the frozen beans in a little salted water. When they are tender drain them, mix them with 2 or 3 tablespoons French dressing and chill. Cut the tomatoes into quarters. Wash the lettuce leaves, dry them well, and toss them in a little French dressing. Arrange the lettuce leaves round the edge of a large bowl. Mix the beans and the tomatoes and put them in the bowl. Arrange over them the tuna fish, the eggs cut into quarters, the anchovy fillets and the olives, and pour 2 or 3 more tablespoons French dressing over the salad before serving.

MARROW

The water content of marrows is high, so they are not worth freezing blanched, but the following ragout makes a very pleasing accompaniment to a meat dish, or can be turned into a light supper or lunch dish by the addition of eggs, a kind of poor man's pipérade. So it is worth making a certain quantity of this, as it keeps very well in the freezer and is useful to have to hand. (See also courgettes au gratin, p. 162.)

[B]   MARROW RAGOUT

1 medium marrow   1 clove garlic
1 oz. butter   6–8 tomatoes
2 tbs. olive oil   salt and pepper
2 large onions

Peel the marrow, take out the seeds and pith and cut it into cubes. Melt the butter and oil in a frying pan or a heavy saucepan and sweat the onions, cut into fine rings, and the finely chopped garlic. When they are transparent add the marrow and the tomatoes and sauté for about 20 minutes, or until all the vegetables are soft and amalgamated. Season liberally.

To serve immediately: serve hot as a vegetable. To make a lunch or supper dish, lightly beat 4 or 5 eggs with a fork, pour them over the ragout and continue to cook over a gentle heat, stirring all the time, until the eggs begin to set to a creamy consistency. Triangles of fried bread go well with this.

To freeze: cool, and freeze in waxed or plastic containers or polythene bags.

To serve after freezing: tip the frozen ragout into a saucepan, warm through gently and serve as above.

PEAS

Home-grown peas, picked fresh and young, are so delicious that they should be eaten and enjoyed straight away. But if you do have a real glut it is worth freezing some, for there is no doubt that though commercially frozen peas are excellent nowadays and very cheap, home-frozen ones are much better. They are especially good frozen cooked, for, though they may become a little soft during the reheating, the taste brings summer to a winter meal.

[A] *To freeze blanched:* shell the peas and blanch them for 2 minutes. Drain, cool and freeze in polythene bags.

To freeze cooked: shell the peas and put them in a saucepan with – for each 1 lb. peas – 1 or 2 tablespoons of water, 3 or 4 sprigs of mint, a knob of butter and a little salt and sugar. After they have come to the boil cook very gently for about 3 minutes. Remove the mint, cool as quickly as possible with the cooking liquid, and freeze both together in polythene bags or waxed containers.

[C] *To serve after freezing blanched:* put the frozen peas in a heavy saucepan with 2 or 3 tablespoons water, a knob of butter, a little salt and sugar and 3 or 4 sprigs of mint, fresh or frozen. Cook very gently until the peas are tender, breaking up the frozen mass carefully with a fork from time to time. Test for seasoning, and add a little more salt and sugar if necessary.

Or cook them *à la française.* Sweat an onion in a generous knob of butter, add a few shredded lettuce leaves or a small bunch of parsley, and then the peas. Add some chicken stock ($\frac{1}{4}$ to $\frac{1}{2}$ pint for each 1 lb. peas) and a little sugar, cover, and simmer gently till the peas are soft. Test for seasoning and serve.

To serve after freezing cooked: put the frozen peas in a heavy saucepan and warm gently until they are heated through, breaking up the frozen mass carefully with a fork as they thaw. They will probably be ready almost as soon as the cooking liquid has come to the boil. Test for seasoning, and add a little more salt and sugar if necessary.

[B] *Pea Soup*

This is a good way of using up peas which are past their best.

2 lb. peas
1 medium onion
knob of butter or chicken fat
1½ pts stock

1 tsp. sugar
pinch of mixed herbs
salt and pepper

2 tbs. cream or top of the milk

Slice the onion and cook it gently in the butter or fat (chicken fat is very good for this soup). When it is soft, add the rest of the ingredients and season. Cook until the peas are soft and put through a blender or a fine mouli.

To serve immediately: heat up again, stir in the cream or top of the milk, test for seasoning and serve.

To freeze: allow to cool, and freeze in waxed or plastic containers.

To serve after freezing: tip the frozen soup into a saucepan and bring gently to the boil. Add the cream or top of the milk, test for seasoning and serve.

TURNIPS

It is worth freezing a few young, tender turnips for using in casseroles.

[A] *To freeze blanched:* wash and trim the turnips and blanch whole for 3 minutes. Drain, cool and freeze in polythene bags.

[B/C] *Glazed Turnips*

1 lb. baby turnips
½ pt water
1 oz. butter

1 oz. sugar
salt and pepper

If you are using frozen turnips, allow them to thaw until they are just soft enough to cut.

Cut the turnips in half and make a few criss-cross incisions in the cut surface to ensure even cooking. Simmer them very slowly in the water, butter, sugar and seasoning until they are cooked and the water has almost all been absorbed, leaving a coating of rich golden sauce on the turnips. Test for seasoning and serve.

To freeze: cool and freeze in waxed containers or polythene bags.

To serve after freezing: tip the frozen turnips into a saucepan and heat gently, stirring from time to time.

CURRANTS: BLACK, WHITE AND RED

Currants are best frozen in small quantities, since their main use is for adding to other dishes, such as summer pudding, or as a basis for ice-cream. Freeze the best berries whole with sugar, and purée any which are squashy.

BLACK CURRANTS

These can be frozen with sugar or as a purée.

[A] *With sugar:* as black currants are so sour when they are cooked, you will need at least 6 oz. sugar to 1 lb. fruit. Strip the berries off the stalks and mix gently with the sugar before freezing in polythene bags.

Purée: strip the berries off the stalks, purée in a blender with 6 oz. sugar to 1 lb. fruit, and put through a nylon sieve. Freeze in waxed or plastic containers. This purée is excellent for making ice-cream, a cold drink in summer or a hot one in winter.

RED AND WHITE CURRANTS

These can be frozen in sugar or syrup or as a purée. If you grow white currants, which have a more delicate taste than the red ones, the two make a pleasant mixture frozen together.

[A] *With sugar*: strip the fruit off the stalks and mix with sugar in the proportion of 4 oz. sugar to 1 lb. fruit. Freeze in polythene bags.

In syrup: strip the fruit off the stalks and put in waxed or plastic containers. Cover with cold syrup made in the proportion of 7 oz. sugar to 1 pint water. Put a piece of crumpled foil over the fruit, under the cover, to keep it below the syrup.

Purée: strip the fruit off the stalks and purée in a blender with 4 oz. sugar to 1 lb. fruit. Strain through a nylon sieve and freeze in waxed or plastic containers.

[C]   *Fuoco nella Neve (Fire in the Snow)*

This is a variation of *vacherin aux fruits*, and is, we think, a more delicious way of amalgamating meringue, fruit and whipped cream. It was 'christened' by an Italian friend who came to dinner and named it on the spot. It is a useful and adaptable dish which can be made all the year round with either fresh or frozen ingredients. Although it takes only a few minutes to assemble, it tastes extremely good, looks very party-like and is very adaptable as regards quantities and the fruit which can be used. Raspberries or red and white currants, or a combination of the two, are particularly good for the filling. The meringue cases can be made beforehand and frozen. They are extremely brittle, and should be packed in tins or cardboard or plastic boxes to avoid damage.

Meringue cases

3 egg whites	¼ tsp. cream of tartar
6 oz. caster sugar	

Filling

about 1½ lb. soft fruit, fresh, or
  frozen in sugar
caster sugar

2 tbs. brandy or kirsch
½-¾ pt double cream

To make the meringues: whip the whites until they are stiff, add the cream of tartar and beat again. Then slowly add the sugar, beating all the time and being careful not to put too much in at once. (This may be one reason why meringues sometimes fail to turn out well – because the sugar is added too quickly, instead of in small quantities, almost as one adds oil in making mayonnaise.) Lightly oil three circular pieces of foil about 8½, 7 and 5 inches in diameter, place them on baking trays, and spread the meringue mixture evenly over them. Cook at the bottom of a very low oven. Start at about 125°F., gas ½, and after ½ hour or so turn the heat down to 100°F., gas ¼. They will take 2 to 2½ hours. Or turn the oven still lower and leave the meringue cases in overnight.

To prepare the filling: if fresh fruit is being used, mix the fruit, sugar and brandy or kirsch together and leave it to stand for an hour or so to draw the syrup out of the fruit. The quantity of sugar depends on individual tastes and the type of fruit used. If fruit frozen in sugar is used, allow it to thaw for 3 to 5 hours before testing for sweetness, and add more sugar if necessary. Pour the brandy or kirsch over it, and leave for a little while so that the liqueur is absorbed by the fruit.

This sweet should be finished off at the last possible moment. Just before dinner put the largest meringue case on a big dish and spread about two thirds of the fruit and juice on top. Repeat with the medium-sized meringue case and the rest of the fruit. Top with the smallest meringue case.

Whip the cream lightly – just enough to give it a fluffy consistency – and pile it on just before bringing the dish to the table.

[B/C]   *Linzer Torte*

This tart can be served as a dessert or as a cake. It may be made
with raspberries or redcurrants, or with a mixture of the two.
The quantities given for the special pastry used are enough for
three 8-inch tarts; it does not have to be used immediately, but
can be kept satisfactorily in the refrigerator for up to a week, or
for several months in the freezer. If you are using frozen fruit,
do not refreeze the tart.

Pastry

8 oz. butter or margarine	14 oz. flour
8 oz. caster sugar	3 tsp. cinnamon
1 egg	1 tsp. ground cloves
grated rind of ½ lemon and ½ orange (or of the whole of either fruit)	8 oz. ground almonds pinch of salt

Filling for each 8-inch tart

½ lb. raspberries or redcurrants   sugar to taste
   or a combination of the two,
   fresh, or frozen in sugar

Cream the butter and sugar, and add the egg and the grated
rind. Sift together the flour and the spices and add them
gradually. Add the ground almonds, knead all well together
and chill for at least 1 hour before using.

Divide the pastry into three equal parts, and if you are not
making three tarts immediately put two balls of pastry into
polythene bags and freeze or refrigerate them.

Roll out the remaining pastry thinly and line a buttered 8-
inch flan-tin, leaving aside enough to make strips for the top.
If the tart is for the freezer, use a foil flan-case or see p. 18.
Spread the fruit over the pastry and sprinkle on sugar to taste.
If you are using frozen fruit spread it on when it has only
slightly thawed. Cut the remains of the rolled-out pastry into
strips about ½ inch wide and criss-cross them diagonally over
the fruit, or make a basket-work lattice (see diagram).

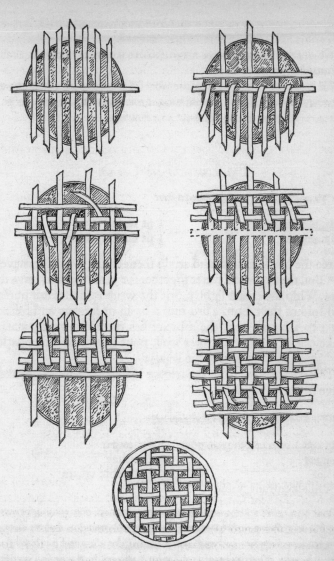

Lattice top for Linzer Torte

To serve immediately: bake in a moderate oven (350°F., gas 4) for 40 to 50 minutes. Serve hot or cold.

To freeze: if you have used a foil flan-case wrap it well. Otherwise see p. 18.

To serve after freezing: place the frozen tart in a hot oven (425°F., gas 7) for ½ hour, then turn heat down to 350°F., gas 4, and cook for a further 40 minutes.

[B/C]   *Blackcurrant Ice-Cream*

[B] *To make with fresh blackcurrants*

1 lb. blackcurrants	¼ pt water
8 oz. sugar	½ pt double cream

Purée the blackcurrants and strain them through a nylon sieve.

* Boil the sugar and water together for 3 minutes and leave to cool. Whip the cream lightly. Stir the syrup into the fruit purée and fold in the cream. Turn into a basin or ice-tray and freeze for 1 to 2 hours, until the mixture has reached a mushy state. Take out of the freezer, beat well, pour into waxed or plastic containers and replace in the freezer.

To serve: remove from the freezer 1 hour before serving and leave in the refrigerator.

[C] *To make from frozen blackcurrants*

1 lb. blackcurrants frozen with sugar	3 oz. sugar
or	¼ pt water
½ pt blackcurrant purée	½ pt double cream

Allow the fruit to thaw at room temperature for 3 to 4 hours, until it is soft enough to purée, and pass through a nylon sieve. If you are using frozen purée this should be allowed to thaw for 2 to 3 hours. Then proceed as from * above, but test for sweetness before freezing and add a little more caster sugar if necessary.

[B/C]   *Blackcurrant Water-Ice*

[B] *To make with fresh blackcurrants*

1 lb. blackcurrants   ½ pt water
8 oz. sugar

Purée the currants and pass them through a nylon sieve. Boil
the water and sugar for 5 minutes and leave to cool.

* Stir the cold syrup into the currant purée, pour into a
basin or ice-tray and freeze for 1 to 2 hours, or until the mixture
has reached a mushy state. Take out of the freezer and beat
well. Freeze in waxed or plastic containers.

To serve: remove from the freezer 10 to 15 minutes before
serving.

[C] *To make from frozen blackcurrants*

1 lb. blackcurrants frozen with   3 oz. sugar
   sugar   ½ pt water
         or
½ pt blackcurrant purée

Allow the fruit to thaw at room temperature for 3 to 4 hours,
until it is soft enough to purée and pass through a nylon sieve.
If you are using frozen purée, it should be allowed to thaw for
2 to 3 hours.

Make a syrup with the water and the 3 oz. sugar, and then
proceed as from * above.

[B/C]   *Redcurrant Ice-Cream*

[B] *To make with fresh redcurrants*

1 lb. redcurrants   ¼ pt water
5 oz. sugar   ½ pt double cream

[C] *To make from frozen redcurrants*

1 lb. redcurrants frozen with sugar	2 oz. sugar
or	$\frac{1}{4}$ pt water
$\frac{1}{2}$ pt redcurrant purée	$\frac{1}{2}$ pt double cream

Make in exactly the same way as blackcurrant ice-cream (see p. 176).

[B/C] *Redcurrant Water-Ice*

[B] *To make with fresh redcurrants*

1 lb. redcurrants	$\frac{1}{2}$ pt water
5 oz. sugar	

[C] *To make with frozen redcurrants*

1 lb. redcurrants frozen with sugar	2 oz. sugar
or	$\frac{1}{2}$ pt water
$\frac{1}{2}$ pt redcurrant purée	

Make in exactly the same way as blackcurrant water-ice (see p. 177).

PINEAPPLE

It is often possible in summer to buy pineapples very cheaply, sometimes with small blemishes which can easily be cut out before the fruit is frozen. They freeze excellently with sugar or in syrup.

[A] *With sugar:* peel the pineapples, remove the eyes and the core, and cut into slices or chunks. Mix with sugar in the proportion of 4 oz. sugar to 1 lb. fruit. Freeze in polythene bags.

In syrup: peel the pineapples, remove the eyes and the core, and cut into slices or chunks. Put in waxed or plastic containers and cover with cold syrup made in the proportion of 7 oz. sugar to 1 pint water. Put a piece of crumpled foil over the top of the fruit, under the cover, to keep it below the syrup.

Pineapple and strawberries, frozen together, make a particularly good combination. Allow about 1 lb. strawberries to a large pineapple. Freeze with sugar in the proportion of 4 oz. sugar to 1 lb. fruit. Mix with a little kirsch or framboise before serving.

[B]   *Pineapple Water-Ice*

1 medium pineapple (approx. weight 2 lb.)	¾ pt water 4–6 oz. sugar

Peel the pineapple, cut out the core and purée the flesh in a blender (there should be approx. ¾ pt. purée). Boil the water and sugar together for 5 minutes – it is difficult to give exact quantities of sugar as pineapples vary greatly in sweetness – and allow to cool. Mix the syrup with the pineapple purée, turn into ice-trays and freeze for 1 to 2 hours, until it has reached a mushy state. Turn the mixture back into the blender or mixing bowl, beat well and freeze in waxed or plastic containers.

To serve: remove from the freezer 10 to 15 minutes before serving.

RASPBERRIES

Raspberries are one of the most successful fruits to freeze, since they keep their flavour and colour unimpaired, and can be used for a great number of dishes. They can be frozen with or without sugar. They can also be frozen in syrup, but since they naturally produce so much juice there is little point in this last method, unless they are later to be used in fruit salad. Slightly over-ripe or squashy fruit is best puréed.

[A] *With sugar:* to 1 lb. fruit allow 4 oz. sugar. Mix the fruit and sugar gently together before freezing in polythene bags.

Without sugar: put a piece of foil on a tray and lay the raspberries singly on this. Freeze, put into waxed or plastic containers and return to the freezer.

In syrup: put the fruit into waxed or plastic containers and cover with cold syrup made in the proportion of 6 oz. sugar to 1 pint of water. Put a piece of crumpled foil over the fruit, under the cover, to keep it below the syrup.

Purée: purée in a blender with 4 oz. sugar to 1 lb. fruit. Put through a nylon sieve and freeze in waxed or plastic containers.

[B/C] *Raspberry Suèdoise*

[B] *To make from fresh raspberries*

1 lb. raspberries   1 oz. gelatine
¼ lb. caster sugar

about 25 tiny meringues – 1 egg white and 2 oz. caster sugar should be enough for this quantity.
½ *pt double cream*

Purée the raspberries and rub them through a nylon sieve. Make a syrup with the sugar and ¼ pt water. Add this to the purée, and make up with water to 1½ pts.

* Soak the gelatine in ¼ pt water, and put over a low heat until it has dissolved. Add to the raspberries and stir well.

To serve immediately: pour into a soufflé dish which has been rinsed out in cold water, and leave in the refrigerator to set. This will take several hours. Then turn the suèdoise on to a serving dish and cover with the lightly whipped cream. Decorate with the meringues and a few fresh raspberries.

To freeze: pour into a foil or plastic mould, allow to cool, cover and freeze. Or see method 4 on p. 17.

To serve after freezing: stand at room temperature for about 4 hours, or in the refrigerator overnight. Turn on to a dish and decorate with whipped cream and meringues as described above.

[C] *To make from frozen raspberries*

½ pt raspberry purée   1 oz. gelatine
  or
1 lb. raspberries frozen with
  sugar

Allow the purée to thaw. If you are using raspberries frozen with sugar, allow to thaw, purée, and put through a nylon sieve. Make up the purée with water to 1½ pints. Test for sweetness, and if necessary add more caster sugar. Then complete the recipe as from * above.

Try this also using a combination of raspberries and red-currants, in the proportion of about ¾ lb. raspberries to ¼ lb. redcurrants.

[B/C]   *Summer Pudding*

This simple pudding is delectable fresh or frozen. It is made from a mixture of whatever soft fruit happens to be available, and everyone has their own favourites – strawberries, cherries, currants, gooseberries – but raspberries and black currants should be included to give the authentic flavour.

[B] *To make from fresh fruit*

approx. ¼ lb. stale white bread   6–8 oz. sugar
1½ lb. mixed fruit   ¼ pt water
whipped cream or custard for serving

Use a basin or soufflé dish which holds about 1½ pints. If you are going to freeze the pudding use a foil basin or see method 4 on p. 17. Cut the bread into thin slices, remove the crusts, and completely line the basin with the slices.

Make a syrup with the sugar and water (the exact quantity of sugar will depend on what fruit you are using), and gently stew the fruit in this until it is soft.

* Test for sweetness, add more sugar if necessary and pour the hot fruit into the prepared basin. Cover with a thin layer of bread. Put a plate or a flat saucer on top which will exactly fit into the basin, and a weight on top of this, so that the pressure will cause the juice to soak into the bread (but see that it doesn't overflow above the rim of the plate). Leave in the refrigerator overnight.

To serve immediately: Turn on to a dish and serve with cream or custard.

To freeze: if you have used a foil basin wrap and freeze. Otherwise see p. 17.

To serve after freezing: stand at room temperature for about 6 hours. Turn on to a dish and serve with cream or custard.

[C] *To make from frozen fruit*

approx. ¼ lb. stale white bread   whipped cream or custard
1½ lb. mixed fruit frozen in
   sugar

Line a basin with the bread as above. Tip the frozen fruit into a saucepan and gently stew it until it is soft. There will probably be enough juice, but if necessary add a little water. Then complete the recipe as from * above.

[B/C]   *Raspberry Ice-Cream*

[B] *To make with fresh raspberries*

1 lb. raspberries   ¼ pt water
5 oz. sugar   ½ pt double cream

[C] *To make with frozen fruit*

1 lb. raspberries frozen with   2 oz. sugar
   sugar   ¼ pt water
     or   ½ pt double cream
½ pt raspberry purée

Make in exactly the same way as blackcurrant ice-cream (see p. 176).

[B/C]   *Raspberry Water-Ice*

[B] *To make with fresh raspberries*

1 lb. raspberries $\frac{1}{2}$ pt water
6 oz. sugar

[C] *To make with frozen raspberries*

1 lb. raspberries frozen with   3 oz. sugar
    sugar $\frac{1}{2}$ pt water
        or
$\frac{1}{2}$ pt raspberry purée

Make in exactly the same way as blackcurrant water-ice (see p. 177).

[B/C]   *Raspberry and Redcurrant Ice-Cream*

These two fruits combine very well to make a fresh-tasting ice-cream. The quantities given below will serve 4 to 6 people.

[B] *To make from fresh fruit*

$\frac{3}{4}$ lb. raspberries $\frac{1}{8}$ pt water
$\frac{1}{4}$ lb. redcurrants $\frac{1}{4}$ pt double cream
5 oz. sugar

Purée the raspberries and redcurrants and put them through a nylon sieve.

* Boil the sugar and water gently together for 3 minutes and leave to cool. Stir this syrup into the fruit purée, and fold in the lightly whipped cream. Turn into a basin or an ice-tray and put in the freezer for 1 to 2 hours, or until the mixture has reached a mushy state. Take out of the freezer, beat well, pour into waxed or plastic containers and replace in the freezer.

To serve: remove from the freezer 1 hour before serving and leave in the refrigerator.

[C] *To make from frozen fruit*

¾ lb. raspberries frozen with sugar	2 oz. sugar
	⅛ pt water
¼ lb. redcurrants frozen with sugar	¼ pt double cream
or	
3 tbs. sweetened redcurrant purée	

Allow the fruit to thaw until it is soft enough to purée and pass through a nylon sieve. Then complete the recipe as from * above. Test for sweetness and stir in a little more caster sugar if necessary.

[B/C]   *Raspberry and Redcurrant Water-Ice*

Use about 3 parts of raspberries to 1 part of redcurrants and follow the method for blackcurrant water-ice, p. 177.

August

BEETROOT

Small young beetroot are worth freezing if you have grown more than you can eat straight away.

[A] *To freeze cooked:* wash the beetroot and cook them in boiling salted water until they are tender – this will take 30 to 50 minutes according to size – cool, and rub off the skins. Freeze in polythene bags.

[C] *To serve after freezing:* Allow to thaw and use in salad, or heat in a little water and serve hot with béchamel sauce.

[B]   *Bortsch*

1 lb. beetroot   a good squeeze of lemon juice
3 pts stock   salt and pepper

1 spoonful of sour cream or yogurt for each serving
a few sweet pickled cucumbers or some chopped parsley (optional)

Peel the beetroot and cook them in the stock until they are tender and the stock has taken on a deep red colour. Lift out the beetroot and set them aside to use later as a vegetable or salad. Test the soup for seasoning and add the lemon juice. Shred one or two of the beetroot and return the slivers to the soup.

To serve immediately: serve hot or chilled, with a teaspoon of sour cream or yogurt in each bowl. Add the slivers of cucumber and the chopped parsley.

To freeze: allow the soup to cool and freeze in waxed or plastic containers.

To serve after freezing:

To serve hot – tip the frozen soup into a saucepan and heat gently. Serve as above.

To serve cold – allow to thaw and serve as above.

CAULIFLOWER

[A] *To freeze blanched:* break up the head into roughly equal flowerlets, wash, and blanch for 2 minutes. Drain, cool, and freeze in polythene bags.

[C] *To serve after freezing:* tip the frozen cauliflower into a little boiling salted water and cook gently until it is soft. Serve with melted butter, béchamel sauce (perhaps enriched with the yolk of an egg), or dried breadcrumbs fried in butter and sprinkled thickly over the cauliflower. Or cover it with a cheese sauce, sprinkle some grated cheese on top, and heat through in a moderate oven for about 15 minutes.

LETTUCE

[B]

Lettuce Soup

This is a practical way of using up lettuces which have bolted.

1 large lettuce (about ¾ lb.)   ¾ pt chicken or veal stock
1 medium onion   ¾ pt milk
1 oz. butter   salt and pepper
2 level tbs. flour

Slice the onion and sweat it in the butter for a few minutes. Shred the lettuce leaves coarsely, add them to the pan, cover, and continue to cook for another 5 minutes or so. Stir in the flour and pour on the boiling stock and milk. Continue to stir until the soup comes to the boil, season, cover, and simmer for about 20 minutes. Pass through a blender or a fine sieve.

To serve immediately: return the soup to the pan and bring back to the boil, test for seasoning and serve.

To freeze: allow to cool, and freeze in waxed or plastic containers.

To serve after freezing: tip the frozen soup into a saucepan and heat gently, stirring from time to time. Test for seasoning and serve.

ONIONS

Since onions store excellently, it is hardly worth freezing them except in cooked dishes. The exception is the small pickling onion, which can usually be bought only in the summer and autumn, is not normally grown in the garden, and is delicious in stews and casseroles. So freeze a few for use in recipes where it makes all the difference to have really small onions.

[A] *To freeze blanched:* peel the onions and blanch them for 3 minutes, drain, cool, and freeze in waxed or plastic containers. This is important, for the smell is so strong that it is not really safe to put them in polythene bags, as the slightest perforation might cause a cross-smell in the freezer.

[B] *Creamed Onion Soup*

1½ lb. onions   1 pt milk
2 oz. butter   1 pt stock
1 oz. fresh white breadcrumbs   salt and pepper
  or rolled oats

fried croûtons or small pieces of diced cheese for serving (optional)

Slice the onions. Heat the butter in a heavy pan and cook the onions in this very gently for an hour, with the pan covered, being careful to see that they do not colour at all. Add the breadcrumbs or rolled oats, the milk and the stock, season, and continue to cook for another ¾ hour. Put the soup through a blender or a mouli.

To serve immediately: return to the pan and bring back to boiling point. Test for seasoning and serve. Fried croûtons or small pieces of diced cheese can be added to the soup just before serving.

To freeze: allow to cool, and freeze in waxed or plastic containers.

To serve after freezing: tip the frozen soup into a saucepan and bring gently to the boil. Test for seasoning and serve as for immediate eating.

[B] *French Onion Soup*

1½ lb. onions	2½ pts stock
3 oz. butter	salt, pepper, ½ tsp. sugar

French bread (1 slice per person)
grated cheddar or gruyère cheese (1 tbs. per person)
1 clove garlic

Slice the onions finely into rings. Melt the butter in a heavy saucepan and cook the onions in it gently for about 20 minutes, stirring from time to time and more frequently towards the end, so that they do not stick to the bottom of the pan, but become creamy and butter-yellow. Then add the salt and pepper, and the sugar which will help the onions to brown, raise the heat a little, and, stirring constantly, cook them for a further 5 minutes, by which time they should be a rich, dark golden colour but not at all burnt. Add the stock, stir well and simmer for ½ hour.

To serve immediately: cut a slice of French bread for each serving, dry it slowly under a grill or in the oven, then rub it with a cut clove of garlic, pile some grated gruyère or cheddar cheese on each slice and quickly melt the cheese under a hot grill. Test the soup for seasoning, pour it, very hot, into soup bowls, and float one piece of the toasted bread and cheese in each bowl.

To freeze: cool and freeze in waxed or plastic containers.

To serve after freezing: tip the frozen soup into a saucepan and heat it, stirring constantly at first, over a gentle heat. Bring it to the boil and serve with the French bread and cheese as above.

[B/C] *Beef and Onion Casserole*

3 lb. beef (chuck or skirt)	bouquet garni
1½ lb. small onions	1½ pts stock
2 oz. seasoned flour	2 tbs. concentrated tomato
1½ oz. dripping	purée
1½ lb. carrots, fresh, or frozen blanched	salt and pepper

Frozen beef should be allowed to thaw before cooking, but carrots may be used straight from the freezer.

Trim the meat and cut it into bite-sized pieces. Roll these in the seasoned flour, leaving on one side 1 heaped tablespoon, and brown evenly in the dripping in a large frying-pan. Transfer the meat to a casserole, and add to it the onions, the carrots, cut into slices if they are large, and the bouquet garni.

Add the remainder of the flour to the fat left in the frying pan, and cook it over a moderate heat until it has browned. Draw off the heat and gradually stir in the stock. Replace on the heat and bring to the boil, stirring all the time. Season, and add the tomato purée. Strain into the casserole. Cover and cook in a slow oven (300°F., gas 2) for about 2½ hours, until the meat is tender.

To serve immediately: test for seasoning and serve.

To freeze: allow to cool and freeze in plastic containers or see method 4 on p. 17.

To serve after freezing: turn straight into a flameproof casserole and warm very gently over a low heat, stirring from time to time. Allow about 1 hour for this quantity.

[B/C] *Coq-au-Vin*

4-lb. chicken, jointed
1 lb. button onions, fresh, or
 frozen blanched or glazed
2 oz. butter
2 tbs. oil
4 oz. streaky bacon
2 cloves garlic
2 oz. flour

1 tbs. concentrated tomato
 purée
1 tbs. brandy
½ bottle full-bodied red wine
thyme, bayleaf
½ lb. button mushrooms, fresh,
 or frozen raw or blanched
salt, pepper and 1 lump sugar

Frozen chicken must be allowed to thaw before cooking, but onions and mushrooms may be used straight from the freezer.

Heat the butter and oil in a flameproof casserole and sauté the diced bacon, the onions and the chopped garlic until they are golden brown. (If you are using frozen glazed onions do not add them yet.) Lift everything out and set aside. Roll the pieces of chicken in the well-seasoned flour and brown them in the casserole. Lift them out and set aside also. Stir in the remains of the flour and the tomato purée and allow to cook for two minutes. Warm the brandy in a spoon, pour it into the casserole and set it alight. Leave it to burn for a moment and then douse the flames with the wine. Stir and allow to bubble for a few minutes, return the chicken and the onions, garlic and bacon to the casserole, add the herbs and the seasoning, cover, and simmer for 1 hour or longer, until the chicken pieces are tender. About ½ hour before the end of the cooking time add the whole mushrooms. If you are using frozen glazed onions add them now. When the mushrooms are tender and the onions are hot, test for seasoning and serve.

To freeze: cool and freeze in a plastic container or see method 4 on p. 17.

To serve after freezing: tip the frozen chicken into the casserole and warm through over a very gentle heat for 45 minutes to 1 hour.

[B] *Onion Tart*

The quantity given below is enough for three 8-inch tarts.

3 lb. onions
1 lb. shortcrust pastry (see p. 28)
3 oz. butter
4 eggs

1 tsp. French mustard
½ pt single cream
3 or 4 bacon rashers (optional)
salt and pepper

Line 3 buttered 8-inch flan-tins with the pastry. If you are freezing the tarts use foil flan-cases or see methods 2 or 3 on p. 18.

Slice the onions, not too finely, and cook them gently in the butter until they are soft. Cool. Beat together the eggs, the mustard and the cream, stir this mixture into the onions, and season. Pour into the pastry cases, and if you are using the bacon rashers cut them into dice and arrange them on top. Bake the tarts in a medium oven (375°F., gas 5) for 30 minutes.

To serve immediately: cook for another 10 to 15 minutes until the pastry is golden brown. Serve very hot.

To freeze: allow to cool. If you have used foil flan-cases wrap the tarts well before freezing. Otherwise see p. 18.

To serve after freezing: put the frozen tart into a hot oven (425°F., gas 7). After 20 minutes turn the oven down to 375°F., gas 5, and cook for a further 20 to 30 minutes, or until the tart is hot right through.

[B] *Onions in White Sauce*

A useful stand-by to keep in the freezer. You can use them to flavour and thicken stews and blanquettes, or serve them as a vegetable.

1 lb. pickling onions
1 oz. butter
1 oz. cornflour

½ pt stock
¼ pt milk
salt and pepper

Blanch the onions for 2 minutes. Bring them to the boil once more in fresh water and simmer until they are just tender but have not lost their shape (about 20 minutes, but this will vary with the size of the onions). Drain them well.

In a separate saucepan make a sauce with the butter, the cornflour, the stock and the milk. Add the onions carefully and test for seasoning before serving.

To freeze: cool and freeze in waxed or plastic containers. It is useful to package the onions in small quantities for use in other dishes.

To serve after freezing: place the frozen onions in a saucepan and heat through gently, stirring carefully. For use in casseroles or other dishes add the frozen onions $\frac{1}{2}$ hour before the end of the cooking time, and stir well until they have thawed and become amalgamated with the dish.

[B]   *Glazed Onions*

These can be served as a vegetable or used in small quantities as a garnish for meat dishes, especially game.

1 lb. small or pickling onions $\frac{1}{4}$ pt chicken stock
1 oz. butter   salt and pepper
2 tsp. sugar

Blanch the onions for 2 minutes. Drain and return them to the pan with the other ingredients and simmer gently, uncovered, for 15 to 20 minutes, or until they are tender but have not lost their shape, and have absorbed all the liquid. They are now ready to serve.

To freeze: cool and freeze in waxed or plastic containers.

To serve after freezing: tip the frozen onions into a saucepan and heat gently.

[B]   *Onions in Cider*

8 fairly large onions   bouquet garni
2 tbs. olive oil   salt and pepper
¼–½ pt cider

Peel the onions and put them in a saucepan which is large
enough to hold all of them on the bottom. Add the olive oil,
put over a moderate heat, and when the oil starts to sizzle pour
in the warmed cider, which should half-cover the onions. Put
in the bouquet garni and season. Cover the pan and cook
steadily but not too fast for ¾ hour.

To serve immediately: uncover the pan and cook the onions for
another 20 minutes or so, until they are very tender and a pale
golden colour.

* Transfer them to a hot dish. Reduce the liquid in the saucepan until it thickens to a syrupy consistency. Take out the
bouquet garni and pour the sauce over the onions.

To freeze: remove the bouquet garni and allow the onions to
cool in the cooking liquor. Freeze together in a rigid container
so that the onions keep their shape – a foil dish is best, as this
will be the easiest to free from the smell of onions when you
come to wash it.

To serve after freezing: put the frozen onions and liquid into a
heavy saucepan and heat gently. Simmer with the pan uncovered for about 20 minutes. Then finish off as from * above.

[B]   *Onions à la Grecque*

These make a very good hors-d'oeuvre.

1 lb. pickling onions   2 tbs. tomato purée
¼ pt water   2 tbs. sugar
¼ pt white wine   a sprig of rosemary
juice of ½ lemon   salt and pepper
4 tbs. olive oil
1 tbs. chopped parsley

Put the onions in a saucepan with all the other ingredients except the parsley. Bring slowly to the boil and simmer for about ½ hour, when the onions should be done. Lift them out carefully and put them in a bowl. Boil the cooking liquid rapidly for 5 to 10 minutes, or until it has reduced by nearly a half. Pour this over the onions and leave to cool.

To serve immediately: sprinkle with the chopped parsley before serving.

To freeze: freeze in plastic or waxed containers.

To serve after freezing: allow to thaw at room temperature for 5 to 6 hours. Serve as above.

RUNNER BEANS

Of all the vegetables in the garden, the useful and prolific runner bean is probably frozen in greater quantities than any other. It is best frozen blanched. Freeze only young, fresh beans.

[A] *To freeze blanched:* cut the ends off the beans, and if necessary pare off the sides. Cut them into slices and blanch for 2 minutes. Drain, cool and freeze in polythene bags.

[C] *To serve after freezing:* put the beans into salted boiling water and heat through, gently breaking up the frozen mass with a fork. They will take between 5 and 10 minutes to cook after they have come to the boil.

MELONS

Melons are often so cheap in August and September that, though they lose a little of their taste when they are frozen, it is worth while putting some in the freezer for later use in fruit salad. They can be frozen with sugar or in syrup; but sugar is preferable from the point of view of taste.

[A] *With sugar:* peel the melon, take out the seeds and cut the fruit into cubes or scoop it into balls. Mix with sugar in the proportion of 4 oz. sugar to 1 lb. melon. Freeze in polythene bags.

In syrup: peel the melon, take out the seeds and cut the fruit into cubes or scoop it into balls. Put into waxed or plastic containers and cover with cold syrup made in the proportion of 9 oz. sugar to 1 pint water. Put a piece of crumpled foil on top of the fruit, under the cover, to keep it below the syrup.

[B]   ## Melon Ice-Cream

2 small ripe melons – the dark-fleshed Italian or Charentais melons are best for this (approx. 1 lb. melon flesh)	½ pt single cream 4 egg yolks 4 oz. sugar

Heat the cream to near boiling point, pour it on to the egg yolks mixed with the sugar and return to the pan. Stir over a gentle heat until the custard thickens, but do not allow it to boil. You may find it easier to do this in a double saucepan. Leave to cool.

Halve or quarter the melons, remove the pips and scoop out the flesh, but be careful not to go too close to the rind or the ice-cream will be bitter. Liquidize the flesh in a blender.

Add the custard and blend for a few more seconds until it is smooth. Taste, and add a little more sugar if necessary. Pour into waxed or plastic containers and freeze.

To serve: remove from the freezer 15 minutes before serving.

PLUMS

Plums are a more doubtful candidate for the freezer than many other fruits, and are really only worth freezing if you have a glut in your own garden or can buy them fresh very cheaply. Choose ripe, firm plums and always stone them before freezing, as they may otherwise acquire an almond-like flavour. Avoid the varieties with tough skins, which may become even tougher in the freezer. Victorias are excellent.

Plums are best frozen in syrup or cooked. Like peaches and apricots, they are inclined to become discoloured, so if you are freezing them raw dip them briefly in a solution consisting of the juice of $\frac{1}{2}$ lemon to 1 pint of water.

[A] *In syrup:* halve and stone the plums and dip them in the lemon solution. Put them in waxed or plastic containers and cover with cold syrup made in the proportion of 9 oz. sugar to 1 pint of water. Put a piece of crumpled foil over the top of the fruit, under the cover, to keep it below the syrup.

Cooked: stone the plums and cook them gently in syrup made with 9 oz. sugar to 1 pint of water. About $\frac{1}{2}$ pint of syrup should be sufficient for 1 lb. fruit (weighed before stoning). When the plums are soft (after about 10 minutes) allow them to cool, and freeze in waxed or plastic containers.

[B]   *Plum Tart*

This is made in exactly the same way as apricot tart (see p. 127).

[B]   *Zwetschgen Torte*

One tart serves 4 to 6 people.

Zwetschgen, or Switzers, as they are sometimes called by greengrocers, are very dark purple plums, with a strong bloom and deep yellow flesh. Their particular combination of sweet flesh and tart skin makes them ideal for flans.

approx. 1 lb. zwetschgen	2–3 oz. sugar
6 oz. sweetened shortcrust pastry (see p. 28)	¼ tsp. cinnamon
	1 oz. flaked almonds
1 tbs. biscuit or sponge cake crumbs	

Line a buttered 8-inch flan-tin with the pastry. If the tart is for the freezer use a foil flan-case or see methods 2 or 3 on p. 18. Bake blind in a hot oven (425°F., gas 7) for 10 minutes. Sprinkle on the biscuit or cake crumbs, which will help to absorb the plum juice and prevent the pastry from getting soggy. Halve and stone the plums and lay them closely on the pastry, skin side upwards. If you have a lot of plums, you can pack them in close ranks, so that they are virtually standing on their sides. Sprinkle on 2 oz. of the sugar combined with the cinnamon and the almonds. Bake in a hot oven (425°F., gas 7) for 40 minutes or until the plums are cooked.

To serve immediately: taste a little piece of plum for sweetness and sprinkle on more sugar if necessary. Serve hot or cold.

To freeze: allow to cool. If you have used a foil flan-case wrap and freeze. Otherwise see p. 18.

To serve after freezing: place the frozen tart in a hot oven (425°F., gas 7) for ½ hour. Serve hot or cold.

September

GROUSE

If you have grouse which you do not want to cook immediately, pluck and draw them and wrap them separately in foil, polythene film or moisture-vapour-proof tissue. Freeze each brace in a polythene bag. The grouse can later be roasted or casseroled.

To roast: allow the frozen grouse to thaw and wipe them inside and out. Place a large lump of butter inside each bird and wrap it in a slice of bacon. Roast in a moderately hot oven (400°F., gas 6) for 30 minutes. Place a piece of toast underneath each bird to absorb the juice, dredge them with a little flour, baste and return to the oven for a further 10 minutes. Serve on the croûtons of toast.

[B/C]   *Casserole of Grouse*

Older, tougher or even slightly 'higher' birds may be used for casseroles.

2 brace of grouse	bouquet garni
1 oz. butter	12 pickling onions or ½ lb.
1 tbs. oil	frozen glazed onions
2 medium onions	½ lb. button mushrooms, fresh,
2 carrots	or frozen raw or blanched
1 clove garlic	juice of ½ lemon
2 tbs. flour	1 tbs. redcurrant jelly
½ pt stock	salt and pepper
½ pt red wine	

If you are using frozen grouse allow them to thaw before cooking. The pickling onions and the mushrooms can be used straight from the freezer.

Melt the butter and oil in a flameproof casserole, wipe the birds and brown them on all sides. Remove them from the casserole and brown in it the diced onions, carrots and garlic. Sprinkle on the flour and continue to cook, stirring constantly, for 2 minutes. Slowly stir in the stock, add the wine, the bouquet garni and the seasoning and replace the grouse. Cover and simmer gently on top of the stove, or place in a moderate oven (350°F., gas 4), for about 1 hour, or until the birds are tender – the time will vary according to their age.

If you are using fresh pickling onions blanch them for 10 minutes.

Add the onions and the whole mushrooms to the casserole about 10 minutes before the end of the cooking time.

When the birds are cooked remove them from the casserole, and unless you wish to serve everyone with a whole grouse cut them in half. Add the lemon juice and the redcurrant jelly to the sauce, and test for seasoning.

To serve immediately: return the birds to the casserole and heat thoroughly before serving.

To freeze: cool and freeze in plastic containers or strong polythene bags.

To serve after freezing: allow to thaw at room temperature for 5 to 6 hours or overnight in the refrigerator. Replace in the flameproof casserole and heat through gently either on top of the stove or in a moderate oven.

VENISON

Venison is not often available in the butcher's, but if you should be offered some, or have the opportunity to buy it, accept gratefully. The meat is tender and extremely tasty, there is hardly any waste and it is relatively inexpensive. It has very little fat, so if you are going to roast it, it will be much improved if you lard it liberally first.

[A] *To freeze:* make sure the meat has been well hung, and if necessary hang it in a cool, airy place for a few days, according to how high you like it, but do not allow it to get too high. Then wash it very well in cold water, scraping off any of the damp sticky substance that may have formed on the outside (use the back of a knife for this) and dry it well. Rub it all over with flour, to keep the surface dry, wrap very well in foil, polythene film or moisture-vapour-proof tissue, and place in an extra thick polythene bag. It is important to insulate the meat very well, so that the smell does not contaminate any of the other contents of your freezer.

[B/C] *Braised Venison*

One of the nicest ways of cooking venison is to marinade the meat for a few days and then to braise it in the marinading juices. This is also the best method if you are going to freeze the left-overs, as it produces a generous amount of richly flavoured sauce in which the venison can be frozen and subsequently re-heated. As with all meat, the larger the joint the better the results, so cook as large a piece as your oven will hold.

¼ haunch of venison (approx. 5 lb.)	6 crushed peppercorns
	6 crushed juniper berries
2 onions	2 oz. butter
2 cloves garlic	1 tbs. flour
2 carrots	1 glass port or madeira
3 tbs. olive oil	2 tbs. redcurrant jelly
1 bottle red wine	salt and pepper
bayleaf, thyme, rosemary	

Frozen venison can be used straight from the freezer, and allowed to thaw as it marinades.

Roughly chop the onions, garlic and carrots and put them in a large bowl. Place the venison on top, pour over 2 tablespoons of olive oil and the wine, add the herbs, the peppercorns and the juniper berries and allow the meat to soak in this marinade for 2 to 3 days, turning it occasionally so that all sides are kept evenly moist.

When you are ready to cook the venison (the longer you leave it in the marinade the gamier it will be) take it out and dry it well. Heat 1 ounce of the butter with the remaining table-spoon of oil in a large flameproof casserole or roasting tin, and sear the meat quickly on all sides. Strain the marinade into a saucepan and bring it to a rapid boil to reduce it by almost half. Pour it over the venison and cover the casserole or, if you are using a roasting tin, cover with a double layer of foil folded firmly over the edges. Cook in a low oven (300°F., gas 2) for anything between 2 and 4 hours, depending on the size of the joint (a 5-lb. joint will take roughly 2½ hours). When the meat is tender remove it from the casserole and keep it warm. Bring the sauce to the boil and reduce it by nearly half. Make a beurre manié with the rest of the butter and the flour, stir this into the sauce and continue to cook until it thickens. Add the port or madeira and the redcurrant jelly, test for seasoning, return the meat to the sauce and serve. Glazed onions (see p. 194) and braised chestnuts (see p. 279) are excellent accompaniments.

To freeze: allow to cool and freeze the meat, whole or sliced, with the sauce in foil or plastic containers, or see method 4 on p. 17.

To serve after freezing: tip the frozen meat into a flameproof casserole or saucepan and heat gently on top of the stove for about 40 minutes.

Note: Unless you have allowed the venison to become very high, be sure to make stock from the bones. This will form the basis of an excellent venison soup, cooked with some root vegetables and onions which have been briefly braised in butter first and put through a blender or mouli. If you have some left-over scraps of the meat and sauce put these in as well, and perhaps another dash of port.

AUBERGINES

The best way of freezing aubergines is cooked, as part of a prepared dish such as moussaka or ratatouille. Before cooking it is advisable to drain them in salt to get rid of any bitterness and excess moisture. Cut them into slices, sprinkle them lightly with salt and leave for about ½ hour. Rinse thoroughly and dry.

However, if you do want to put a few bags in the freezer for using later on, or have the chance of buying some cheaply but no time to cook them before they are past their prime, they do freeze moderately well blanched, and there is then no need to carry out the salting.

[A] *To freeze blanched:* choose firm aubergines with dark, smooth, glossy skins. Wash them and cut them into slices. Blanch for 4 minutes, drain, cool and freeze in polythene bags. To avoid discoloration, the blanching should be done as soon as possible after you have sliced the aubergines.

[B] *Moussaka*

This rich Mediterranean mixture of lamb and aubergines is a considerable trouble to prepare but a great pleasure to eat. So make a large quantity at a time. The amounts given here will fill two 2-pint dishes. Strictly speaking the dish should be made with raw minced lamb, but you can also use minced or diced cooked lamb or a combination of lamb and beef. If you are using cooked meat you may need to add a little stock to the ingredients listed below.

2 lb. minced lamb (see above)
3 lb. aubergines
½ lb. onions
2 cloves garlic
approx. ½ pt olive oil
herbs – preferably a little of each of the following:
thyme, rosemary, marjoram

spices – a pinch each of ground coriander, mace and allspice
2 tbs. concentrated tomato purée
salt and pepper

Sauce

2 pts milk
6 egg yolks
3 tsp. cornflour

2 oz. grated cheese
salt, pepper and a little grated nutmeg

Start by making the sauce, as this can cook very slowly while you prepare the rest of the ingredients. Scald the milk, beat up the egg yolks with the cornflour and gradually pour on the milk, stirring all the time. Season with salt, pepper and nutmeg. Leave this mixture in a double saucepan or a bowl set in a saucepan of simmering water at the back of the stove, and stir it from time to time. It should thicken to a rich smooth custard. Stir in the cheese towards the end.

Take the green stalks off the aubergines, cut them into thin slices and prepare them as described on p. 206.

Slice or chop the onions and garlic very finely and cook them slowly in 2 tablespoons of the olive oil in a heavy frying pan till they become soft and transparent. They should not be allowed to brown. Add the meat, the herbs, spices and seasoning, and continue to cook gently until the meat is done. Add the tomato purée; if you have used cooked meat you may also need to add a little stock at this point. Set this mixture aside.

Heat some olive oil in a heavy frying pan and cook the aubergine slices very gently, a few at a time – they should become a translucent golden yellow but not be allowed to brown. Take each batch out when it is ready and drain it on absorbent paper. This will take longer, absorb more oil and use more kitchen paper than you will believe possible.

When all the aubergine slices have been cooked, assemble the moussaka. Line the bottom of an oven-proof dish with aubergines (use foil pie-dishes or line the dishes with foil if the moussaka is destined for the freezer). Follow with a layer of the meat mixture, and continue to alternate the two until both mixtures have been used up, ending with a layer of aubergines. Pour the custard mixture over the top.

To serve immediately: bake in a medium oven (350°F., gas 4) for about 1 hour and serve.

To freeze: the dish may be frozen cooked or uncooked.

To freeze uncooked – if you have used a foil pie-dish wrap the dish securely and freeze. Otherwise see method 2 on p. 17.

To freeze cooked – cook as for immediate eating, cool, and freeze as above.

To serve after freezing: unless you have used a foil dish, strip the foil off the frozen moussaka and replace in the casserole. Cook in a hot oven (425°F., gas 7) for 20 minutes and then turn the oven down to 350°F., gas 4. If the moussaka was frozen cooked, bake for a further 20 to 30 minutes. If it was frozen uncooked, bake for a further 40 to 50 minutes.

[B]   *Ratatouille*

This colourful medley of Mediterranean vegetables can be eaten hot or served cold as an hors d'oeuvre. It goes particularly well with a robust meat dish, such as a beef casserole, or with grilled mackerel or mullet.

2 medium aubergines	2 pimentoes (red or green)
2 tbs. olive oil	½ lb. tomatoes
2 Spanish onions	salt, pepper and a pinch of
1 large clove garlic	sugar

Heat the oil in a flameproof casserole or heavy saucepan. Sauté the finely sliced onions and garlic over a low heat until they become transparent, and add the thickly sliced, prepared aubergines (see p. 206). When these have cooked together for about 10 minutes add the pimentoes, cut into strips and with the seeds taken out, and finally, after another 10 minutes' cooking, add the tomatoes cut into quarters. Season and continue to cook over a low heat for 30 to 40 minutes, until all the vegetables are soft, but have not lost their individual colour and identity. Test for seasoning and serve.

To freeze: cool, and freeze in plastic or waxed containers or polythene bags.

To serve after freezing

To serve hot – return the frozen ratatouille to a saucepan or casserole, heat gently and serve.

To serve cold – allow to thaw for about 6 hours at room temperature or overnight in the refrigerator.

[C]   *Pipérade*

Served in this way, ratatouille can be turned into a pleasant light supper dish. The pipérade can be eaten by itself or with fried croûtons or fried bacon or ham.

ratatouille (the quantity given   4–6 eggs
  on p. 209)   salt and pepper
1 tbs. olive oil

Warm the olive oil in a deep frying pan or a flameproof earthenware dish. Add the frozen ratatouille and heat through gently. Beat the eggs lightly with a fork, and when the ratatouille is quite hot pour them into the pan and stir gently until they have just set but are still creamy. Test for seasoning and serve at once.

[B]   *Stuffed Aubergines*

These may be served cold as an hors d'oeuvre or hot as a vegetable dish.

4 aubergines   1 lb. tomatoes
4 tbs. olive oil   2 tbs. chopped parsley
2 Spanish onions   salt, pepper and 1 lump sugar
2 cloves garlic

Cut the aubergines in half lengthwise. Scoop out a little of the flesh from each half, but be careful not to cut the skin. Salt the aubergines and leave them skin side up, to drain off the excess moisture, for at least ½ hour. Rinse and dry them and fry them gently in half the olive oil until they are soft and transparent.

Drain them and place them, skin side down, in a shallow baking dish so that they do not overlap. Sauté the finely sliced onions and chopped garlic in the rest of the olive oil until they are transparent, add the scooped-out aubergine flesh and finally all but 2 large or 3 small tomatoes, seeded and chopped. Season and add the lump of sugar. Continue to cook the mixture until it is completely soft and stir in the parsley.

Spoon this mixture into the aubergine halves and top each one with slices of the reserved tomatoes. Pour a little water around the aubergines in the baking dish and bake in a slow oven (300°F., gas 2) for 1 hour. Serve hot or cold.

To freeze: allow to cool, and wrap the aubergines in foil before freezing, being careful not to overlap them or they will lose their shape. Or freeze in smaller quantities in foil flan-tins.

To serve after freezing

To serve hot – place the frozen aubergines in a medium oven (350°F., gas 4) and heat through. Allow about 40 minutes for this.

To serve cold – leave the aubergines to thaw at room temperature for about 5 hours or overnight in the refrigerator.

[B]   *Turkish Stuffed Aubergines*

This is a spicier variation of the previous recipe.

4 aubergines	½ lb. tomatoes
4 tbs. olive oil	1 tsp. allspice
½ lb. Spanish onions	1 tsp. pine kernels (optional)
2 cloves garlic	salt and pepper

Proceed exactly as for the previous recipe, but use all the tomatoes for the filling and add the allspice and the pine kernels to the mixture before stuffing the aubergines.

Cook, and serve or freeze as for the previous recipe.

[B]   *Aubergines Provençales*

¾ lb. aubergines   ¾ lb. onions
1 tbs. flour   1 lb. tomatoes
7 or 8 tbs. olive oil   salt and pepper

¼ *pt stock*
½ *tsp. chopped basil*
2 oz. grated cheese

Cut the aubergines into ½-inch slices and prepare them as described on p. 206. Dip the slices in the flour and sauté them in the olive oil in a heavy pan until they are golden brown all over. It is difficult to judge exactly how much oil they will take, so start with about 4 tablespoons and add more as you need it. Take the aubergines out of the pan and put them on absorbent paper to soak up any excess oil.

Gently sauté the sliced onions until they are quite tender. Skin the tomatoes and slice them.

If the aubergines are to be frozen, either use a foil dish or see method 2 on p. 17. Put in a layer of aubergines, then of onion and then of tomato, and continue until the vegetables are finished. Season each layer.

To serve immediately: pour over the stock and sprinkle on the basil and finally the grated cheese. Cook in a moderate oven (375°F., gas 5) for about 1 hour. The dish is now ready to serve.

To freeze: allow the vegetables to cool. If you have used a foil dish, wrap and freeze. Otherwise, see p. 17.

To serve after freezing: heat the frozen aubergines in a moderate oven (375°F., gas 5) for about ½ hour. Pour over the stock, sprinkle on the basil and cheese, and continue to cook for about another hour.

MUSHROOMS

Mushrooms freeze excellently, and are one of the best stand-bys to have in the freezer. For short-term storage it is a good idea to stock up with some of the cellophane-wrapped pannets which can be bought at most supermarkets and greengrocers. As they are airtight they keep excellently in the freezer. For longer-term storage it is best to blanch or sauté the mushrooms before freezing them.

They can be chopped as soon as they come out of the freezer. But if they must be sliced it is best to leave them for about ½ hour.

[A] *To freeze blanched:* wash the mushrooms, quarter them if they are large, and blanch them for 4 minutes. Drain, cool and freeze in polythene bags.

To freeze sautéed: wash and slice the mushrooms and sauté them in butter until they are soft. Allow them to cool, and freeze them with the cooking liquid in waxed cartons.

[B/C]   *Mushroom Soup (1)*

This is a very rich soup, but a little of it goes a long way, and the quantities given below are enough for 6 to 8 people.

1 lb. mushrooms, fresh, or frozen raw or blanched	approx. 1¼ pts milk
4 oz. butter	1 oz. flour
	salt and pepper

3 or 4 tbs. cream

Roughly chop or slice the mushrooms. Frozen mushrooms can be used straight from the freezer and left whole. Cook them gently in about half the butter in a covered pan until they are soft, and put them through a coarse mouli. You can also blend them, but if so do not purée them, as this makes the soup too bland and smooth. Strain off the juice and make it up to $1\frac{1}{2}$ pints with the milk. Make a sauce with the remainder of the butter, the flour, and the milk and mushroom liquid. Add the mushrooms, season, bring to the boil, and simmer for two or three minutes.

To serve immediately: stir in the cream, test for seasoning and serve.

To freeze: allow to cool and freeze in waxed or plastic containers.

To serve after freezing: tip the frozen soup into a saucepan and bring it gently to the boil, stirring from time to time. Add the cream, test for seasoning and serve.

[B/C]   *Mushroom Soup (2)*

½ lb. mushrooms, fresh, or frozen raw or blanched	2 oz. butter
1 pt water or chicken or veal stock	1½ level tbs. flour
	1 pt milk
	salt and pepper

Chop the mushrooms roughly and cook them in the water or stock for 5 minutes or so. Frozen mushrooms can be used straight from the freezer and left whole, but they will take a little longer to become soft. When the mushrooms are cooked purée them in a blender with the cooking liquid, or put them through a fine mouli. Make a sauce with the butter and flour and milk, add the mushroom purée and season. Return to the pan, bring to the boil and serve.

To freeze: allow to cool, and freeze in waxed or plastic containers.

To serve after freezing: tip the frozen soup into a saucepan and bring it gently to the boil, stirring from time to time. Test for seasoning and serve.

[B/C] *Boeuf Stroganoff*

This fragrant mixture of beef and mushrooms is an excellent way of stretching one of the more expensive cuts of beef. The quantities given will serve 6 generously.

1½ lb. rump steak
½ lb. mushrooms (or more), fresh, or frozen sautéed
1 clove garlic
4 oz. butter

2 onions
squeeze of lemon juice
1 glass white wine
½ pt sour cream
salt and pepper

If you are using frozen meat, it is easiest to slice it before it has completely thawed. Frozen sautéed mushrooms can be used straight from the freezer.

Slice the beef as thinly as possible. Rub each slice with a cut clove of garlic, salt and pepper them on both sides, and then beat them out very thin with a rolling pin. Cut each slice into strips ½-inch wide and 3 to 4 inches long. Melt half the butter in a frying pan and fry the fingers of beef very quickly on both sides. Set them aside and keep them warm. Put the rest of the butter in the pan and fry the finely chopped onions gently. When they are soft add the sliced mushrooms and a squeeze of lemon juice and cook for 5 minutes. If you are using frozen sautéed mushrooms, you will need rather less butter. Add the wine and let it bubble over a raised heat, then stir in the sour cream and the strips of beef, being careful not to lose any of the juice of the meat.

To serve immediately: heat all well together, test for seasoning and serve with rice.

To freeze: cool quickly, and freeze in foil or plastic containers.

To serve after freezing: tip the frozen stroganoff into a saucepan, heat very gently, stirring frequently, and bring to near simmering point, but do not allow to boil. This will take about 20 minutes. You may need to add a little more cream, sour cream or top of the milk.

[C]   *Mushrooms in Cream Sauce*

This simple concoction of cream and mushrooms makes a delicate accompaniment to chicken or fish. A little of the mixture placed in a cocotte dish, topped with an egg and a spoonful of cream or top of the milk and baked briefly in a moderate oven, makes a delicious start to a meal, or it may be served on toast or used as an omelette or vol-au-vent filling to provide a quick supper dish.

½ lb. mushrooms frozen sautéed	approx. ⅛ pt double cream or sour cream, or a combination of the two
2 onions	salt and pepper
1 oz. butter	
squeeze of lemon juice	

Sauté the finely chopped onions in the butter. Add the frozen mushrooms and heat through gently. When they are warm add a squeeze of lemon juice, stir in the cream and test for seasoning. Bring briefly to the boil and serve.

[B/C]   *Mushroom Sauce*

This sauce goes well with chicken, fish, eggs or pasta.

4 oz. mushrooms, fresh, or frozen blanched	2 oz. flour
1 medium onion	1 pt stock
2 oz. butter	4 tbs. double cream
	salt and pepper

2 tbs. parsley

Frozen mushrooms should be left for about ¼ hour until they are soft enough to chop.

Chop the onion finely and sauté it in the butter for a few minutes. Add the mushrooms, chopped finely or put through a coarse mouli. Cook for a few more minutes and stir in the flour. Gradually pour on the stock, season, and stir until the sauce boils. Continue to cook for a minute or two and stir in the cream.

To serve immediately: add the chopped parsley, test for seasoning and serve.

To freeze: when the sauce is cold, freeze in waxed or plastic containers.

To serve after freezing: tip the frozen sauce into a saucepan, heat gently, add the chopped parsley, test for seasoning and serve.

PIMENTOES, RED, GREEN
AND YELLOW

Pimentoes freeze best blanched. They can also be frozen unblanched, but they do not taste as good, and are in any case too soft to be used for salad. So it is worth the small amount of trouble involved in blanching them.

Freeze them in small quantities, as you are not likely to need more than two or three at a time. It is a good idea to mix the colours.

[A] *To freeze blanched*: wash the pimentoes, cut them in half and remove the seeds. This is very important, as if any of the seeds remain the pimentoes will be unbearably hot. Cut them into quarters or slices, depending on the dishes for which they will later be needed – it is useful to have a few bags of each – and blanch for 2 to 4 minutes, according to size. Drain, cool and freeze in polythene bags.

[B/C]   *Braised Beef with Pimentoes*

3 lb. braising beef (flat top or   2 onions
   topside) in one piece   2 tomatoes
1 lb. pimentoes   1 wineglass of red or white
1 oz. butter   wine
1 tbs. olive oil   salt and pepper
1 clove garlic

If you are using frozen beef it should be allowed to thaw at least partially before cooking. Pimentoes and tomatoes can be used straight from the freezer.

Melt the butter and oil in a flameproof casserole. Wipe the meat and rub it with the cut clove of garlic, salt and pepper it and sear it quickly on all sides. Remove it from the casserole, add the chopped onions and garlic and fry them gently for 5 minutes. Return the meat to the casserole and add the peeled and chopped tomatoes, the pimentoes cut into strips and with the seeds taken out, and the wine. Bring to the boil and allow to bubble for a few moments, then cover the casserole and leave it on a very low heat or in a low oven (300°F., gas 2) for 1½ to 2 hours. The exact time will depend on how well cooked you like your beef.

To serve immediately: remove the meat from the casserole and carve it. Reduce the sauce by quick boiling if necessary, and serve it with the meat.

To freeze: allow to cool and freeze the meat – sliced or left in a piece – and the sauce in foil or plastic containers.

To serve after freezing: return the frozen meat and sauce to the flameproof casserole and heat through gently on top of the stove. Proceed as for immediate eating.

[B/C]   *Beef Goulash with Pimentoes*

This is a good hearty dish. It has a much stronger flavour than the veal goulash given on p. 65, and is considerably less expensive. It is easy to make in large quantities, and is ideal for a teenage party.

3 lb. braising beef or best quality stewing beef	3 tbs. flour
1 lb. pimentoes	1 dsp. paprika (or more)
¼ lb. paprika speck or streaky bacon	1 pt stock
	½ lb. tomatoes
1 lb. onions	bayleaf, pinch of oregano and thyme
2 cloves garlic	salt and pepper
1 tbs. caraway seeds (optional)	

1 lb. potatoes
¼ pt sour cream

Frozen beef should be allowed to thaw before preparing. Pimentoes and tomatoes can be used straight from the freezer.

Cut the speck or bacon into small cubes and fry them gently in a flameproof casserole. Add the sliced onions and garlic, the caraway seeds and the meat cut into bite-sized cubes, and sauté until the vegetables are golden brown. Sprinkle on the flour and paprika (exactly how much paprika you use depends on your taste and how fresh the paprika is, as it loses some of its pungency with time) and cook gently for 2 more minutes, stirring well. Then add the stock, the peeled and roughly chopped tomatoes, the pimentoes cut into strips and with the seeds taken out, and the herbs and seasoning. Simmer on a low heat for about 1½ hours or until the meat is tender.

To serve immediately: peel the potatoes, cut them into ½-inch slices and parboil them for 6 to 8 minutes. Add them to the goulash, simmer for another 10 minutes or until they are cooked but not mushy, gently stir in the sour cream, heat through and serve.

To freeze: cool quickly and freeze in plastic containers or polythene bags or see method 4 on p. 17.

To serve after freezing: return the frozen goulash to the casserole and heat gently. When the meat is warmed through (allow about ¾ hour) continue as for immediate eating. You may need to add a little more water to the goulash before adding the potatoes, if the sauce is too thick.

[B/C]   *Chicken Casserole with Pimentoes*

4-lb. chicken, jointed	1 clove garlic
2 pimentoes	½ lb. tomatoes
1 oz. butter	¼ pt white wine
1 tbs. olive oil	salt and pepper
2 onions	

Frozen chicken must be allowed to thaw before cooking, but pimentoes and tomatoes can be used straight from the freezer.

Wipe the pieces of chicken and season them well. Melt the butter and oil in a flameproof casserole, sear the chicken pieces quickly on all sides and lift them out. Lower the heat and sauté the sliced onions and chopped garlic for 10 minutes. Replace the chicken joints, add the pimentoes, cut into strips and with the seeds taken out, and the peeled and roughly chopped tomatoes. Add the wine and seasoning and leave to simmer, covered, over a very low flame for 1½ hours, by which time the chicken should be cooked and the vegetables soft and amalgamated into a thick sauce. If after 1 hour the sauce still seems rather watery, leave the lid off for the last ½ hour. Check for seasoning and serve hot with rice.

To freeze: cool, and freeze in a plastic container or see method 4 on p. 17.

To serve after freezing: return the frozen chicken to the casserole and heat slowly, stirring gently from time to time. Allow about 45 minutes for this. Serve with rice.

[B/C]   *Chicken Paprika*

4-lb. chicken, cut into serving pieces	approx. 1 tsp. paprika
	1 lb. tomatoes
2 pimentoes, preferably 1 red and 1 green	½ pt stock, chicken or veal
	1 tbs. concentrated tomato purée
1–2 tbs. flour	
2 tbs. olive oil	bayleaf
2 onions	salt and pepper
1 or 2 cloves garlic	
½ pt sour cream	

Frozen chicken must be allowed to thaw, but pimentoes and tomatoes can be used straight from the freezer.

Season the flour well and coat the pieces of chicken in it. Fry them in the oil over a good heat in a flameproof casserole for 10 minutes. Add the chopped onion, the crushed garlic, and the pimentoes, sliced and with the seeds taken out. Next stir in the paprika. It is impossible to give exact quantities, as its strength varies so greatly, but be careful not to put in too much at the beginning, and taste as you go. Cook for another 10 minutes or so before adding the skinned and roughly chopped tomatoes, the stock, the concentrated tomato purée, the seasoning and the bayleaf. Cover, and cook for about 45 minutes to 1 hour either on top of the stove over a gentle heat or in a moderate oven (350°F., gas 4).

To serve immediately: 10 minutes before the chicken is ready, add the sour cream. Stir in well, and test for seasoning before serving.

To freeze: cool and freeze in a plastic container or see method 4 on p. 17.

To serve after freezing: return the frozen chicken to the casserole and heat slowly for about 45 minutes, stirring gently from time to time. Add the sour cream, test for seasoning and serve.

[B/C]   *Pimento and Tomato Tart*

2 red pimentoes	2 tbs. olive oil
1 green pimento	3 eggs
1 lb. tomatoes	⅜ pt milk
10 oz. shortcrust pastry (see p. 28)	2 oz. fresh breadcrumbs
1 large onion	2 tbs. grated cheese, preferably Parmesan
2 cloves garlic	salt and pepper
1 oz. butter	

Pimentoes and tomatoes can be used straight from the freezer.

Line a 10-inch buttered flan-tin, or two 7-inch tins, with the pastry. If the tart is to be frozen use foil flan-cases or see methods 2 or 3 on p. 18.

Chop the onion and the garlic finely and fry them gently in the butter and oil in a large frying pan. After a few minutes add the sliced pimentoes and continue to cook for another 15 minutes until they are soft. Beat the eggs and the milk together in a large basin and stir in the breadcrumbs. Add the peeled and roughly chopped tomatoes and the pimento mixture and mix well together. Stir in the cheese and season. Pour into the pastry cases and cook in a medium oven (375°F., gas 5) for about 45 minutes, until the filling has set. Serve hot.

To freeze: allow to cool. If you have used a foil flan-case wrap well before freezing. Otherwise see p. 18.

To serve after freezing: put the frozen tart in a hot oven (425°F., gas 7) for 20 minutes, then turn down the oven to 375°F., gas 5, and cook for another 20 to 30 minutes, depending on the size of the tart, until it is hot right through.

[B]   *Stuffed Pimentoes*

These can be eaten hot as a main course, with tomato sauce, in which case allow 2 pimentoes per person, or cold as an hors d'oeuvre, when one each should suffice.

8 pimentoes
1 lb. minced beef or lamb, raw or cooked
2 onions
1–2 cloves garlic
4 tbs. olive oil
½ lb. cooked rice
1 tbs. concentrated tomato purée
1 tbs. currants (optional)
a sprinkling of chopped rosemary leaves
1 pt tomato sauce (optional) (see p. 231)
salt and pepper

Sauté the chopped onions and garlic in 2 tbs. of the olive oil, add the meat and stir over a gentle heat until the meat is cooked, if you are using raw mince, or until it is well mixed in, if you are using cooked meat. Add the rice, the tomato purée, the currants, the rosemary and the seasoning, and heat well through.

Meanwhile cut across the tops of the pimentoes with a sharp knife, and with a little twist lift out the top with the core and seeds attached. Rinse out the insides and the tops of the pimentoes very well, making sure that none of the pith or the seeds remain, and being careful not to injure the pimento cases. Sometimes a grapefruit knife is useful for this.

Stuff the pimento cases with the meat mixture, place them upright in an ovenproof dish and replace the tops. Sprinkle the remains of the olive oil over and round the pimentoes, cover the dish with a lid or foil, and bake in a moderate oven (375°F., gas 5) for 40 minutes.

To serve immediately: serve hot with tomato sauce, or leave to cool and serve as an hors d'oeuvre.

To freeze: cool and freeze in waxed or plastic containers, with or without tomato sauce.

To serve after freezing: place the frozen pimentoes in a medium oven (350°F., gas 4) and heat through. Allow about 40 minutes for this.

[B]   *Peperonata*

A dish from Italy which makes a pleasant and unusual vegetable. It is quite strong-tasting, so not much of it is needed.

2 lb. red pimentoes	1 clove of garlic (optional)
2 lb. ripe tomatoes	3–4 tbs. olive oil
1 large onion	salt

Slice the onion and garlic and cook them in the olive oil until they are golden brown. Remove the seeds from the pimentoes, and cut them into strips. Add them to the pan, cover, and continue to cook gently for 15 minutes. Skin the tomatoes, chop them roughly and put them in the pan. Salt, and cook for a further 30 to 40 minutes, until the tomatoes have turned into a thick sauce and the peppers are quite soft. The liquid should all be absorbed by the peppers, so if the dish is still too runny towards the end of the cooking leave the lid off for the last few minutes. Add more salt if necessary. The dish is now ready to serve.

To freeze: allow to cool and freeze in small quantities in waxed containers or polythene bags. It is better not to use plastic containers, since the taste and smell of the pimentoes are difficult to remove.

To serve after freezing: tip the frozen peperonata into a saucepan and heat gently.

SWEET CORN

Sweet corn are excellent frozen, but they must be allowed to thaw before they are cooked.

[A] *To freeze blanched:* remove the husks and silk and trim the ends. Blanch for 4 to 8 minutes, according to size. Drain, cool and freeze in polythene bags.

[C] *To serve after freezing:* allow the cobs to thaw before cooking. This will take quite 3 or 4 hours – longer if the weather is very cold. Plunge them into a saucepan of salted boiling water and simmer for 12 to 15 minutes. Drain, rub liberally with butter all over, and serve.

[C]   *Sweet Corn Fritters*

These are nice on their own, and an excellent accompaniment also to cold meat, especially ham. They can be varied by adding a little minced or chopped ham to the mixture before frying.

1 sweet corn	2 eggs
1 tbs. flour	lard for frying
½ tsp. baking powder	salt
¼ tsp. paprika	

Allow the corn to thaw, and boil it in salted water until it is quite tender, which will take 10 to 15 minutes. Drain, and cut the corn off the cob. Chop it coarsely and mix it with the dry ingredients. Stir in the egg yolks, which have been beaten until they are thick, and then fold in the stiffly beaten whites. Heat some lard in a large frying pan until it is smoking hot, and put the sweet corn mixture into the pan in small spoonfuls, cooking them quickly on both sides. Drain them on absorbent paper and serve very hot.

TOMATOES

Although tomatoes are available all the year round, their price fluctuates enormously, so it pays to freeze as many as you can. Since their water content is high, they are not suitable for freezing for later use in salads. However, they are excellent frozen raw, either whole or puréed, for subsequent cooking. And they can be used in many dishes which are assembled or cooked before freezing.

Unless you grow enough tomatoes yourself, it is particularly worth while to look out for the small English ones which are often to be found very cheaply in shops and markets, especially towards the end of September. They are quite adequate for sauces and soups.

[A] *To freeze raw:* choose firm, ripe tomatoes. Put them in hot water for a few seconds, drain, plunge immediately into cold water, and take off the skins. Freeze in polythene bags.

If you are in a hurry, you can freeze the tomatoes without skinning them first. When you come to use them, drop the frozen tomatoes into boiling water for a few seconds and the skins will come off very easily.

[B] *To freeze cooked (puréed):* use imperfect or slightly over-ripe tomatoes for this. Cut them up roughly and take out any imperfect bits – there is no need to skin them – and put them in a heavy saucepan with a little salt and pepper and sugar. Stew gently for about 15 minutes and put through a nylon sieve. Cool, and freeze in waxed or plastic containers.

Tomato purée is excellent as a flavouring for soups, stews and sauces, and is delicious mixed with winter vegetables such as artichokes or celeriac.

[B/C]   *Tomato Soup (1)*

This is a thick and substantial soup.

1 lb. tomatoes	1 tsp. flour
1 medium onion	1½ pts water
¼ lb. bacon scraps	2 oz. rice
½ oz. butter or chicken fat	salt, pepper and sugar

chopped parsley (optional)

If you are using frozen tomatoes, there is no need to wait for them to thaw.

Slice the onions finely, dice the bacon, and fry both gently in the fat until the onions are lightly browned. Sprinkle in the flour and stir until it is blended. Skin the tomatoes, chop them roughly and add them to the saucepan, together with the boiling water. If you are using frozen tomatoes, heat them up in the water, skin them, and chop them before adding them to the soup. Season and put in a little sugar. Bring to the boil and add the rice. Simmer, covered, for about an hour, stirring occasionally.

To serve immediately: test for seasoning and add more water if the soup is too thick. Serve with chopped parsley sprinkled over each helping.

To freeze: allow to cool, and freeze in waxed or plastic containers.

To serve after freezing: tip the frozen soup into a saucepan and heat slowly. Test for seasoning, add a little water if necessary, and serve with parsley as above.

[B/C] *Tomato Soup (2)*

This is a creamier, lighter soup than the previous one.

2 lb. tomatoes
1 oz. butter
1 dsp. olive oil
2 medium potatoes
2 onions

½ pt milk
cream
parsley ⎫ optional
basil ⎭

2–3 sprigs parsley
a little basil
1 pt water or light chicken
   stock
salt, pepper and 2 tsp. sugar

If you are using frozen tomatoes, there is no need to wait for them to thaw.

Melt the butter and oil in a heavy saucepan, add the peeled and diced potatoes and onions and cook them gently for 5 minutes. Then add the skinned tomatoes and the herbs, sugar and seasoning, and continue to cook gently until all the vegetables have softened. Add the water or a very light chicken stock – the tomato taste should predominate – and simmer until all the vegetables are well cooked. Pass the soup through a blender or mouli and sieve it.

To serve immediately: dilute the soup with the milk, reheat, but do not allow it to boil. Test for seasoning and serve with a spoonful of cream and a sprinkling of chopped parsley and basil in each bowl.

To freeze: cool and freeze in waxed or plastic containers.

To serve after freezing: turn the frozen soup into a saucepan, reheat gently, and proceed as above.

[B] *Pizza*

This is a quickly made recipe which does not need yeast. (You can, of course, also make pizza with a yeast dough – see p. 30.)

The basic cheese and tomato topping can be added to in any number of ways – with black olives or anchovies, bits of bacon or ham, or mushrooms sliced and previously cooked in a little butter.

¾ lb. tomatoes	6–10 anchovy fillets (optional)
½ lb. flour	¼ lb. black olives (optional)
¼ pt milk	1 tsp. chopped marjoram or
4 tbs. olive oil	more to taste
1 tsp. baking powder	salt and pepper
6 oz. cheese	

Oil a baking tin about 11 inches in diameter, or two 8-inch tins. If the pizza is to be frozen, use foil tins or see method 3 on p. 17. Stir together the flour, the milk, the oil and the baking powder, and season generously. Spread this mixture on the dish, working at it till it is spread thinly and evenly – it will be quite springy. Grate or slice the cheese on top, and over this put the sliced tomatoes. Arrange the anchovy fillets and the olives over the tomatoes, and sprinkle on the marjoram. You may want more or fewer anchovies and olives, according to your taste. Or if the dish is for children you may prefer to omit these altogether, and have simply the cheese and tomatoes, or some blander addition like ham or mushrooms.

Cook in a hot oven (450°F., gas 8) for about 25 minutes, or until the dough is cooked through and the cheese is melting and bubbly. The pizza is now ready to serve.

To freeze: take out of the oven about 5 minutes before you would do if you were going to eat the pizza at once. Allow to cool. If you have used foil flan-cases wrap and freeze. Otherwise see p. 17.

To serve after freezing: take the pizza out of the foil in which it was cooked, and replace in the original baking tin. Put it while still frozen in a hot oven (450°F., gas 8) and heat through for 45 minutes to 1 hour.

Note: as well as large pizzas, it is useful to have a supply of smaller ones in the freezer, enough for one person. These will take only about 20 to 25 minutes to heat through.

[B] *Stuffed Tomatoes*

Use the large Mediterranean tomatoes for this dish, if possible, as they have so much more taste than the ubiquitous Money-makers most often found in shops here.

6 large tomatoes	peel of 1 lemon
¼ lb. cooked rice	1 tbs. olive oil
3 shallots or 2 small onions	salt and pepper
parsley and marjoram	

Cut the tops off the tomatoes and scoop out the pulp. Mix this with the cooked rice, add the finely chopped shallots or onions and herbs, and the grated lemon peel. Season, and fill the tomatoes with this mixture. Arrange them on a shallow baking dish, dribble a little olive oil over each tomato and bake in a moderate oven for about 40 minutes, or until the tomato cases are softened.

To serve immediately: serve hot as a vegetable with meat or fish or cold as an hors d'oeuvre, perhaps sprinkling a little more olive oil on them before serving.

To freeze: cool, and put in single layers on a foil-covered baking tray, freeze for 24 hours, wrap well and return to the freezer. Or freeze in smaller quantities in foil flan-tins.

To serve after freezing

To serve hot – put the frozen tomatoes in a medium oven (350°F., gas 5) and heat through for ¾ hour.

To serve cold – allow to thaw at room temperature for 5 to 6 hours.

[B] *Tomatoes Provençales*

1 lb. tomatoes	2 tbs. breadcrumbs
2 medium onions	1 tbs. olive oil
2 cloves garlic	salt and pepper
parsley and basil	

Cut the tomatoes in half. Score each cut surface with a sharp knife and sprinkle on salt and pepper. Chop the onions, garlic and herbs very fine, mix them with the breadcrumbs, and put a good teaspoon of the mixture on to each tomato, pressing it in as much as possible. Sprinkle a little olive oil over the tomatoes and grill them for 15 to 20 minutes, by which time they should be cooked and the tops even a little charred.

To serve immediately: serve hot as a vegetable dish or as a starter.

To freeze: cool, and freeze in foil flan-tins well wrapped. Or put in single layers on a foil-covered baking tray, freeze for 24 hours, wrap well and return to the freezer.

To serve after freezing: place the frozen tomatoes in a medium oven (350°F., gas 5) and heat through for $\frac{1}{2}$ hour. Serve as above.

[C]   *Creamed Tomatoes*

These can be served with almost any poultry, meat or fish dish. A couple of tablespoons for each person adds an unusual flavour, as well as looking pretty.

1 lb. tomatoes	1 tbs. chopped basil (optional)
1 tbs. seasoned flour	$\frac{1}{4}$ pt double cream
2 oz. butter	salt and pepper
1 tbs. brown sugar	

Skin the frozen tomatoes, and as soon as they have thawed sufficiently chop them roughly and dredge them with the seasoned flour. Put them in a frying-pan with the butter, and sprinkle over the sugar and basil. Season lightly. Cook very gently for 10 to 15 minutes, until the liquid has almost evaporated. Add the cream and stir it in well.

[B/C] *Tomato Sauce*

These quantities will make about 2½ pints of sauce.

2 lb. tomatoes
4 medium onions
4 cloves garlic
8 tbs. olive oil
8 tbs. concentrated tomato
  purée (10 oz.)

½ pt red wine
2 tbs. sugar
basil (optional)
salt and pepper

If you are using frozen tomatoes, you need only skin them – there is no need to wait for them to thaw.

Chop the onions and garlic finely and sauté them in the olive oil in a heavy saucepan until the onion is transparent. Add the skinned tomatoes and all the other ingredients. Cover the saucepan and let the sauce simmer for 2 to 3 hours over a very low heat, stirring from time to time. Test for seasoning. By the time the sauce is ready to serve it should be quite thick.

To freeze: cool, and freeze in waxed containers in the quantities which you will need for each meal. It is difficult to remove the smell of tomato sauce from the container in which it was frozen, so use old cream or yogurt pots which are expendable.

To serve after freezing: tip the frozen sauce into a pan and heat very gently, stirring from time to time. Test for seasoning before serving.

[B/C] *Sauce Bolognese*

2 lb. tomatoes
1 lb. minced beef *or* ½ lb.
  minced beef and ½ lb.
  minced pork
2 onions
2 cloves garlic
1 carrot

4 tbs. olive oil
¼ pt stock or red wine
4 tbs. concentrated tomato
  purée (5 oz.)
thyme and basil
salt and pepper

Frozen meat should be allowed to thaw for 2 to 3 hours if possible. Tomatoes can be used straight from the freezer and need only be skinned.

Sauté the finely chopped onions, garlic and carrot in the oil for 10 minutes. Add the meat and continue to cook very gently until it changes colour. Add the skinned tomatoes and all the other ingredients. Simmer very slowly, without a lid, stirring from time to time, until the sauce has reduced to a thick purée. Test for seasoning.

To freeze: cool, and freeze in waxed containers in the quantities your family use per meal. It is very difficult to remove the smell of tomato sauce from the container in which it was frozen, so use old cream or yogurt pots.

To serve after freezing: tip the frozen sauce into a pan and heat very gently, stirring from time to time. Test for seasoning before serving.

BLACKBERRIES

Blackberries freeze extremely well, and preserve their fresh, hedgerow taste almost indefinitely. Freeze the best berries with sugar and purée the less perfect ones.

[A] *With sugar:* mix the berries gently with sugar in the proportion of 3 to 4 oz. sugar to 1 lb. fruit. Freeze in polythene bags.

Purée: purée the blackberries in a blender with 3 oz. sugar to 1 lb. fruit, and rub through a nylon sieve. Freeze in waxed or plastic containers.

[C]   *Blackberry Fluff*

1 lb. blackberries frozen with sugar	2 tbs. water
	a little caster sugar (optional)
½ oz. gelatine	3 egg whites
juice of ½ lemon	

whipped cream for serving (optional)

Simmer the frozen blackberries until they are soft – about 15 to 20 minutes – and put them through a nylon sieve. Sprinkle the gelatine over the lemon juice and water, leave for a few minutes, and heat gently until the gelatine has dissolved. Add this to the purée, test for sweetness, and stir in a little caster sugar if necessary. Leave in a cool place until the mixture thickens and begins to set. Fold in the stiffly beaten egg whites. Chill for 3 to 4 hours and serve with whipped cream.

[B/C]   *Blackberry Ice-Cream*

[B] *To make with fresh blackberries*

1 lb. blackberries	¼ pt water
5 oz. sugar	½ pt double cream

[C] *To make from frozen fruit*

1 lb. blackberries frozen with sugar	2 oz. sugar
	¼ pt water
or	½ pt double cream
½ pt blackberry purée	

Make in exactly the same way as blackcurrant ice-cream (see p. 176).

[B/C]   *Blackberry Water-Ice*

[B] *To make with fresh blackberries*

1 lb. blackberries	½ pt water
6 oz. sugar	a good squeeze of lemon juice

[C] *To make with frozen blackberries*

1 lb. blackberries frozen with sugar	3 oz. sugar
	½ pt water
or	
½ pt blackberry purée	

Make in exactly the same way as blackcurrant water-ice (see p. 177).

October

BEEF

Late September or early October is the best time to buy home-produced beef for the freezer. It may be only marginally cheaper then – the seasonal price of beef does not fluctuate much – but the quality will be at its best at this time of the year, when the cattle have enjoyed their summer diet of rich fresh grass.

Whether you buy a whole side, half a side or a smaller quantity still will depend on the size of your family, your freezer and your bank balance, but in any case a bulk purchase of beef is likely to be the biggest investment in food for the freezer that you will make, so it is most important that you invest wisely. Whereas most families will get through a lamb in a few months, you may well be eating your beef for a whole year, so you want to be certain that you will enjoy it. (See also general notes on the bulk purchase of meat on p. 20).

Discuss with your butcher what quantity you will buy, and give him at least a week's notice. In deciding on the quantity, bear in mind not only the size of your freezer, but also the fact that you will not want to live on beef alone for the next six months. Very roughly, a whole side of beef will weigh 280 lb. and take up 8 cubic feet of freezer space. Half a side, whether the forequarter or the hindquarter, will weigh half as much. The hindquarter is more expensive than the forequarter and the price per lb. of a side of beef will be somewhere between the two. The hindquarter consists largely of the more expensive cuts, such as topside, sirloin and silverside for roasting, rump-steak and half the fillet for frying or grilling, and skirt, and leg for casseroles, stews and pies or puddings.

The forequarter also has some very good meat for roasting but not as much as the hindquarter – i.e. the forerib, back rib and top rib. It will also include chuck steak for casseroles, brisket for slow braising and shin and neck for stewing.

The forequarter flank can be rolled, for slow roasting, or minced, and the hindquarter flank is usually minced (from a whole side of beef you will get in the region of 18 lb. minced beef). It is useful also to have the butcher cut up the kidney and some of the better stewing or braising steak for you, so that you have a few bags of steak and kidney in the freezer, ready for pies or puddings.

As there are many different ways of cutting up a side of beef, and, unlike a leg or shoulder of lamb, the size of the joints is very much a matter for individual choice, it is especially desirable that you should be able to watch the cutting up process. Only you know how many pieces of steak you want in each bag, whether you prefer sirloin joints or porterhouse steaks and how big you would like each piece of topside to be.

When a piece like the topside or sirloin is being cut up, allow not only for your normal family consumption, but have a few pieces cut larger for parties, remembering that the bigger the piece of meat, the better it cooks. The aitchbone will make one excellent, huge joint for a special occasion, but do not be carried away by visions of grandeur, and keep in mind the size of your roasting tins and oven.

The fat which is trimmed off during the cutting up can be rendered down, and most butchers have a special vat for this. From a whole side of beef you will probably get about 10 lb. dripping.

And do not leave behind the bones. You may not want to keep them all, but ask the butcher to pick out the marrow bones and any of the meatier ones, and to chop them up into manageable pieces. They may be kept in a polythene bag in the freezer until you are ready to use them for stock, consommé or a pot-au-feu.

[B/C]   *Beef Stock*

beef bones   bayleaf, thyme, marjoram,
2–3 onions   parsley
2–3 carrots   salt and pepper
1–2 cloves garlic

Put some of the bones in a large saucepan (do not use the marrow bones for this, as they should be kept for better things, such as a pot-au-feu) and cover them with cold water. Bring very slowly to simmering point and skim off the scum which will rise to the top. Continue to skim for about 5 minutes, add the rest of the ingredients and season. Pour over enough cold water to cover the contents of the pan by at least 1 inch, and leave to simmer very gently for 4 to 5 hours. Skim off any further scum from time to time, and wipe the side of the pan where the water has evaporated with kitchen paper. Taste the stock, and when it seems to have sufficient body strain it into a bowl and adjust the seasoning. Allow it to cool and leave in the refrigerator overnight – you will then be able to lift off the lid of fat. Freeze in ½-pint cream cartons.

[B/C]   *Beef Consommé*

beef bones   1–2 cloves garlic
shin of beef   bayleaf, thyme, marjoram,
pig's trotter or calf's foot   parsley
  (optional)   2 egg whites
2–3 onions   salt and pepper
2–3 carrots

white wine ⎫
lemon juice ⎬ optional
sherry ⎭

You can make this by using only bones, as for beef stock, but the consommé will have a better taste and colour if you add some meat to the ingredients. Shin of beef is particularly suitable, as it is slightly gelatinous and will help the stock to set. So will a pig's trotter or a calf's foot.

The method is exactly the same as for making stock, but when you have removed the lid of fat – and for consommé it is particularly important that not a speck of fat should remain – you should, for perfection, clarify the stock. Heat it up again in a clean saucepan, beat two whites of egg to the soft-peak stage and whisk them into the hot stock. Bring it just to the boil, remove the pan from the heat and whisk well; repeat this procedure three or four times. Then pour it through a sieve or colander which has been lined with a cheese cloth or a clean white teatowel, wrung out in hot water. The egg whites should remain in the cloth, with any particles from the stock adhering to them, leaving it transparent and clear.

To serve immediately: a little white wine, some lemon juice and sherry may now be added to improve the flavour. Test for seasoning and serve hot, or chill for 5 to 6 hours for serving en gelée.

To freeze: allow to cool and freeze in waxed or plastic containers.

To serve after freezing: tip the frozen consommé into a saucepan, heat and boil briskly for 1 minute. Serve hot or cold as for immediate eating.

[C] *Pot-au-feu*

This classic French housewife's dish is an excellent way of using some of the large quantity of topside and some of the bones, particularly the marrow bones, which come with your half or quarter of beef. It provides two courses for a good family meal; the stock can be served first as a clear soup, and the meat and vegetables will make up the main course. It should be cooked in as large a quantity as your biggest saucepan can hold. The meat is also excellent cold, and the stock may be used for any number of purposes later. The quantities given here are a minimum, as any smaller piece of beef would probably disintegrate during the long cooking.

2–3 lb. beef bones – shin and marrow bones

3-lb. piece topside

1 onion
1 carrot } for the stock

garlic

a large bouquet garni

a piece of lemon peel

1 lb. onions

1 lb. carrots, fresh, or frozen blanched whole

1 lb. leeks, fresh, or frozen blanched whole

some slices of French bread (optional)

salt and pepper

For this recipe both meat and vegetables may be used straight from the freezer.

Put the frozen bones in a very large saucepan and cover them with cold water. If you are using marrow bones and like to eat the marrow, tie them first in a muslin cloth so that the marrow does not drop out. If you do not care for the marrow, simply put them in the saucepan with the other bones and the marrow will enrich the stock. If you have any chicken carcasses in the freezer, put those in also. Bring the water very slowly to boiling point, and as it continues to simmer skim off the scum which will form on top. When the water seems clear add the frozen piece of topside, skim again, and when no more scum rises add one onion, one carrot, the garlic, the bouquet garni, the lemon peel and the seasoning, and continue to simmer very, very slowly, so that the water is just barely moving, for about 4 hours. At the end of this time take out the meat, set it aside, take out the bones and strain the stock. Allow the stock to cool and remove the fat.

Return the meat to the stock, test for seasoning and add more salt and pepper and another bouquet garni if necessary. Add the onions and the whole carrots, simmer for another 30 minutes and add the whole leeks. When these are cooked the dish is ready to serve.

To serve: start by serving the soup. If you have kept the marrow bones separately you can toast some pieces of French bread, spread the marrow on them and float one piece in each bowl of soup.

Serve the meat, surrounded by the vegetables, for the second course. You can serve it with a little of the stock, or you can make some gravy by thickening some of the stock with a little beurre manié and boiling it for 5 minutes.

Any meat that is left over will taste excellent served cold, with horseradish sauce or mayonnaise, or diced and mixed into a rice salad.

The remainder of the stock may be frozen for use later.

[C]   *Brisket*

3-lb. roll of brisket	2 tbs. olive oil
a bunch of mixed herbs (mar-joram, thyme, parsley, rose-mary)	1–2 onions
	1 carrot
	stock, wine or water
1 clove garlic	salt and pepper

Allow the meat to thaw for 3 to 4 hours, spread it with some of the herbs and tie it into a roll. If the brisket has already been rolled, it should be possible to poke the herbs into the roll, provided it has been allowed to thaw sufficiently. Rub the joint all over with a cut clove of garlic and some salt and pepper, and brown it quickly in the oil in a flameproof casserole. Add an onion or two, a carrot and the rest of the herbs, and enough stock, wine or water to come up about 2 inches in the casserole. Cover and simmer over a very low heat until the meat is cooked – about 1½ to 2 hours, depending on the size of the joint.

Serve hot, with the cooking liquid. The remainder will be excellent cold, sliced thinly.

[B/C]   *Carbonnade de Boeuf Flamande*

2 lb. braising beef (chuck or skirt) or best quality stew-ing beef	1 lb. onions
	½ pt dark ale or stout
2 tbs. flour	bouquet garni
1 tbs. butter or dripping	salt and pepper

If you are using frozen beef it should be allowed to thaw before preparing.

Trim the fat off the meat and cut it into large cubes. Season the flour liberally with salt and pepper and roll each piece of meat in it. Heat the butter or dripping in a heavy pan or flame-proof casserole and cook the sliced onions gently until they are soft but not brown. Remove the onions, raise the heat, and quickly brown the pieces of meat on all sides. Remove the meat, add any of the seasoned flour which may be left over, slowly pour the ale or stout into the casserole, and stir well to dissolve any browned sediment at the bottom of the pan. Return the meat and onions, add the bouquet garni, cover, and cook in a slow oven (300°F., gas 2) or over a very low heat for 2 hours, by which time the meat should be tender and the sauce quite thick. Remove the bouquet garni.

To serve immediately: test for seasoning and serve.

To freeze: allow to cool, skim any fat from the top, and freeze in plastic containers or polythene bags, or see method 4 on p. 17.

To serve after freezing: return the frozen carbonnade to the flameproof casserole and heat through very gently on top of the stove, stirring from time to time. Allow about 1 hour for this quantity.

[B/C] *Boeuf en Daube*

This dish is economical and simple to prepare, and so is suitable for a family meal; but it is also tasty enough to make an excellent dinner-party main course.

3 lb. braising beef (chuck or skirt)	bouquet garni
	2 cloves
3 tbs. olive oil	thin strip of orange peel
1–1½ lb. onions	piece of celery, sliced
2 cloves garlic	1 pt red wine (it doesn't matter how cheap or old)
1 carrot	
3 tomatoes roughly chopped or 1 tbs. concentrated tomato purée	approx. ¼ lb. black olives (optional)
	salt and pepper

If you are using frozen beef it should be allowed to thaw before preparing.

Trim the fat off the meat and cut into bite-sized pieces. Heat the oil in a flameproof casserole and brown the meat. Slice the onions and garlic, cut the carrot into strips, and add them to the casserole. When they begin to brown, put in the rest of the ingredients (except for the olives), and season. The wine should threequarters cover the contents of the casserole; if necessary, make up with stock. Bring to the boil, cover, and transfer to a low oven (250°F., gas 1) for 3 to 4 hours. The liquid does not thicken, but remains of a gravy-like consistency. The olives should be added about ½ hour before the end of the cooking time.

To serve immediately: test for seasoning and serve. Ribbon noodles or boiled potatoes are a good accompaniment.

To freeze: allow to cool, skim any fat from the top, and freeze in plastic containers, or see method 4 on p. 17.

To serve after freezing: return the frozen daube to the flameproof casserole and heat through very gently on top of the stove, stirring from time to time. Allow about 1 hour for this quantity.

[B/C]   *Beef Olives*

This is a useful recipe for stretching a limited amount of meat. The quantities given will feed 8 generously.

2 lb. beef (topside or rumpsteak or, at a pinch, the best quality braising steak)
¼ lb. fresh breadcrumbs
2 onions
½ lb. mushrooms, fresh, or frozen blanched
peel of 1 lemon

large handful of parsley
1 egg
1 tbs. flour
approx. ½ pt stock
1 clove garlic
1 tbs. French mustard
salt and pepper

If you are using frozen meat it is easiest to slice it before it has completely thawed and while it is still quite hard at the centre. Frozen mushrooms can be used straight from the freezer.

Trim the fat off the beef and slice it very thinly. Beat out each piece as thinly as possible with a rolling pin, salt and pepper them and trim into convenient squares or oblongs, large enough to roll up over a spoonful of stuffing.

Mix the breadcrumbs with the chopped onions and chopped mushrooms, add the thinly pared and finely chopped lemon peel and parsley, season, and bind with the egg.

Place one dessertspoonful of the mixture on each piece of meat, roll them up into little sausage shapes and either secure with a toothpick or wind round with a little thread (these may be removed before serving). Meanwhile in a heavy saucepan or flameproof casserole render down the fat trimmed off at the beginning, then take out the pieces and pour off all but 2 tablespoons of the fat. Brown each beef olive rapidly on all sides and remove on to a plate. Sprinkle the flour into the pan and allow it to brown gently, then return the beef olives and cover with the stock, to which you have added the crushed clove of garlic. Simmer gently, uncovered, over a low heat for 45 minutes, by which time the meat should be cooked and the sauce thickened. Add the French mustard to the sauce and test for seasoning – it should be fairly sharp to make a pleasant contrast with the fresh taste of the stuffing. The dish is now ready to serve.

To freeze: allow to cool and freeze in foil or plastic containers, or see method 4 on p. 17.

To serve after freezing: return the frozen beef olives to the flameproof casserole and heat through very gently on top of the stove. Allow about 40 minutes for this. You may need to add a little stock or water.

[B/C] *Steak and Kidney Pudding*

Suet puddings are not improved by two long periods of steaming, before and after freezing. So if this pudding is to be frozen, it is better to cook the meat first before putting it in the uncooked suet crust.

Filling

1¼ lb. chuck steak	1½ tbs. seasoned flour
8 oz. ox kidney	¼ pt stock or water
1 medium onion	

Crust

6 oz. flour	salt and pepper
3 oz. suet	

If you are using meat out of the freezer, allow it to thaw before preparing.

Butter a 2-pint pudding basin, or, if the pudding is to be frozen, use a foil basin or see methods 2, 3 or 4 on p. 17.

Mix the flour and the suet together, and add enough cold water to make a very stiff paste. Roll this out fairly thinly, leaving aside enough for the top, and line the basin.

Trim the fat off the steak, and remove the skin and the core from the kidney. Cut both up, and roll in the seasoned flour. Chop the onion finely and mix with the meat.

To serve immediately: put the meat in the basin, add the stock or water, cover with the rest of the suet crust and put a piece of foil over the top, tucking it securely down over the rim. Steam for 3 hours. Serve with a very good gravy, which is made more interesting by the addition of chopped and sautéed mushrooms.

To freeze: put the meat and the onion in a casserole, add the stock, and cook in a fairly slow oven (300°F., gas 2) for about 2 hours, until the meat is tender. Cool as quickly as possible. When it is quite cold, put the meat into the suet-lined basin, together with the juice in which it was cooked, and cover with the suet crust. If you have used a foil basin, wrap and freeze. Otherwise, see p. 17.

To serve after freezing: thaw at room temperature for about

6 hours or in the refrigerator overnight. Cover the basin securely with a piece of foil and steam for 2 hours. Serve with gravy as described above.

[B/C] ## *Steak and Kidney Pie*

2 lb. steak (rump, skirt or chuck)	½ pt stock
½ lb. kidney	bay leaf, marjoram and 2 cloves
10 oz. flaky pastry	1 tbs. sherry
2 oz. flour	a few drops of Worcestershire or Tabasco sauce
2 oz. butter	salt and pepper
2 onions	

If you are using meat out of the freezer, allow it to thaw before cooking.

Cut the meat into bite-sized pieces and roll them in the well-seasoned flour. Melt the butter in a heavy saucepan, sauté the chopped onions, and brown the meat quickly. Sprinkle in any flour that is left over, allow it to cook for 1 minute, and add the stock, herbs and seasoning. Cover and simmer for about 1 hour or until the meat is tender. Remove the bayleaf, add the sherry and sauce, and test for seasoning.

Turn the meat into well-greased pie-dishes. For freezing it is best to use foil dishes, and the quantities given will make one large (2-pint) dish or three small ones (7½ × 5½ inches).

To serve immediately: cover the meat with the pastry, make one or two incisions in the top and cook in a hot oven (425 °F., gas 7) for ½ hour or until the pastry is golden brown.

To freeze: the pie may be frozen with the pastry cooked or uncooked. If you are freezing it uncooked, allow the meat to cool before covering it with pastry. Wrap the pie in foil and freeze. If you are freezing it cooked, cook as for immediate eating, allow to cool, wrap and freeze.

To serve after freezing: place the frozen pie in a hot oven

(425°F., gas 7). If it was frozen uncooked, make one or two incisions in the pastry. After ½ hour turn the oven down to 350°F., gas 4, and cook for a further 20 minutes if the pastry was frozen cooked, or 40 minutes if it was frozen uncooked. Cover with a piece of foil or greaseproof paper towards the end of the cooking time, if the pastry is getting too brown.

PARSNIPS

One has to be a real addict to want to freeze parsnips, but for those who are, or who have a glut of them in the garden, here are two basic methods. Use only young, tender parsnips.

[A] *To freeze blanched:* peel the parsnips and cut them into quarters. Blanch for 2 minutes. Drain, cool and freeze in polythene bags.

To freeze cooked: boil the parsnips in salted water for 10 minutes or so, until they are just tender. Drain them well and cook them in a covered saucepan with plenty of butter for another 10 minutes. Allow to cool and freeze in polythene bags.

[C] *To serve after freezing blanched:*

1. Cook the frozen parsnips in salted water until they are just tender. Drain well, add plenty of butter, cover the saucepan and leave over a gentle heat until they are quite soft. Serve with plenty of freshly ground pepper.

2. Place the frozen parsnips round the joint and roast, just as you would roast potatoes.

To serve after freezing cooked: tip the frozen parsnips into a saucepan and heat through gently. Add a little more butter if necessary and serve with freshly ground pepper.

APPLES

Coping with a glut of apples can seem a nightmare at the time, but it is wonderful to have a supply of them in the freezer. They are best frozen cooked, in almost any apple dessert or as sweetened purée, and seem to preserve their taste indefinitely. Purée is a good way of using up summer apples, or any of the main crop which are not sound enough to store. Apples can also be frozen sliced and blanched, but although we give the method below we find that they become rather tasteless and flabby if they are treated in this way.

[A] *To freeze puréed:* 1. Peel, core and slice the apples and put them in a saucepan with just enough water to keep them from burning: 2 or 3 tablespoons should be enough. Cover, and cook steadily until they are soft and frothy. Stir in sugar in the proportion of about 3 oz. sugar to 1 lb. apples (weighed before peeling and coring). It is not possible to be exact about the quantity of sugar, for the tartness of apples varies so much. Cool the purée and freeze in waxed cartons or polythene bags.

2. This method saves time if you have a lot of small apples. It makes a tarter purée, more suitable for apple sauce. Quarter and core the apples and take out any bad pieces, but do not peel them. Cook them with a little water until they are soft, and pass them through a nylon sieve. Sweeten to taste, cool, and freeze in waxed cartons or polythene bags.

To freeze blanched: peel, core and slice the apples. Unless you can blanch them immediately, put them into a salt solution to prevent discoloration – 1 tablespoon of salt to 1 quart of water. Do not leave them in this solution for longer than 10 minutes, and rinse them well in cold water afterwards. Blanch for 1 minute. Drain, cool and freeze in polythene bags.

To freeze baked: apples are very good frozen baked, so if you like them cooked in this way bake a few extra whenever it is convenient, leave them to get cold, and store them in the freezer for heating up later on.

Chicken with Apples

[B/C]

4-lb. chicken, jointed
1¾ lb. cooking apples
2 tbs. olive oil
2 oz. butter
1 tbs. flour

¾ pt cider
bouquet garni
salt and pepper

½ pt chicken stock (after freezing only)

Frozen chicken must be allowed to thaw before cooking.

Melt the oil and 1 oz. of the butter in a flameproof casserole or a heavy saucepan and brown the chicken pieces all over. Lift them out of the pan and put in about one third of the apples, peeled, cored and cut into thin slices. Allow them to cook gently for 5 minutes, stirring from time to time, add the flour and let it brown, and pour in ½ pint of the cider. Season and bring slowly to the boil. Return the chicken pieces and add the bouquet garni. Cover, and cook in a medium oven (375°F., gas 5) for about 1 hour.

While the chicken is cooking, peel, core and quarter the remaining apples and sauté them in the rest of the butter for about 5 minutes in a flameproof casserole, stirring them from time to time so that they do not stick. Add 2 tablespoons of water, cover, and place in the lower part of the oven. They should cook down to a thick purée.

When the chicken is tender, take it out of the casserole and for immediate eating arrange on a dish and keep warm. Pour the rest of the cider into the casserole, boil rapidly until the liquid has reduced by half, and strain it into the second casserole containing the apples. Test for seasoning.

To serve immediately: serve the chicken with the sauce poured over it or handed round separately.

To freeze: allow the chicken and the sauce to cool, and freeze them separately in foil or plastic containers.

To serve after freezing: return the frozen chicken to a flameproof casserole, pour over the stock, cover, and warm over a very gentle heat for about 45 minutes. The apple sauce should be heated separately but will take only about 20 minutes. Lift the chicken out of the stock and serve as above.

[B]   *Covered Apple Tart*

1 lb. apples   3–4 oz. sugar
10 oz. shortcrust pastry (see   grated rind of 1 lemon
  p. 28)

icing sugar

Line a buttered 8-inch flan-tin with two thirds of the pastry. If the tart is for the freezer, use a foil flan-case or see p. 18. Peel, core and quarter the apples and cut them into thin slices. Fill the flan-case with these, sprinkle on the sugar and the grated lemon rind and cover the flan with the remaining pastry. Seal the edges well.

To serve immediately: bake in a hot oven (425°F., gas 7) for 20 minutes, then lower the temperature to 350°F., gas 4, and continue baking for another $\frac{1}{2}$ hour or until the pastry is golden brown. Turn the tart out and serve hot or cold, liberally dredged with icing sugar.

To freeze: if you have used a foil flan-case wrap and freeze. Otherwise see p. 18.

To serve after freezing: put the frozen tart in a hot oven (425°F., gas 7) for 30 minutes, then turn the oven down to 375°F., gas 5, and bake for a further 40 to 50 minutes. Serve as above.

Note: you can also freeze this tart after it has been cooked, if this is more convenient. In that case, when you take it out of the freezer it will only need 20 minutes in a hot oven, and a further 20 minutes after you have turned the oven down.

[B]   *Apple Flan*

One tart serves 4 to 6 people.

8 oz. apples	2 oz. sugar
6 oz. shortcrust pastry (see p. 28)	1 tbs. apricot jam
	1 tbs. water

Line a buttered 8-inch flan-tin with the pastry. If the flan is for the freezer use a foil flan-tin or see methods 2 or 3 on p. 18. Bake blind in a hot oven (425°F., gas 7) for 10 minutes. Meanwhile peel, quarter and core the apples and cut them into very fine slices. Arrange these overlapping in circles on the pastry, sprinkle on the sugar and bake in a hot oven (425°F., gas 7) for $\frac{1}{2}$ hour. By this time the apples should be cooked and slightly juicy, and they should be a little browned at the edges.

When the tart has cooled make the glaze by boiling the jam and the water together for 1 minute, strain and allow to cool a little, and brush over the flan.

To serve immediately: allow the glaze to set, and serve.

To freeze: if you have used a foil flan-case, wrap and freeze. Otherwise see p. 18.

To serve after freezing: place the frozen tart in a hot oven (425°F., gas 7) for $\frac{1}{2}$ hour. Serve hot or cold.

[B]   *Creamy Apple Flan*

One tart serves 4 to 6 people.

1 lb. apples	3–4 oz. sugar
6 oz. sweetened shortcrust pastry (see p. 28)	$\frac{1}{4}$ pt double cream

Line a buttered 8-inch flan-tin with the pastry. If the flan is for the freezer use a foil flan-tin or see methods 2 or 3 on p. 18. Bake blind for 10 minutes in a hot oven (425°F., gas 7). Peel, core and quarter the apples and cut them into thin slices. Arrange these very closely together, standing upright, in the pastry case. Sprinkle on the sugar, pour on the cream and cook the flan in a moderate oven (375°F., gas 5) for 40 minutes.

To serve immediately: this flan can be served hot or cold, but it is best hot.

To freeze: cool. If you have used a foil flan-case, wrap and freeze. Otherwise see p. 18.

To serve after freezing: place the frozen flan in a hot oven (425°F., gas 7) for ½ hour. Serve hot or cold.

[B] *Apple Cheese-Cake*

2 large cooking apples   4 oz. butter
12 oz. shortcrust pastry (see   2 eggs
  p. 28)   2 lemons
8 oz. caster sugar

Line two buttered 8-inch flan-tins with the pastry. If the cheese-cakes are for the freezer use foil flan-cases or see methods 2 or 3 on p. 18.

Cream the sugar and the butter. Add the beaten eggs, the apples, peeled and coarsely grated, and the rind and juice of the lemons. Put the filling into the flan-cases and bake in a hot oven (400°F., gas 6) for 20 to 25 minutes. Then turn the oven down to 325°F., gas 4, and cook for a further 25 minutes or so (about 50 minutes in all) until the filling has set.

To serve immediately: serve warm or cold.

To freeze: allow to cool. If you have used foil flan-cases wrap and freeze. Otherwise see p. 18.

To serve after freezing: place the frozen tart in a hot oven (400°F., gas 6) for ½ hour. Serve warm or cold.

[B] *Toffee Apple Tart*

One tart serves 4 to 6 people.

1 lb. apples   4 oz. sugar
5 oz. sweetened shortcrust   1 oz. butter
  pastry (see p. 28)   1 tbs. water

Melt the sugar with $\frac{1}{2}$ ounce of the butter and the water in a saucepan until it turns to a golden toffee colour. Pour it quickly into a buttered 8-inch flan-tin, turning the tin so that the whole surface becomes coated with the toffee. If you are freezing the tart you must use a foil flan-case unless you can leave the tart in its tin while it is in the freezer.

Peel and core the apples, cut them into fine slices and arrange them closely on the toffee. Dot them with the remaining butter, and, if they are very sour, sprinkle on a little more sugar. Cover with the pastry, sealing the edges down well. Prick the pastry and bake in a hot oven (425°F., gas 7) for 40 minutes.

To serve immediately: allow to cool for a few minutes, then put a plate on top of the tin and turn the tart out carefully, so that the toffee is on top. Be careful not to spill the juice. Serve hot or cold.

To freeze: allow to cool, wrap and freeze.

To serve after freezing: place the frozen tart in a hot oven (425°F., gas 7) for 20 minutes. Serve as for immediate eating.

[B]   *Apples in their Dressing-Gowns*

A great favourite with children and grown-ups alike.

8 medium cooking apples	**approx. 4 oz. demerara sugar**
1 lb. shortcrust pastry (see	**1 oz. butter**
p. 28)	

icing or caster sugar

Peel the apples and core them, but leave them whole. Roll out the pastry, cut it into 8 equal squares and place one apple on each. Stuff the centre of each apple with as much sugar as it will hold and dot with a small knob of butter. Pick up the four corners of each square of pastry to meet at the top of the apple, pinch them together and pinch together the edges of the pastry, to make a neat parcel of each apple.

To serve immediately: place the apples on a buttered baking tray and bake in a hot oven (425°F., gas 7) for 15 minutes. Turn the oven down to 375°F., gas 5, and bake for a further ½ hour. Serve hot or cold, dredged with a little icing or caster sugar.

To freeze: wrap each apple in foil or moisture-vapour-proof tissue, pack in a polythene bag and freeze.

To serve after freezing: place the frozen apples on a buttered baking tray and bake in a hot oven (425°F., gas 7) for ½ hour. Lower the oven to 375°F., gas 5, and cook for a further ½ hour. Serve as for immediate eating.

Note: you can also freeze the apples after they have been cooked, if this is more convenient. In that case, when you take them out of the freezer they will only need 20 minutes in a hot oven, and a further 20 minutes after you have turned the oven down.

[B] *Apple Strudel*

Though this traditional Austrian dish is not difficult to make, it takes rather a long time, so it is a good idea to make a number of strudels at once. The following quantity will make 4 medium-sized strudels.

3 lb. cooking apples	2 oz. butter
1 lb. flour	6 oz. caster or demerara sugar
½ tsp. salt	squeeze of lemon juice
2 small eggs	a handful of raisins ⎫
4 tbs. olive oil	2 oz. chopped ⎬ optional
approx. ¼ pt warm water	blanched almonds ⎭
4 oz. fresh breadcrumbs	

icing sugar

Sift the flour and salt into a bowl. Whisk the eggs and oil together and pour them into a well in the middle of the flour. Work this gradually into the flour, together with as much warm water as is needed to form a stiff dough which comes away clean from the sides of the bowl. Flour a pastry board and knead the dough on this until it begins to form bubbles. Leave it to rest in a warm place for ½ hour.

Meanwhile fry the breadcrumbs in the butter to a crisp golden colour. Peel and quarter the apples and cut them into paper thin slices.

Divide the dough into four equal parts and make one strudel at a time. Spread a clean teatowel on a flat surface, sprinkle it liberally with flour and on this roll out the first quarter of pastry until it is a about the same shape and size as the teatowel, very thin

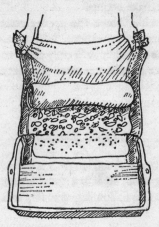

Apple Strudel (rolling)

indeed and transparent. It is important to use the rolling pin from the centre outwards, as otherwise you are likely to end up with thin pastry at the edges, but a thick section in the middle. You can also pull and stretch it by hand, but this is best done with two people. Sprinkle on 1 oz. breadcrumbs and cover the whole surface closely with about a quarter of the apple slices, leaving a 1 inch margin at the edges. Sprinkle on about $1\frac{1}{2}$ oz. sugar, a squeeze of lemon juice, and a few raisins and almonds if you are using them. Lift up one end of the tea-towel and gently allow the strudel to roll itself up as it falls away from the towel. Have a greased baking tin ready at the other end, with the teatowel just overlapping on to it, so that the strudel will finally roll on to the tin. Seal the edges with a little water.

To serve immediately: brush a little melted butter over the top of the strudel and bake in a hot oven (450°F., gas 8) for 15 minutes. Turn the oven down to 375°F., gas 5, for another 40 minutes. Sprinkle liberally with sieved icing sugar before serving hot or cold.

To freeze: put the uncooked strudel into the freezer on the baking tin and leave for about 24 hours. It is important that it should go into the freezer straight away, before the apples begin to ooze their juice. When it is frozen wrap well and replace in the freezer.

To serve after freezing: brush the frozen strudel with a little melted butter and cook in a hot oven (450°F., gas 8) for ½ hour, then turn the oven down to 375°F., gas 5, and cook for another 45 minutes to 1 hour. Serve as for immediate eating.

[C]   *Friar's Omelette*

This quantity is enough for 3 to 4 people.

½ pt apple purée	1 egg and 1 yolk
1 oz. flour	2 oz. butter
1 tsp. sugar	grated rind of 1 lemon
⅛ pt milk	approx. 2 tbs. rum

Make a batter with the flour, the sugar, the milk and 1 egg. Beat it well and leave for at least 1 hour. When you are ready to make the omelette gently warm the apple purée and beat into it the egg yolk, the lemon rind and 1 oz. butter. Taste for sweetness and add more sugar if necessary. Keep the mixture hot. Melt the rest of the butter in a large frying pan (about 10 inches), beat the batter once more, pour it into the pan and cook gently. When the first side is done turn the pancake over, and while the second side is cooking spread the apple mixture over the top. When the pancake is thoroughly cooked fold it over, sprinkle with the rum and sieve over it plenty of caster sugar. Serve very hot.

[C]   *Danish Apple Pudding*

¾ pt apple purée	2 oz. chopped almonds
4 oz. coarse white bread- crumbs	3 oz. butter 2 tbs. sherry
1 oz. sugar	¼ pt double cream

Allow the purée to thaw. Test for sweetness and add more sugar if necessary. Mix the breadcrumbs with 1 oz. sugar and the almonds and fry them gently in the butter. When they are crisp and golden leave them to cool. Arrange a layer of the apple purée in a bowl, cover with a layer of the crumbs and repeat until both the crumbs and the apple have been used up, finishing with a layer of the crumbs. Sprinkle on some sherry and top with whipped cream.

[C]   *Apple Snow*

This is a favourite with children, and with the addition of sherry makes a pleasant pudding for adults too.

¾ pt apple purée	2 eggs
5–6 trifle sponges	approx. 2 tbs. sugar
1 pt milk	4–5 tbs. sherry (optional)
1 heaped tbs. custard powder	

Allow the apple purée to thaw. Test for sweetness and add more sugar is necessary. Meanwhile slice each of the sponges into about six pieces and put them in a dish. Make a custard with the milk, the custard powder and the egg yolks, and sweeten to taste.

If the pudding is for adults add 2 or 3 tbs. of sherry to the custard, and sprinkle the rest over the sponge. Pour the hot custard over the sponge and leave to get cold. An hour or two before eating, beat the egg whites very stiffly and fold them into the apple pulp. Pile on top of the sponge, and chill until needed.

[B] *Swedish Apple Cake*

This can be served as a cake, or with whipped cream as a dessert. If it is not being made for the freezer it should if possible be stored in a tin for 3 or 4 days before eating.

3 large cooking apples	8 oz. self-raising flour
3 oz. margarine	1 tbs. chopped candied orange
6 oz. caster sugar	peel
2 eggs	1 dsp. grated fresh orange peel
2 tbs. milk	2 oz. chopped almonds

Grease a shallow baking tin about 10 inches square, or line it with buttered greaseproof paper. Cream the margarine and the sugar until they are fluffy. Add the beaten eggs and the milk. Sieve in the flour and add the candied peel, the fresh orange peel and the almonds. Peel and core the apples, cut them into very small dice and mix them in well. Put into the tin and bake in a moderate oven (350°F., gas 4) for 40 to 50 minutes. Turn on to a cake rack and allow to cool.

To freeze: as soon as the cake is cool, wrap in foil or moisture-vapour-proof tissue and freeze.

To serve after freezing: thaw at room temperature for 5 to 6 hours before serving.

[B] *Apfelkuchen*

2 lb. cooking apples	2 eggs
½ lb. margarine	¾ lb. self-raising flour
½ lb. butter	2 or 3 drops vanilla essence
approx. ½ lb. sugar	½ tsp. cinammon (optional)

whipped cream

Cream the margarine and butter with ¼ lb. of the sugar. Add the well-beaten eggs, the flour and the vanilla essence.

Line a shallow baking tin with buttered greaseproof paper and spread the mixture in this. It should be about $\frac{1}{2}$ inch thick, and a rectangular tin measuring about 12 × 8 inches, or a round one about 11 inches in diameter, can be used.

Peel and core the apples, quarter them and cut them into very thin slices – they should be about $\frac{1}{8}$ inch thick at the outer edge – and press them, rounded side upwards, into the cake mixture. Every centimetre of it should be covered, and in the end you should have a pattern of half-moons sticking up cheek by jowl. Dredge the rest of the sugar on top (you can if you like mix $\frac{1}{2}$ teaspoon of cinnamon with this), and bake in a moderately hot oven (400°F., gas 6) until the apples are pale brown and juicy, and the cake mixture well cooked. When the cake has cooled a little, turn it on to a cake rack and allow it to become quite cold.

To freeze: Wrap in foil, polythene film or moisture-vapour-proof tissue and freeze. This quantity will give you a big cake, so it is better to cut it in two and freeze the two halves separately.

To serve after freezing: thaw for 5 to 6 hours at room temperature. Cut into slices and serve with whipped cream.

PEARS

Pears do not freeze well raw, but they are very successful frozen cooked.

[A] *To freeze cooked:* peel and halve the pears and take out the core. Drop them at once into slightly salted water to prevent discoloration. Make a syrup with $\frac{1}{2}$ pint water and 4 oz. sugar – this is sufficient for 2 lb. pears. Rinse the pears and poach them gently in the syrup for about 30 minutes or until they are quite soft. Leave to cool in the syrup and freeze in waxed or plastic containers, with a piece of crumpled foil over the top, under the cover, to keep the fruit below the syrup.

[B]   *Pears in Red Wine*

This is the simplest possible dessert, and one of the most refreshing.

2 lb. dessert pears   4 oz. sugar
¼ pt water   ¼ pt red wine

whipped cream for serving

Make a syrup with the water and sugar and boil it for 3 minutes. Peel the pears but leave on their stalks. Put them in the smallest saucepan which will hold them all on the bottom, and pour over the syrup and the wine, which should nearly cover them. Put the lid on the pan and poach gently until the pears are quite soft, which will take anything from 30 minutes to 1 hour, according to how ripe they are. Lift them out of the pan and put them in a bowl. Boil the juice hard, with the lid off, until it has reduced by about half, then pour it over the pears and leave them to get cold, turning them over from time to time so that each side absorbs the syrup. Serve with whipped cream.

To freeze: freeze the pears and juice together in waxed or plastic containers, with a piece of crumpled foil on top, under the cover.

To serve after freezing: thaw at room temperature for 5 to 6 hours. Serve with whipped cream.

QUINCES

Quinces add a very special flavour to apple and pear desserts. They cannot be stored for more than a week or two, but they freeze well blanched, so if you like their taste keep some in the freezer for adding to apple pies, puddings and tarts. They also make the most delicious and surprising ices.

[A] *To freeze blanched:* peel, quarter and core the quinces, being very careful to take out all the hard pieces round the core. Cut into chunks and blanch for 2 minutes. Drain, cool and freeze in polythene bags. Only put a very small quantity into each bag, as you will not want to use many at a time.

[C] *To use after freezing:* the frozen quinces can be used in most apple or pear desserts, but as they will take longer to become soft they should be cooked on their own first. Stew them very gently in a saucepan with a little sugar and a tiny bit of water – just enough to keep them from burning – until they are tender, and add them to the apples or pears when you make the dessert.

[B]   *Quince Water-Ice*

2 lb. quinces   14 oz. sugar

Peel and core the quinces, being careful to take out all the gritty bits which surround the core. Cut into small pieces and put in a large saucepan with just enough water to cover. Cook over a low heat until they are quite soft – this may take 40 minutes or more, and you may need to add a little more water halfway through the cooking. When they are soft pass them through a blender, mouli or sieve. You should have approximately 1 pint of purée.

Boil 1 pint of water with the sugar for 10 minutes, by which time it should be reduced to 1 pint of syrup. Allow this to cool, then stir it into the quince purée, pour into ice-trays or plastic containers, and freeze for 1 to 2 hours, until the mixture has reached a mushy state. Remove from the freezer, beat well, pour into waxed or plastic containers, and replace in the freezer.

To serve after freezing: remove from the freezer 10 to 15 minutes before serving.

[B]   *Quince Ice-Cream*

1 lb. quinces   ¼ pt water
6 oz. sugar   ¼ pt cream

Make a purée of the quinces as in the previous recipe. Boil the sugar and water for 3 minutes, add this syrup to the purée and allow to cool.

Whip the cream lightly and fold it into the quince purée. Pour into ice-trays or plastic containers, and freeze for 1 to 2 hours, until the mixture has reached a mushy state. Remove from the freezer, beat well, pour into waxed or plastic containers and replace in the freezer.

To serve after freezing: remove from the freezer 1 hour before serving and leave in the refrigerator.

November

Scallop and Artichoke Soup

This is a delicious variation on artichoke soup. The delicate flavour of the scallops blends particularly well with the very distinctive but subtle taste of the artichokes.

2 scallops
2 pts artichoke soup (see p. 45)

⅛ pt white wine
⅛ pt water

Poach the scallops in the wine and water mixture for 5 minutes, by which time they will be just barely cooked, and slice them into small pieces (you should get about 8 to 10 pieces from each scallop, according to their size). Heat the artichoke soup and add the scallops and the liquid in which they have been cooked. Do not allow the soup to boil again once the scallops have been added. Test for seasoning and serve.

To freeze: allow to cool, and freeze in waxed or plastic containers.

To serve after freezing: tip the frozen soup into a saucepan and heat through very gently. Do not allow it to boil as the scallops will become tough.

[B] *Scallops au Gratin*

6–8 scallops (one per person)
approx. ½ pt white wine ⎱ to make 1 pt liquid
approx. ½ pt water ⎰
1 onion
slice of lemon peel
bouquet garni
½ lb. button mushrooms

squeeze of lemon juice
1 oz. butter
1 oz. flour
a dash of sherry (optional)
approx. ¼ pt single cream
1 tbs. parsley
1 shallot (or ¼ onion)
2 oz. fresh white breadcrumbs

Detach the scallops from the shells and wash both in cold water. Make a court-bouillon by boiling together the wine, the water, the roughly chopped onion, the slice of lemon peel and the bouquet garni until the liquid has reduced by about half. Add the scallops and poach them for 5 to 10 minutes or until they are cooked. Drain them and strain the cooking liquid. Meanwhile simmer the mushrooms briefly in a little water with a squeeze of lemon juice in it. Leave them whole if they are very small, otherwise slice them. Make a beurre manié with the butter and flour, add it to the cooking liquid and simmer gently, stirring, until the sauce is smooth and thick. Season and add a dash of sherry. Pour in the cream gradually, but if the sauce seems to be becoming too thin do not use the whole ¼ pint. Slice the scallops and arrange them evenly on the shells. Add the mushrooms and pour over the sauce. Sprinkle with a mixture of the finely chopped parsley, shallot and breadcrumbs.

To serve immediately: dot with a little butter and place under a hot grill until the top is lightly browned.

To freeze: put the scallops on a baking tray and freeze them for 24 hours. Then wrap each shell in foil, polythene or moisture-vapour-proof tissue and pack together in a polythene bag.

To serve after freezing: if possible, allow to thaw for an hour or two. Dot with butter and place under a medium grill until the scallops are heated through. This will take between 15 and 20 minutes. You can also reheat straight from the freezer, but this will take longer, and you must be careful to see that the top doesn't become charred.

[B]   *Fruits de Mer in Cream Sauce*

This is a particularly useful recipe if you have some cooked white fish. The mixture may be used as a filling for vol-au-vents or as a stuffing for crêpes de fruits de mer. The proportions of fish given are approximate, and any combination of white fish and shell fish may be used.

4 scallops	6 peppercorns
½ lb. any cooked white fish	a little fennel or thyme
¼ pt prawns (preferably with the shells)	1 oz. flour
	½ oz. butter
½ pt white wine	small glass of sherry or a dash
½ pt water	of Pernod
1 onion	¼ pt cream
a slice of lemon peel	salt and pepper

Make a court-bouillon by boiling the white wine and the water, together with the shells of the prawns and the roughly chopped onion, the lemon peel, the peppercorns and the fennel or thyme. When the liquid has reduced by half, strain it, and gently poach the scallops in it for 10 minutes. Lift them out, slice them fairly thinly and mix them with the flaked white fish and the prawns.

Make a beurre manié by working the flour into the butter and drop this into the cooking liquid. Heat gently and stir until the beurre manié has dissolved, and continue to simmer until the sauce has thickened. Season, add the sherry or the Pernod and the cream and fold the fish mixture into the sauce.

To serve immediately: either fill the mixture into hot vol-au-vent cases and serve; or, for crêpes de fruits de mer, make some pancakes with a batter using half milk and half beer, and adding a good pinch of curry powder. Roll each pancake round a spoonful of the hot mixture and serve.

To freeze: allow to cool and freeze in waxed or plastic containers.

To serve after freezing: tip the frozen mass into a saucepan and heat through very gently. You may need to add an extra spoonful of cream at this stage. Serve as above.

BRUSSELS SPROUTS

These are extremely satisfactory to freeze, and it is a joy to have several bags in the freezer in the late winter when there are no green vegetables in the garden and they are expensive and scarce in the shops. Red brussels sprouts are an interesting variation of the ordinary green kind. The seeds are not easy to get, but Suttons generally stock them or Thomson & Morgan, Ipswich. They are smaller than the green sprouts, and have a very special, nutty flavour. Their great virtue for many gardeners is that pigeons don't eat them.

[A] *To freeze blanched:* trim off any coarse or discoloured leaves and cross-cut the stalks. Wash and blanch for 2 to 3 minutes, depending on the size of the sprouts. Drain, cool and freeze in polythene bags.

[C] *To serve after freezing:* tip the frozen sprouts into boiling salted water – about 1 inch in the saucepan should be enough – and cook fairly briskly until they are soft, which will take 10 to 15 minutes. Break up the mass of sprouts gently with a fork from time to time. Serve with a generous knob of butter. They are also excellent mixed with braised chestnuts (see p. 279).

CELERY

Celery cannot be frozen for subsequent use in salads, but blanched celery is excellent for using as a vegetable.

The outer sticks can be frozen without blanching for flavouring soups. Put several together in a polythene bag, and use them as you need them.

[A] *To freeze blanched:* leave the hearts whole or quarter them or cut the celery sticks into 2 to 3 inch pieces. Wash thoroughly and blanch for 4 to 5 minutes for the hearts, or 3 minutes if the celery has been cut into pieces. Drain, cool and freeze in polythene bags.

[C] *To serve after freezing:* put the frozen celery in boiling salted water and separate gently as it warms through. It should be soft in about 15 minutes from the time it comes to the boil. Serve with a béchamel sauce made with milk and a little of the celery liquid. Or put the celery in a shallow heatproof dish, completely cover with dry breadcrumbs, small pieces of butter and grated cheese, and put under the grill for a few minutes until a golden crust has formed on top.

[B] ## *Celery Soup*

1 lb. celery	½ oz. cornflour
1 large onion	¼ pt milk
1 oz. butter	2 tbs. cream or top of the milk
1¼ pts veal or chicken stock	1 egg yolk (optional)
bouquet garni	salt and pepper

chopped parsley (optional)

Cut the celery into 1-inch pieces. You can use the outside stalks and some of the green leaves as well. Chop the onion roughly. Sauté the celery and the onion in the butter for a few minutes, but do not let them brown. Add the stock, the bouquet garni and the seasoning, cover the pan and simmer for about 20 minutes, until the vegetables are soft. Put through a blender or mouli and then through a nylon sieve. Return to the pan. Mix the cornflour with the milk and add to the soup. Bring to the boil and simmer for a few minutes, stirring all the time. Add the cream or top of the milk. Beat it first with the yolk if you are using one, and in this case do not allow the soup to boil again.

To serve immediately: test for seasoning, and serve with a little finely chopped parsley or celery leaves sprinkled over each helping.

To freeze: allow to cool and freeze in waxed or plastic containers.

To serve after freezing: tip the frozen soup into a saucepan and warm gently. If you have used an egg yolk be careful that the soup does not boil. Serve as for immediate eating.

RED CABBAGE

Red cabbage freezes excellently cooked and tends, if anything, to improve with reheating. It should be frozen in expendable containers, since it is difficult to free them afterwards from the smell of the cabbage.

[B]

2½–3 lb. red cabbage
1 large onion
1 clove garlic
2 oz. chicken fat or 2 tbs. olive oil
2 large cooking apples
2 cloves (optional)
approx. ¼ pt red wine or a mixture of wine vinegar and water
1–2 tbs. brown sugar
salt and pepper

Slice the onion and garlic and cook them very slowly in the fat or olive oil in a large saucepan for about 10 minutes. Add the cabbage, cut into ¼-inch slices, and when this has cooked down in the saucepan – after about 15 minutes – add the peeled, cored and sliced apples, the cloves, the wine and a tablespoon or so of sugar. Season and cook gently for about 3 hours. Test for seasoning, and if necessary add more salt or sugar. The dish is now ready to serve. To freeze, see opposite page.

[B]   RED CABBAGE WITH ORANGE

About a quarter of an hour before the end of the cooking time, add the juice and the finely grated peel of an orange.

[B]   RED CABBAGE WITH CHESTNUTS

Prepare 1 lb. chestnuts (see p. 278) and add them to the cabbage for the last 2½ hours of the cooking. If you are using dried chestnuts, they should first be boiled for 30 minutes or so in plenty of water before they are added to the cabbage.

[B]   BRAISED RED CABBAGE

To the basic ingredients for red cabbage add:

¼ pt red wine   ½ pt stock

Use a large flameproof casserole and follow the basic recipe
until all the ingredients have been added, including the addi-
tional wine and the stock. Give the cabbage a good stir, cover
the casserole, and transfer to a slow oven (325°F., gas 3) for
about 3 hours. Test for seasoning, and if there seems to be too
much cooking liquid strain off a little before serving the cabbage. But if the cabbage is to be frozen leave all the liquid,
especially if you are going to use it for pork with red cabbage.

To freeze (*for all these recipes*): allow to cool, and freeze in
waxed cartons.

To re-heat: turn the frozen cabbage into a heavy saucepan and
cook gently until it is hot all through (which will take ½ hour at
least, unless the quantity is small). It may have become a little
dry during the freezing; if so, add a small quantity of stock.

[C]   *Pork with Red Cabbage*

3-lb. piece of boned pork for   2 generous tsp. chopped fresh
  roasting   herbs – a mixture of any you
2½–3 lb. braised red cabbage   have available – or 1 tsp.
  (see above)   dried herbs
1 tsp. salt   1 clove garlic
¼ tsp. pepper   ½ lb. chestnuts (optional)

Start by marinading the pork. This is not essential, but it is
quick and easy to do and gives the meat a spicy taste.

Mix together the salt, pepper, herbs and crushed garlic and
spread them all over the pork. Leave it in a covered bowl for
several hours, turning it over from time to time so that the
herbs blend into the meat juice.

Tip the frozen red cabbage into a flameproof casserole and

warm through gently, stirring from time to time, until it is hot. Add the chestnuts if you are using them (see p. 278 for method of preparing).

Wipe a little of the marinade off the pork and brown it briskly on all sides in some good fat. Place it on the cabbage, cover the casserole and put in a slow oven (325°F., gas 3) for about 2¼ hours, by which time the meat should be well cooked. Lift the pork out, put it on a large warmed dish and arrange the cabbage round it, together with the cooking liquid. You may not need all the liquid, but be generous with it as there is no gravy.

ALMONDS

[B] *Charlotte Malakoff*

This is a rather extravagant pudding, but luckily it is so rich that no one can eat very much of it. The quantities given here are enough to fill two small (1 pint) moulds, each of which will serve 6 people amply. It is particularly delicious served with a rather tart fruit, such as raspberry or redcurrant purée.

8 oz. ground almonds	8 oz. unsalted butter
2 tbs. Grand Marnier	8 oz. caster sugar
1 tbs. water	½ pt double cream
½ lb. sponge fingers (or more)	

Mix 1 tablespoon of the Grand Marnier with the water in a plate and dip the smooth sides of the sponge fingers briefly in the liquid. Line the charlotte moulds or pudding basins with the biscuits, standing them round the sides, sugar side outwards, and trim them to size.

Cream the butter and sugar until they are white and fluffy and add the rest of the Grand Marnier and the ground almonds. Whip the cream lightly and fold it in also. Pour this mixture into the lined moulds and tap them sharply on the table three times to get rid of any air bubbles.

To serve immediately: chill for 3 to 4 hours, turn out mould and serve.

To freeze: freeze for 24 hours, turn out of the mould, wrap and replace in the freezer.

To serve after freezing: allow to thaw at room temperature for 6 hours. Serve as above.

You can also make the following variations of this pudding.

[B/C]   RASPBERRY CHARLOTTE MALAKOFF

Add ½ lb. raspberries to the list of ingredients. Pour one-third of the Malakoff mixture into the prepared mould, cover with a layer of raspberries, repeat the process and finish with the Malakoff mixture.

You can use fresh or frozen raspberries for this. If you are using frozen ones, use those which were frozen without sugar, and do not allow them to thaw if you are freezing the Malakoff.

[B]   WALNUT CHARLOTTE MALAKOFF

Make exactly as for Charlotte Malakoff, substituting finely ground walnuts for the ground almonds. This is only for those with a passion for walnuts, as the taste is very strong.

[B]   CHOCOLATE CHARLOTTE MALAKOFF

Add 4 oz. plain chocolate and 2 tablespoons of strong coffee to the basic ingredients. You can also substitute Tia Maria for the Grand Marnier. Dip the sponge fingers in a mixture of the liqueur and 1 tablespoon of coffee. Melt the chocolate with the other tablespoon of coffee over a gentle heat or in a double saucepan, and add it to the well-beaten butter and sugar mixture.

[B] *Frozen Almond Cream*

This is not exactly an ice-cream but more what the Italians call a semi-freddo, which never becomes quite hard. Like the previous recipe it is very rich, and the following quantities are enough for 8 to 10 portions. You could make it in conjunction with the praline ice-cream to use up the egg whites.

4 oz. blanched almonds	4 tbs. water
4 egg whites	4 tbs. Marsala
4 oz. sugar	½ pt double cream

Roast the almonds in a hot oven or under a grill until they are dark brown but not burnt. Leave them to cool and then crush them to a fine powder with a rolling pin or in a blender.

Whip the whites of egg until they are stiff. Melt the sugar with the water, and when it turns golden brown pour it in a thin thread into the egg whites, continuing to whisk until all has been amalgamated. Stir in the powdered almonds, keeping aside a little for decoration if you like. Add the marsala and finally fold in the whipped cream.

This cream is best served in individual portions. You can pour the mixture into small cocotte dishes, freeze them for 24 hours and turn them out of the dishes by dipping them very briefly in hot water. Wrap them in foil and replace in the freezer. Alternatively, pour them into yogurt or small mousse or cream pots, and freeze them in those. If you are using cocotte dishes you can sprinkle some reserved crushed almonds on the top for decoration; if you are using yogurt pots, sprinkle some almonds in the bottom before pouring in the cream.

To serve: these creams should be eaten straight from the freezer. If you have used cocotte dishes they can be returned to these for serving; if you have used yogurt pots they can be turned out on to plates.

[B] *Praline Ice-Cream*

This quantity will serve 8 to 10 generously.

Praline

6 oz. blanched almonds	**2 tbs. water**
3 oz. sugar	

Ice-cream

4 egg yolks	**½ pt single cream**
5 oz. sugar	**½ pt double cream**

To make the praline : put the sugar and water in a saucepan and boil them gently together until they turn golden brown. Remove from the heat, add the almonds and stir them with a wooden spoon so that they become evenly coated with the toffee. Pour the mixture on to a wooden board or baking tray and leave to cool.

To make the ice-cream : lightly beat the egg yolks with the sugar, heat the single cream and add it, stirring well. Return the custard to the pan and stir over a gentle heat, or in the top of a double boiler, until it thickens. Leave to cool.

Meanwhile crush the praline mixture to a powder with a rolling pin or in a blender. Stir this into the cooled custard, whip the double cream lightly and fold it in also. Freeze in waxed or plastic containers.

To serve : remove from the freezer 15 minutes before serving.

CHESTNUTS

Chestnuts are not suitable for long-term freezing (except as part of cooked dishes), as they tend to acquire a slightly musty flavour. However, they are quite all right for three or four weeks, so if you like chestnut stuffing for turkey you can make it before the Christmas rush starts. (See p. 299.)

Fresh chestnuts are at their best at this time of year, but their preparation involves a lot of time and trouble. A useful alternative are the dried chestnuts which can be bought at health-food stores and at many large groceries.

To prepare fresh chestnuts: make a cross in the shells and cook them in plenty of boiling water for about 10 minutes. Take them out three or so at a time and peel off the shell and the brown skin.

To prepare dried chestnuts: soak in a large basin of cold water for 24 hours and drain. Dried chestnuts generally have shreds of the brown inner skin sticking to them which must be removed before they are cooked. They need about twice the amount of cooking time that you would give fresh chestnuts.

[B]   *Chestnut Soup*

1 lb. chestnuts	1 small potato
1 oz. butter	2 pts stock – pheasant or beef
1 onion	salt and pepper
1 carrot	

parsley
cream
sherry (optional)

Prepare the chestnuts (see above). Melt the butter in a large saucepan, sauté the diced onion, carrot and potato for 2 to 3 minutes, add the chestnuts and the stock, and season. Simmer all together for about ½ hour, or until the chestnuts are tender. Pass through a blender, mouli or sieve.

To serve immediately: reheat the soup, test for seasoning, and serve with a good sprinkling of parsley and a swirl of cream in each bowl. A dash of sherry adds a pleasant kick, but be careful not to put in too much as it can easily dominate the delicate chestnut taste.

To freeze: allow to cool and freeze in waxed or plastic containers.

To serve after freezing: tip the frozen soup into a saucepan and heat gently. Serve as above.

[B] *Braised Chestnuts*

These are particularly good served as a garnish with venison or game.

1 lb. chestnuts	1 oz. butter
½ pt stock	salt and pepper

Prepare the chestnuts (see p. 278). Put them in a heavy saucepan with the rest of the ingredients and simmer, covered, for 40 to 50 minutes, until the chestnuts are tender but have not disintegrated, and the liquid has all been absorbed. Leave the lid off the saucepan for the last 15 minutes if necessary. Test for seasoning and serve hot.

To freeze: cool and freeze in waxed or plastic containers.

To serve after freezing: tip the frozen chestnuts into a saucepan and heat through gently. You may need to add a knob of butter or a tablespoon of stock or water.

HAZELNUTS

[B] *Nut Bread*

The following quantities will make one 3-lb. loaf or an equivalent number of smaller ones.

2 oz. yeast	8 oz. butter
3 oz. sugar	3 tbs. milk
3 tbs. warm water	pinch of salt
1 lb. plain flour	

Filling

8 oz. shelled hazelnuts	2 eggs
8 oz. sugar	2 tbs. water
6 plain or chocolate digestive biscuits	melted butter
	icing sugar

279

Mix the yeast, a teaspoon of the sugar and the warm water to a smooth paste and leave them to rise in a warm place for 10 to 15 minutes. Sift the flour and the salt into a large bowl, sprinkle on the remaining sugar, make a well in the centre and pour in the yeast ferment. Soften the butter over a very low heat, warm

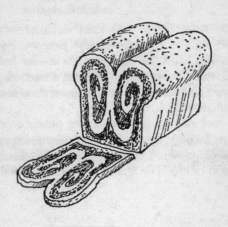

the milk, and make a dough by gradually working all the ingredients together. When it comes away clean from the side of the bowl sprinkle a little flour over the ball of dough, cover the bowl with a clean cloth, and set it in a warm place again to rise for at least 1 hour.

Meanwhile make the filling. Roast the hazelnuts for 20 minutes in a low oven (300°F., gas 2), rub off the skins and crush them with a rolling pin. Mix them with the sugar and the crushed biscuits and add the eggs and water to make a soft paste.

When the dough has risen divide it into equal parts if you wish to make more than one loaf. Roll it out into an oblong just over ⅛ inch thick, as wide as your bread tin is long, and as long as possible. Spread the corresponding proportion of the filling over this, getting as near to the edges as possible, and then roll it up into a kind of Swiss roll. Or roll from both ends towards the middle until they meet in the centre, so that when you cut the loaf you have an attractive double swirl effect.

Place the loaves in the buttered bread tins, leave them to rise once more in a warm place for ½ hour and then bake them in a low oven (300°F., gas 2) for 45 minutes to 1 hour, depending on the size of the loaves. When they come out of the oven leave them to stand for 10 minutes, take them out of their tins and put them on a cake rack. Brush with melted butter and dust liberally with icing sugar.

To freeze: as soon as the loaves are cold freeze wrapped in foil, polythene film or moisture-vapour-proof tissue.

To serve after freezing: allow to thaw for 4 to 5 hours.

[B]   *Chocolate Hazelnut Gâteau*

This gâteau is very rich and the quantities given below will be enough to provide a dessert for 8, especially if you cover the cake with whipped cream.

4 oz. shelled hazelnuts	4 oz. plain chocolate
4 oz. butter	1 tbs. strong coffee
4 oz. caster sugar	1 tbs. rum
4 eggs	

¼ pt double cream (optional)

Grind the hazelnuts. Beat the butter and sugar until they are light and fluffy, add the egg yolks one by one and then the hazelnuts. Melt the chocolate over a low heat with the coffee and beat this into the mixture. Add the rum, and finally fold in the stiffly beaten whites of egg.

Pour into a buttered 8-inch sponge or flan-tin and bake in a slow oven (250°F., gas 1) for 1½ hours, or until a skewer inserted into the cake comes out clean.

Allow to cool on a cake rack. Serve with whipped cream.

To freeze: wrap in foil or moisture-vapour-proof tissue.

To serve after freezing: allow to thaw at room temperature for 4 to 5 hours.

[B] *Hazelnut Ice-Cream*

4 oz. shelled hazelnuts   4 oz. sugar
½ pt single cream   2 tbs. marsala (optional)
4 egg yolks   ½ pt double cream

Grind the hazelnuts or chop them very finely and roast them for 10 minutes in a hot oven. Put them in a saucepan with the single cream and bring very slowly to simmering point. Lightly beat the egg yolks with the sugar and add the cream, stirring well. Return the custard to the pan and stir over a gentle heat or in the top of a double boiler until it thickens. Allow to cool. Add the marsala and fold in the lightly whipped double cream. Freeze in waxed or plastic containers.

To serve: take out of the freezer 15 minutes before serving.

WALNUTS

[B] *Walnut Soup*

8 oz. walnuts   salt and pepper
1 large clove garlic
2 pts stock, preferably chicken
   or veal

a little cream

Blend the walnuts together with the clove of garlic and a little stock. When they have been reduced to a thick cream add the rest of the stock gradually, pour into a saucepan and heat gently. Season to taste.

To serve immediately: Pour into bowls with a little swirl of cream for each serving.

To freeze: cool and freeze in waxed or plastic containers.

To serve after freezing: tip the frozen soup into a saucepan, reheat very gently and serve as above.

[B] *Walnut-Toffee Tart*

8 oz. walnuts
14 oz. sweetened shortcrust pastry (see p. 28)
8 oz. sugar
2 tbs. water
6 oz. (one small tin) evaporated milk or cream

2 oz. butter
3 tbs. double cream
2 egg whites
4 oz. icing sugar

Line one 10-inch or two 7-inch buttered flan-tins with about two thirds of the pastry rolled out thinly, keeping aside enough to make a lid. Put the sugar in a heavy saucepan with two tablespoons of water and boil it, stirring continuously, until it is pale gold. Remove from the heat and quickly stir in the milk, butter and cream. Return to the heat and cook, stirring, until it turns a rich golden brown. Stir in the roughly chopped walnuts and pour on to a wooden board or baking tin to cool. Spread this soft toffee mixture into the pastry-lined flan-cases, cover with the rest of the pastry, prick the top a few times with a fork and bake at 325°F., gas 3, for about 30 minutes, until the pastry is cooked but not brown. Turn out of the tins and leave to cool upside down on a wire rack.

When the tarts are cold whip the egg whites with the icing sugar in a basin placed over a pan of boiling water, or in the top of a double boiler, until the icing thickens and has doubled in bulk. Pour this icing over the inverted tarts and leave to set.

To freeze: when the icing is quite dry, freeze wrapped in foil or polythene.

To serve after freezing: allow to thaw for 4 to 5 hours.

December

Hare is one of the cheapest varieties of meat, and it loses none of its characteristic flavour in freezing. With two hares you can make any three of the following recipes. If it is more convenient to freeze the hare raw, either joint it or leave it whole, but be sure to wrap it very well.

[B]   *Hare Soup*

This soup can be made from the bones and all the left-overs of hare – if you have roasted a saddle, for instance, or cooked hare fillets with mushrooms, and have not used the rest of the carcass. These quantities will serve 8 to 10 people.

left-overs and bones of hare	bouquet garni
2 oz. butter	approx. 4 pts stock, or stock
1 onion	and water
1 carrot	12 peppercorns
1 turnip	1 small glass port
1 celery stalk	salt
1 tbs. cornflour	

Melt the butter in a large pan, and quickly fry all the bones and pieces of hare and the roughly chopped vegetables. Stir in the cornflour, add the bouquet garni, the stock, the peppercorns and some salt, put the lid on the pan and simmer gently for about 3 hours. Remove the meat from the bones and put it through a blender or a mouli, with the vegetables. Return to the pan, add the port, test for seasoning, reheat and serve.

To freeze: allow to cool and freeze in waxed or plastic containers.

To serve after freezing: tip the frozen soup into a saucepan and heat slowly.

[B/C] *Roast Saddle of Hare*

1 saddle of hare
4 oz. sliced streaky bacon
2 oz. lard or beef dripping
½ pt red wine or preferably the
  reduced cooking liquid from
  the hare pâté (see p. 292)

1 tbs. port or madeira
1 tbs. redcurrant jelly
salt and pepper

Frozen hare must be allowed to thaw before roasting.

Wrap the saddle of hare in the bacon and place it in a roasting tin with the lard or beef dripping. Roast it in a hot oven (425°F., gas 7) for ½ hour, then allow it to cool a little. Take all the meat off the bones, remove the skin, and carve the meat into thick slices.

Skim off any excess fat from the roasting pan and add the red wine or the reduced cooking liquid, together with the port or madeira and the redcurrant jelly. Season if necessary. Return the meat to the tin and continue to cook in a moderate oven (350°F., gas 4) for a further 20 minutes or until the meat is completely cooked. The dish is now ready to serve.

To freeze: allow to cool and freeze in foil or plastic containers.

To serve after freezing: tip the frozen meat into a flameproof casserole and warm through gently for about ½ hour or until the meat is hot right through.

[B/C] *Jugged Hare*

When making this recipe, you may like to keep the saddle for roasting (see above). Preserve the blood carefully – ask your butcher to keep it for you if he is jointing the hare.

1 hare, jointed
2 oz. butter
4 oz. streaky bacon
1 lb. small onions or 4 medium
  onions
2 oz. flour
1 pt red wine
bouquet garni

2 cloves
1 lb. button mushrooms (optional), fresh, or frozen raw
  or blanched
1 tbs. redcurrant jelly
1 tbs. port or madeira
salt and pepper

Frozen hare must be allowed to thaw before cooking, but mushrooms may be used straight from the freezer.

Melt the butter in a heavy saucepan or a flameproof casserole and brown the joints of hare. Remove them from the pan and fry the diced bacon and the onions (roughly chopped into quarters if they are large) until they are golden brown. Remove them from the pan. Stir in the flour and when it is slightly browned slowly pour on the wine, stirring to prevent lumps. Add the salt, pepper, bouquet garni and cloves and return the meat, bacon and onions to the pan. Cover and simmer slowly for 2 hours or place in a low oven (300°F., gas 2). Add the whole mushrooms and continue to cook for a further 20 minutes or until the meat is tender.

Take out the meat, bring the sauce to a rapid boil for 5 minutes to reduce it and add the redcurrant jelly, the port or madeira, and lastly the blood, adding it very slowly and taking care not to allow it to come to the boil as it would curdle.

To serve immediately: replace the meat in the casserole, test for seasoning and serve.

To freeze: allow to cool and strip the meat off the bones as far as possible, since they are quite large and take up a lot of freezer space. Freeze in foil or plastic containers, or see method 4 on p. 17.

To serve after freezing: tip the frozen hare into a heavy pan or flameproof casserole and warm through gently for about 40 minutes or until the meat is hot. Test for seasoning and serve.

[B/C]   *Hare Casserole with Forcemeat Balls*

The marinading and the slow cooking of the hare makes this the richest and most aromatic of all the hare dishes, while the herbs in the forcemeat balls add a very pleasant freshness.

1 hare
6 cloves garlic
6 bay leaves
peel of 1 lemon
¼ pt olive oil
1 bottle red wine – this may be as cheap and as rough as you like

3 oz. flour
10 cloves or 1 tsp. powdered cloves
2 rashers streaky bacon *or* 1 oz. butter and 1 tbs. olive oil
salt and pepper

Frozen hare must be allowed to thaw before preparing.

Cut the meat of the hare off the bones and put it into a large bowl. Add the roughly chopped garlic, the bay leaves, the thinly pared rind of lemon, the olive oil and as much of the wine as you have room for in the bowl, and leave all to marinade overnight.

The next day drain the pieces of meat and roll them in the flour, which has been liberally seasoned with salt, freshly ground black pepper and the crushed or powdered cloves. Melt the chopped rashers of bacon or the oil and butter in a flame-proof casserole, quickly brown in it each piece of meat, add any of the seasoned flour that remains, stir well and allow to cook for a few minutes. Pour on the strained marinading liquid and any remaining wine, raise the heat and bring the liquid to boiling point. Put the lid on the casserole, place it in a slow oven (300°F., gas 2) and leave it to cook for 5 to 6 hours, by which time the meat and sauce will have reduced to a rich stew. Test for seasoning.

To serve immediately: serve with forcemeat balls (see below), with baked potatoes and if possible with quince, medlar or crab-apple jelly.

To freeze: cool and freeze in foil or plastic containers, or see method 4 on p. 17.

To serve after freezing: tip the frozen hare into a heavy pan or flameproof casserole and warm gently, stirring from time to time (allow about 40 minutes for this). Serve as above.

[B]   FORCEMEAT BALLS

4 oz. fresh breadcrumbs	1 egg
1 tsp. chopped parsley	2 tbs. milk
1 tsp. chopped marjoram	1–2 oz. butter
½ tsp. thyme	1 tbs. oil
finely grated rind of 1 lemon	salt and pepper

1 oz. butter
1 tbs. oil

Mix the breadcrumbs with the herbs, the seasoning and the lemon peel. Add the egg lightly beaten with the milk, and the just melted butter. Mix all well together and roll little balls of the mixture, about the size of a walnut.

For immediate eating: fry quickly in the butter and oil and drop into the hare casserole just before serving.

To freeze: wrap in a polythene bag and freeze separately.

To serve after freezing: fry the frozen forcemeat balls in the butter and oil and drop them into the hare casserole just before serving.

[B/C]   *Hare Casserole with Mushrooms*

a saddle of hare and the back legs	1 wineglass white wine
1 tbs. lemon juice	¼ lb. mushrooms, fresh, or frozen raw or blanched
1 tbs. flour	½ pt stock
2 medium onions	3 tbs. cream
1 oz. butter	salt and pepper

Frozen hare must be allowed to thaw before preparing. Mushrooms should be left for ½ hour until they are soft enough to slice.

Strip the flesh from the saddle and legs of the hare and cut it into small strips. Sprinkle the lemon juice over the fillets and roll them in the seasoned flour. Slice the onions and cook them gently in the butter in a flameproof casserole or heavy pan. When they are soft add the hare fillets and brown them, pour on the wine and cook for a few minutes. Slice the mushrooms and put them in the pan, together with the stock, and simmer for a further 15 to 20 minutes. When the hare is tender stir in the cream. Test for seasoning and serve.

To freeze: allow to cool and freeze in a foil or plastic container.

To serve after freezing: tip the frozen hare into a flameproof casserole or saucepan and heat through gently. Allow 30 to 40 minutes for this.

[B] *Hare Pâté*

When making this recipe you may like to keep the saddle and use it for roasting (see p. 288).

1 hare, jointed	bay leaves, marjoram, thyme
1 lb. streaky bacon	and rosemary
1 large onion	1 pt red wine
2–3 cloves garlic	salt and pepper

Place the pieces of hare in a casserole – leaving the saddle on one side if you are going to roast it – together with three quarters of the bacon, the roughly chopped onion, the garlic and the herbs. Add the red wine, cover the casserole and place it in a slow oven (325°F., gas 3) for about 1 hour. Remove the casserole from the oven and allow to cool. Lift out the pieces of hare and strip the meat off the bones. Strain the juice and set it aside.

Mince the meat and the bacon or, if you like a fine pâté, chop roughly and put in a blender with some of the cooking liquid. Season the mixture with plenty of pepper and a little salt – you may find the bacon makes this unnecessary – and more crushed garlic and herbs.

Line a terrine with some of the remaining bacon cut into slices. If the terrine is for the freezer, use a foil dish or see methods 2 or 4 on p. 17. Put in the pâté, top with the rest of the bacon and a fresh bay leaf, and pour in as much of the cooking liquid as the dish will hold. Place the terrine in a bainmarie and cook in a very low oven (250°F., gas 1) for 1½ hours.

To serve immediately: allow the pâté to cool, pour a little melted butter over the top to seal it, and leave in a refrigerator for several hours.

To freeze: cool. If you have used a foil container wrap and freeze. Otherwise see p. 17.

To serve after freezing: allow to thaw at room temperature for 5 to 6 hours or overnight in the refrigerator.

CELERIAC

Celeriac is an extremely useful vegetable, and it freezes excellently blanched or cooked.

[A] *To freeze blanched:* peel the celeriac and cut it into large dice. Blanch for 4 minutes. Drain, cool and freeze in polythene bags.

To freeze puréed: peel the celeriac and cut it up roughly. Put it into a saucepan with some good stock – ½ to ¾ pint of stock for 2 lb. celeriac – and a little salt, cover and simmer gently until the stock has been absorbed. If necessary, leave the cover off the pan for the last 10 minutes or so. Put through a blender or mouli, allow to cool and freeze in waxed or plastic containers.

[C] *To serve after freezing blanched:* tip the frozen celeriac into a saucepan with a little salted water or stock and cook gently until it is soft. Serve with butter or béchamel sauce. Or else braise the celeriac (see p. 295).

To serve after freezing puréed: tip the frozen purée into a saucepan, add plenty of butter and heat through gently. Stir in a little cream, test for seasoning and serve.

The purée can also be combined with mashed potatoes beaten up with plenty of butter, hot milk and pepper. It doesn't matter how much potato you add, so long as there is not more than there is celeriac.

[B/C]   *Celeriac Soup*

1 lb. celeriac   1 lb. potatoes
1 large onion   1½ pts chicken stock
1 oz. butter   salt and pepper

½ pt milk
2–3 tbs. chopped parsley

If you are using frozen celeriac there is no need to wait for it to thaw.

Peel and dice the celeriac. Slice the onion and sauté it for a few minutes in the butter. Add the celeriac and cook for a further 5 minutes. Peel and dice the potatoes and add them to the saucepan, together with the chicken stock. Season. Cook until the vegetables are soft and put through a blender or a fine mouli.

To serve immediately: return to the pan, add the milk and bring to the boil. Test for seasoning, and add some more milk if the soup is too thick. Like other root vegetables celeriac sometimes tastes a little sweet: the remedy for this is lots of seasoning and above all parsley, which adds a delicious flavour.

To freeze: allow to cool and freeze in waxed or plastic containers.

To serve after freezing: tip the frozen soup into a saucepan and heat gently. Add the milk and parsley as above.

[B/C] *Braised Celeriac*

2 lb. celeriac
1 large onion
1 oz. butter
¼ pt stock

⅛ pt white wine (or all stock can be used)
salt and pepper

Peel the celeriac and cut it into dice or ½-inch slices. Blanch for 5 minutes and drain. If you are using frozen celeriac there is no need to wait for it to thaw or to blanch it.

Slice the onion and cook gently in the butter in a flameproof casserole until it is soft. Add the celeriac and pour on the stock, or the stock and wine. Any stock will do but the tastier it is the better the celeriac will be (pheasant stock is delicious). The liquid should about two thirds cover the celeriac. Season. Bring to the boil, cover, and put into a medium oven (350°F., gas 4) for about ½ hour.

To serve immediately: cook for a further ¼ hour or so and serve.

To freeze: cool and freeze, with the cooking liquid, in a plastic container or a polythene bag.

To serve after freezing: put the frozen celeriac into a heavy pan or flameproof casserole and gently heat through on top of the stove or put into a fairly warm oven for about an hour.

Christmas

TURKEY

Turkey on Christmas Day, fresh from the oven, is a pleasure, cold on Boxing Day it can still be enjoyed, but as the days after Christmas wear on it is generally greeted by groans. So, while it is still fresh and long before the family have reached saturation point, strip the meat off the bones, make a good stock from the carcass, with plenty of tarragon and lemon peel to counteract the slight sweetness of turkey stock, and freeze one or both of the following dishes. They will be welcome for a party or family meal long after Christmas has been forgotten.

[B]   *Chaud-Froid of Turkey*

This makes an excellent dish for a cold lunch or buffet. Use the best slices of meat for this – strictly speaking, it should be the white meat only – and keep the smaller pieces and the scraps for the turkey in cream sauce.

3–4 lb. sliced turkey meat
½ pt. double cream (or ¼ pt double and ¼ pt single)
¾ pt turkey stock
2 good sprigs of tarragon or 1 tsp. dried tarragon

¼ oz. gelatine
2 tbs dry white wine or dry white vermouth
juice of ½ lemon
salt and pepper

If you are freezing this dish, line a large meat platter with foil or polythene film, and arrange the slices of turkey on it neatly.

Simmer the cream and the stock together for 15 minutes, with the tarragon. Remove from the heat and take out the tarragon if you have used whole sprigs. Dissolve the gelatine in the wine or vermouth and the lemon juice, and stir it into the sauce. Season the sauce and add more finely chopped tarragon leaves if you like. Leave the sauce to cool and thicken a little, and then spoon it carefully over the meat. It is best to do this several times, so that the sauce does not merely run to the bottom of the dish but forms a thick coating over the meat.

To serve immediately: chill until the sauce is set and serve.

To freeze: allow to cool. Cover with a piece of foil or plastic film and freeze for 24 hours. Lift it off the dish, wrap well and replace in the freezer.

To serve after freezing: unwrap, replace on the original platter and allow to thaw at room temperature for at least 6 hours. It is important that this dish should not be too cold when eaten or the delicate flavour will suffer.

[B] ## *Turkey in Cream Sauce*

Use the dark meat and any scraps of turkey meat for this. It is a useful stand-by to have in the freezer, and may be used as a filling for vol-au-vents, omelettes and pancakes, or served with rice as a supper dish.

For 1 lb. turkey meat:

2 oz. butter	½ tsp. chopped tarragon
1 onion	a dash of dry white vermouth
2 oz. flour	(optional)
½ pt milk	salt and pepper
½ pt turkey stock	

Dice the meat. Melt the butter and sauté the finely chopped onion. Add the flour and make a sauce with the milk and the stock. Flavour with tarragon and vermouth, and season well. Stir the meat into the sauce.

To freeze: allow to cool and pour into waxed or plastic containers. It is useful to freeze this in small quantities.

To serve after freezing: tip the frozen mass into a saucepan, warm gently and serve as suggested above.

STUFFINGS

Stuffings for the turkey can be prepared weeks in advance of Christmas and stored in the freezer, so saving much of the frenzy of the days immediately before Christmas. Any recipe for stuffing can be frozen, and we give below three which we have found extremely good. They are all quite different and complement one another very well.

[B]   *Rich Stuffing*

Any of this stuffing that is left over will be excellent served cold
as a pâté, so, if you are making more than you think will be
eaten on Christmas day, do not stuff it into the turkey but cook
it separately.

½ lb. mushrooms	1 clove garlic
2 oz. butter	small tin pâté de foie
6 oz. streaky bacon	finely grated rind of 1 lemon
6 oz. loin of pork	1 tbs. chopped parsley
liver from the turkey or ¼ lb. chicken livers	pinch each of thyme and marjoram
1 large Spanish onion	salt and pepper
4 anchovy fillets	

Sauté the chopped mushrooms in 1 ounce of the butter.
Roughly chop all the meat and the onion and put them, with
the rest of the ingredients, through a coarse mincer or a
blender. Melt the remaining ounce of butter before adding it.
Fry a small pat of the mixture in a little butter, taste, and adjust
the seasoning as necessary.

To freeze: freeze in a polythene bag, or, if the stuffing is to be
cooked separately, in a foil dish or in a casserole (see methods 2,
3 or 4 on p. 17).

To cook after freezing

For cooking inside the turkey – allow to thaw for 4 to 5 hours
at room temperature or overnight in the refrigerator before
stuffing into the bird.

For cooking separately – place the frozen stuffing in the oven
and cook for 2 to 3 hours. If you are cooking the turkey in a
very low oven, it may need a little longer. Baste it from time to
time with a little of the turkey juice, or, if the turkey is being
cooked in foil, dot with butter before placing in the oven and
baste liberally with turkey juice at the end.

[B] *Forcemeat Stuffing*

8 oz. fresh breadcrumbs   rinds of 2 lemons, finely grated
4 oz. suet   3 eggs
3 tbs. chopped parsley   salt and pepper
2 tsp. mixed herbs

Mix together all the dry ingredients. Beat the eggs and stir into
the mixture, and press all well together into a ball. Season. This
quantity is sufficient for a 15-lb. bird (dressed weight).

To freeze: freeze in a polythene bag.

To thaw: leave at room temperature for 2 to 3 hours, or in the
refrigerator overnight, before using to stuff the tail-end of the
turkey.

[B] *Chestnut Stuffing*

2 lb. fresh chestnuts or 1 lb.   2 oz. butter
  dried   1 tsp. sugar
½ pt milk   salt and pepper
½ pt water

Prepare the chestnuts (see p. 278) and simmer them in the milk
and water until they are soft. The time required varies a great
deal according to the chestnuts. They may be done in about
20 minutes or may take double that time. Dried chestnuts will
probably need at least an hour. Add a little more liquid if
necessary.

Put the chestnuts and any cooking liquid that is left through
a blender, a fine mouli or a sieve. Add the melted butter and the
sugar, season to taste and squeeze into a ball. This quantity is
sufficient for a bird of about 15 lb. (dressed weight).

To freeze: allow to cool and freeze in a polythene bag.

To thaw: thaw at room temperature for 3 to 4 hours or in the
refrigerator overnight before using to stuff the breast of the
turkey.

Note: if you have cooked more chestnuts than you need for

the stuffing, you can use the surplus for one of the simplest and most delectable sweets in the world. Put them through a fine mouli and serve with masses of whipped cream and caster sugar – but you will need literally spoonfuls and spoonfuls of both.

[B]   *Bread Sauce*

1 pt milk   1 large onion
6 oz. fresh breadcrumbs   1½ oz. butter
3 cloves   salt and pepper

knob of butter
2 or 3 tbs. cream or top of the milk

Do not use a sliced loaf for this sauce, as the breadcrumbs will not have enough body.

Stick the cloves in the onion and simmer in the milk for 15 minutes. Take out the onion and pour the milk over the breadcrumbs. Add the seasoning and the butter and cook gently for a further 5 minutes or so, stirring from time to time. Do not overcook, as the sauce should have a roughish consistency. For this reason also we do not recommend making it in a blender.

To freeze: cool and freeze in waxed or plastic containers.

To serve after freezing: turn the frozen sauce into a heavy saucepan or a double pan. Add a knob of butter and a spoonful or two of the top of the milk or cream, and heat gently. Add more salt if necessary and – very important – plenty of freshly ground pepper.

[B]   *Christmas Pudding*

Most families have their favourite recipe for Christmas pudding, but this is a useful one because it is rich without being too dark and heavy. The quantities given below will fill two 2-pint pudding basins (each enough for about 8 people). Save time by making two at once, and freeze one for next year. It will keep perfectly in the freezer, with no risk of mould forming on top, as sometimes happens in even the best store-cupboards.

1 lb. cooking apples	6 oz. sultanas
1 large carrot	2 oz. flour
4 oz. mixed peel	⅛ nutmeg finely grated or a
12 oz. fresh breadcrumbs	couple of shakes of pow-
8 oz. suet	dered nutmeg
1¼ lb. demerara sugar	3 eggs
8 oz. seedless raisins	1 wineglass brandy
6 oz. currants	

Peel, core and mince the apples and finely shred the carrot and the peel. Mix with all the other dry ingredients, and add the beaten eggs and the brandy. Stir very thoroughly and put into well-buttered pudding basins. Put a piece of buttered grease-proof paper over the top and then a piece of cloth and tie securely, making sure that the pudding has room to expand. Steam for 5 or 6 hours.

To serve immediately: turn out on to a warmed dish, and as you bring the pudding to table pour over it a couple of tablespoons of warmed brandy and set it alight. Serve with brandy butter.

To freeze: turn out the pudding and allow to cool. Wrap well and freeze.

To serve after freezing: replace the pudding in the basin and thaw at room temperature for about 8 hours. Put a piece of foil on top of the pudding, tucking it securely over the sides of the basin, and steam for 3 hours. Serve as above.

ALTERNATIVES
TO CHRISTMAS PUDDINGS

Here are recipes for several puddings which look very festive and will be welcomed by those – especially children – who find the traditional Christmas pudding too heavy at the end of a big meal.

[B]   *Christmas Ice-Pudding*

This is strictly for adults, and is no less rich than the traditional Christmas Pudding.

6 oz. of a combination of any of the following: raisins, currants, glacé orange, glacé cherries, marrons glacés	5 egg yolks
	5 oz. caster sugar
	4 oz. (2 good tbs.) unsweetened chestnut purée (tinned)
4 tbs. rum	4 oz. bitter chocolate
½ pt single cream	½ pt double cream

Chop the dried and glacé fruits roughly, and soak them in the rum.

Heat the single cream to near boiling point, pour it on to the egg yolks mixed with the sugar and return to the pan. Stir over a gentle heat till the custard thickens, but do not allow it to boil. You may find it easier to do this in a double saucepan. When the custard has thickened add the chestnut purée and the chocolate and stir well until they have dissolved and the custard is quite smooth. Test for sweetness and leave to cool. Mix in the rum-soaked fruits and finally fold in the whipped double cream.

Line a pudding basin with foil or polythene film. Pour in the mixture, wrap and freeze. If you cannot spare the basin until the pudding is eaten lift it out after 24 hours, wrap, and replace in the freezer.

To serve: remove from the freezer about 1 hour before serving. Unwrap the pudding and leave it in the refrigerator until you are ready to eat it.

[B]   *Ice-Cream Yule Log*

This can be the children's alternative to Christmas pudding or the ice-cream can be laced with a liqueur and served to adults also. The quantities given will make 8 to 10 good servings.

1 pt vanilla ice-cream	½ lb. chocolate cake glaze
1 pt chocolate ice-cream	

Fill a long, narrow loaf or cake tin with the slightly softened vanilla ice-cream, which can first be laced with liqueur. Return it to the freezer for a few hours to harden. Invert the tin on a foil-covered tray or dish, wrap a teatowel wrung out in hot water round it and lift off the tin. Cover the vanilla ice with the slightly softened chocolate ice, round off the edges to make a log shape and smooth it well. Spread only a little chocolate ice-cream over the ends of the log and mix it with the vanilla ice to make a pale brown. Make a swirl in the ends with a fork and return the log once more to the freezer for about 1 hour. Melt the chocolate glaze over a low heat, allow it to cool a little, spread it gently over the log with a palette knife and draw a fork along it lengthwise, to give a rough surface. Finally you can decorate the log with sprigs of holly, robins and pinecones. Return the finished log to the freezer and take it out 15 minutes before serving.

Baked Alaska

This is a very easy-to-make spectacular which can be brought flaming to the table and yet is light and easy to digest. It can be prepared two or three days before Christmas, stored in the freezer and put straight into the oven only 15 minutes before it is to be served. Any flavour of ice-cream and liqueur can be used, but we have found the combination of vanilla ice-cream and marsala particularly good, as the tart edge of the marsala counteracts the sweetness of the meringue. For children it is of course better to use a flavoured ice-cream and to omit the alcohol. The following quantities will serve 6, but it can be made in almost any size.

4 oz. trifle sponges	3 egg whites
4–6 tbs. marsala	3 oz. caster sugar
1 pt vanilla ice-cream	

1 tbs. sugar
1–2 tbs. brandy

Halve the sponge cakes and use them to line a shallow oven-proof dish, making sure that the bottom and sides of the dish are completely covered. Dribble on about half the marsala. Mix the remainder of the marsala into the slightly softened ice-cream and pile this on to the sponge cakes, leaving a good 1-inch margin at the edges, and smoothing it off on top. Place the dish in the freezer while you prepare the meringue mixture. Beat the egg whites until they are stiff and add the caster sugar gradually, while continuing to beat. Pile this over the ice-cream and sponge cakes so that everything is covered in a thick layer of meringue. Return to the freezer immediately, and wrap or cover lightly when it has frozen. (The meringue mixture never becomes completely hard.)

To serve: take the alaska out of the freezer 15 minutes before you are ready to serve it. Place in a hot oven (425°F., gas 7) for 15 minutes, then sprinkle with sugar, pour on the warmed brandy and set it alight. (You may find it is easiest to do this by setting light to the second spoonful of brandy before you pour it over.) Bring to the table at once, while it is still flaming.

[B] *Mince-Pies*

Mince-pies frozen uncooked and put into the oven straight out of the freezer are light and tasty. Mincemeat can be frozen separately, also, and will keep better in this way than in the store-cupboard.

Mincemeat

3 oz. almonds	4 oz. sultanas
6 oz. mixed peel	1¼ lb. demerara sugar
1¼ lb. apples	rind and juice of 1 lemon
8 oz. suet	rind and juice of 1 orange
12 oz. raisins	⅛ pt brandy
6 oz. currants	

Blanch and chop the almonds and shred the peel finely. Peel and core the apples and mince them with all the other dry ingredients except the currants, which should be left whole. Add the rind and juice of the lemon and orange and the brandy, and stir thoroughly. Freeze in waxed cartons. This quantity will yield a little over 4 lb. mincemeat.

Mince-pies

12 oz. shortcrust pastry (see p. 28)
1 lb. mincemeat

Roll out the pastry and line about 24 patty-pans. Fill them with mincemeat and cover with the rest of the pastry. Put in the freezer for 24 hours. The mince-pies will then slip easily out of the patty-pans and can be replaced in the freezer, preferably in a cardboard box or a tin, so that there is no risk of their getting damaged. If you are likely to be using them in small quantities, it is worth wrapping each one separately in moisture-vapour-proof tissue or polythene film.

To serve after freezing: replace the frozen mince-pies in the patty-pans and pop them into a hot oven (425°F., gas 7) for 20 to 25 minutes, until the pastry is cooked but not brown. Sprinkle generously with caster sugar and serve hot.

INDEX

MORE ABOUT PENGUINS
AND PELICANS

Penguinews, which appears every month, contains details of all the new books issued by Penguins as they are published. From time to time it is supplemented by *Penguins in Print*, which is a complete list of all titles available. (There are some five thousand of these.)

A specimen copy of *Penguinews* will be sent to you free on request. For a year's issues (including the complete lists) please send 50p if you live in the British Isles, or 75p if you live elsewhere. Just write to Dept EP, Penguin Books Ltd, Harmondsworth, Middlesex, enclosing a cheque or postal order, and your name will be added to the mailing list.

In the U.S.A.: For a complete list of books available from Penguin in the United States write to Dept CS, Penguin Books Inc., 7110 Ambassador Road, Baltimore, Maryland 21207.

In Canada: For a complete list of books available from Penguin in Canada write to Penguin Books Canada Ltd, 41 Steelcase Road West, Markham, Ontario.

FRESH FROM THE FREEZER

MARYE CAMERON-SMITH

Whether you speak of a freezer or, (as many do incorrectly), a deep-freeze, this handbook will persuade you how much time, work, and money can be saved in the home by an appliance which (with a capacity of four or five cubic feet) need cost no more than £60.

Cooling food rapidly to a lower temperature than that of a refrigerator, a freezer will store most fruit and vegetables for up to a year, fish or shellfish for periods between three and nine months, and most meats (other than offal) for between four and eight months.

Marye Cameron-Smith gives expert advice here on the best type of appliance to buy, and on the selection, preparation, and air-tight packaging of fish, meat, vegetables, pastry, pies, cooked dishes, puddings and other foods, so that they can be kept for months with very little loss of freshness, colour, flavour or quality. Many of her directions are presented in handy tables and they cover both home-grown produce and the range of quick-frozen foods which can be bought.

ELIZABETH DAVID

Elizabeth David is well known for the infectious enthusiasm with which she presents her recipes.

'She has the happy knack of giving just as much detail as the average cook finds desirable; she presumes neither on our knowledge nor on our ignorance' – Elizabeth Nicholas in the *Sunday Times*

MEDITERRANEAN FOOD

A practical collection of recipes made by the author when she lived in France, Italy, the Greek Islands and Egypt, evoking all the colour of the Mediterranean but making use of ingredients obtainable in England.

FRENCH COUNTRY COOKING

Some of the splendid regional variations in French cookery are described in this book.

FRENCH PROVINCIAL COOKING

'It is difficult to think of any home that can do without Elizabeth David's *French Provincial Cooking* . . . One could cook for a lifetime on the book alone' – *Observer*

ITALIAN FOOD

Exploding once and for all the myth that Italians live entirely on minestrone, spaghetti and veal escalopes, this exciting book demonstrates the enormous and colourful variety of Italy's regional cooking.

SUMMER COOKING

A selection of summer dishes that are light (not necessarily cold), easy to prepare and based on the food in season.

ENGLISH COOKING ANCIENT AND MODERN 1
Spices, Salt and Aromatics in the English Kitchen

Elizabeth David presents English recipes which are notable for their employment of spices, salt and aromatics. As usual, she seasons instruction with information, explaining the origins and uses of her ingredients.